UNVEILING
THE SONG of SONGS

Jill Shannon

www.xulonpress.com

OTHER BOOKS BY JILL SHANNON

Coffee Talks with Messiah: When Intimacy Meets Revelation
Evergreen Press, 2007

A Prophetic Calendar: The Feasts of Israel
Destiny Image Publishers, 2009

The Seduction of Christianity:
Overcoming the Lukewarm Spirit of the Church
Destiny Image Publishers, 2010

Israel's Prophetic Destiny: If I Forget Jerusalem (Psalm 137)
Destiny Image Publishers, 2012

ACKNOWLEDGMENTS

I thank my Father in Heaven, who has entrusted me with this intimate and holy assignment. Abba, I felt unqualified to write this book, but that didn't stop You from being faithful to help me every step of the way. Thank You, my loving, kind Father.

My thanks to my family, who always give me the freedom to complete all these holy tasks. I love you and bless you, dear Dror, Keren, Ariela, Raviv and Amber, and my precious grandsons, Caleb and Jacob.

I am indebted to Steven Francis, who prophetically called forth this book. Thank you for faithfully sharing what the Lord desired of me. He has honored this Word.

I bless and thank the teaching ministries of Sadhu Sundar Selvaraj, Mike Bickle, Neville Johnson, Sid Roth, Robert Misst, Pastor Joe Sweet, Paul Keith Davis, Pastor Steven Brooks, Nita Johnson, Pastor Steven Shelley, and Rick Joyner. I am privileged to have grown and learned under your sacrificial ministries unto the Lord.

My thanks to my dear brother, David J. Michael, who has been a faithful friend, intercessor and teacher, in some of my most difficult moments. Thank you, David, for your contribution to this teaching and for your steadfast love.

To my faithful sister, Cathy Minnick, who has helped to edit this book, and prayed for the fullness of the message to be released. You have carried me on the wings of prayer for a long time. Bless you, faithful friend.

To my beautiful sister, Nancy DeWind: Thank you with all my heart for the profoundly beautiful artwork, which you created just for these newest projects on the Song. It expresses the bridal love in such an intimate and golden way. I am honored to have the joy of joining your art to my music and writings. May the Lord shine continually on your precious family.

To beloved Suzette and John, you have sacrificially tended the garden that the Lord planted in me. There is no value I can place on what you have done to make this ministry possible. I can only thank you with words I do not even have. Bless you and your destiny in our Beloved.

My loving thanks to my dear friends, intercessors, and helpers. To the Newman family: I can't imagine being here without you. My deepest love and appreciation to Tracy, Bob and Marinelle, Bernard and Vivien, my dear Israeli intercessors, and all the pastors, First Nation chiefs, and friends who have hosted me and supported this ministry in many diverse ways. Thank you for your lavish generosity and love.

To my Lamb of God, Yeshua: You are the One I cling to, in this broken world. You are everything to me, and I can't imagine going on without You. You have shown me unfailing love and kindness, and it is to You that I dedicate this book about Your Bridegroom heart of love. Please don't stay away, Beloved. We are waiting for You.

ENDORSEMENTS

I n Jill's book you will see the Song of Solomon presented to you
in High Definition. Jill writes from a scholarly perspective by
drawing upon her Hebrew heritage and rich understanding of the
Jewish culture. She lives in Israel full-time and applies her knowledge and insight of the Holy Land and the Middle Eastern people
to open up this unique book in a way that God intended for it to be
understood. "Unveiling the Song of Songs" makes the Song come
alive in color, context, and majesty.

As brilliant as Jill is in her research and presentation of historical
facts surrounding the Song of Solomon, it is still her keen prophetic
insight that leaves the reader staggering from the reality of the intense
love that Christ has for His bride. This book is loaded with thought
provoking truths that require a reassessment of our spiritual priorities.
Jill doesn't pull any punches but presents the responsibility of the
bride, in light of having received such remarkable favor. This great
kindness from the King demands that we respond with a seeking first
of His kingdom and the entire laying down of our lives to Him.

As you move through each chapter of "Unveiling the Song of
Songs," don't be surprised to feel that you are sitting on a romantic
powder keg. The Song of Solomon is an intense book of divine love
that is intentionally descriptive in its language. Jill takes the match of
the Holy Spirit and is bold enough to light the fuse of intimacy with
God. This book will cause your heart to be on fire for Yeshua like
never before!
Pastor Steven Brooks
Moravian Falls, North Carolina
www.stevenbrooks.org

When you understand how to have greater intimacy with Jesus from a One New Man, Hebrew, historic, and even botanical perspective, your intimacy with Messiah will become *normal* – normal as defined by the Bible.

Sid Roth,
Host, *It's Supernatural!*

Our dear sister Jill has broken the seals of the riches of God's heart in this book. Since the creation of man it has been the Lord's yearning to be intimate with each one of His people. The Lord is asking us to remove the veil that we use to hide from Him. He is pursuing us with jealous love, and arranging every detail of our lives, even the trials and sufferings, to bring us into a place of bridal readiness. He longs to hear our voice, our tears and passionate cries.

The Bridegroom will only marry a bride who has prepared herself for the Marriage with the Lamb. The true church must be equally yoked to this intense and holy King. I pray that the truths in this book will help us to make ourselves ready for the Bridegroom King.

Sadhu Sundar Selvaraj
Jesus Ministries

In the "The Parable of the Wise and Foolish Virgins" found in Matthew's Gospel, the Lord Yeshua Himself said *"the kingdom of heaven shall be likened to ten virgins who took their lamps and went out to meet the Bridegroom."* **While all of the virgins, both wise and foolish,** slumbered, *"at midnight a cry was heard: 'Behold the Bridegroom is coming; go out to meet Him!'"*

We are now living in the dark days of *"the midnight hour"* of history. This book is a cry from heaven to the bride to awaken and be prepared to meet our Bridegroom. The Lord Yeshua is coming soon!

Just as John the Baptist was a *"burning and shining lamp"* sent to prepare the way of the Lord, Jill Shannon is burning with a prophetic message that will truly help awaken, equip and prepare the reader for our soon-coming Bridegroom King.

Joe Sweet, Senior pastor
Shekinah Worship Center
Lancaster, California

We are now on a countdown to the end of the age and the physical return of Jesus back to this earth. The journey is almost complete our race is almost finished. Living in these End -Times confers on us a responsibility that previous generations have not had to face.

Generations of Christians have come to this earth, lived their lives and returned home, but many of this generation will live to see the return of Jesus. This places a responsibility on us to be ready for Jesus the bridegroom's return. Past generations of Christians looked forward to the day when they would be taken home through death to be with the Lord. This generation is anticipating the Lords return and is becoming more aware of the need to prepare for this great event.

Jill's book lays out a clear pathway for the heart preparation that is needed in order for us to be ready for the coming of the Lord. You will be blessed and challenged by this book, and the revelatory insights it contains will motivate and help you prepare you for the greatest historic event since the birth, death, and resurrection of Jesus. The bridegroom is coming.

Neville Johnson
Living Word Foundation

Jill has once again written another book with the fragrance of the Son, our Lord Jesus. Her passion for Jesus and His Bride can be felt in the different passages where she has reflected upon her dealings of the Spirit in her inner life. The advantage of her Jewish heritage has given the edge in interpreting this beautiful book. It is my prayer that many who read this book will be able to smell the fragrance of the Beloved in the Garden of fellowship and the incense of worship that rises in the temple of God. Be ready for the coming of Jesus!

Dr. Steven Francis
Founder, Rivers of Life Ministries & College of Prophets
Singapore

CONTENTS

Chapter 1

MARRIAGE AND GOVERNMENT

The Song of Songs, authored by King Solomon, has long been a subject of great fascination to students of the Bible, rabbis, and Israelis, and there are several key ways that it has been interpreted.

Solomon was a prolific songwriter like his father David before him. Scripture records that he composed 1,005 songs (1 Kings 4:32). And yet he titled this one, "The Song of Songs," which carries the same superlative meaning as "King of Kings," or "Holy of Holies." Solomon believed that this song was his crowning legacy, his highest musical and literary achievement as a composer. The literary beauty of this Hebrew poetry would grant the Song a lofty status among a vast body of compositions throughout history.

Sadly, we have no recordings of the musical sounds of this song, but only the lyrics remain. This has allowed great freedom for other songwriters through the ages to compose new love songs for the Bridegroom, taken from the lyrics of this Song. In the Millennial Kingdom, I'm sure we'll finally get to hear the ultimate Song of Songs, sung by the Lord Himself to His Bride. That will be the Song of all Songs to our hearts. When the Lord sings it, each one of us will feel as if we are the only one in the room.

Interpreting this Book

Because of the highly romantic content, there have been numerous debates about whether this is a natural story of love and marriage, or a parable of God's love for His people. Within the last few generations, the natural interpretation of this book has become popular. In this view, the reader would understand it as a natural love story between King Solomon and his bride, the Shulamite maiden. Or, on a broader level, this view would treat it as an expression of all courtship, love and marriage between a man and a woman. In this natural view, the Song emphasizes the God-given beauty of marital friendship, love and intimacy. Some churches even use the Song as a "marriage manual."

While believers are free to hold a natural view, this book will approach it as a spiritual parable of our developing relationship with the Lord; to this I have added the "spices" of the story line, as well as historic, Hebrew, botanical and sociological research for depth of background.

Since its composition nearly 3,000 years ago, it has been widely accepted by the rabbis, and later by the early believing communities, to be an allegory (or parable), depicting the intense love shared between the Lord and His covenant people. There were some rabbinic debates in the 2nd century, as to whether this book should be included in Sacred Scriptures, due to its content. These debates were recorded, and the ruling was: "All the writings are holy, but the Song of Solomon is the Holy of Holies."[1]

The rabbis even considered it too holy to be quoted at weddings, as merely "love words" to inspire the new couple. They believed that "the kisses of His mouth," were the Divine revelation given at Mt. Sinai, as His word came down to kiss His people with truth. We know that the kisses of His Word go beyond Mt. Sinai, and allow us even to hear His heart, and to partner with Him in His purposes on the earth and in our nations.

Designed for Loving Partnership

We were made in the image and likeness of God, destined to rule and reign with Yeshua, equally yoked in love. Having dominion was part of our original mandate (see Gen. 1:26-28). If we lack this understanding of our governmental partnership with the Lord, we will sleepwalk through this brief life without grasping the Lord's purposes for placing each of us on this earth. He desires a committed partner, with whom He can overcome the darkness and prepare the earth for His Kingdom.

When the Lord comes to fully establish His earthly reign, we must have already prepared ourselves to be wise, humble and righteous leaders over the earth. The Lord will partner with these trusted ones to subdue the earth, and all of its rebellious infrastructures. This is our time to practice partnering with Him, and we cannot do so without experientially knowing His emotions, His desires and affection for us.

> *The heaven, even the heavens, are the Lord's; But **the earth***
> ***He has given to the children of men**.* (Psalm 115:15-17)

After the fall, the Lord began to develop the human Seed of redemption, through one who would be born of a woman (Gen. 3:14). Over the generations, the Lord selected a particular genealogy from which to birth the Redeemer of mankind. This Seed would come through Abraham, Isaac and Jacob.

This people would end up coming out of Egypt, into the wilderness, after hundreds of years of slavery. The Lord raised up Moses, who was one of the children of Israel, to be their deliverer. They came out in great number, not having yet learned how to be a loyal people under Creator God and His requirements.

The Lord saw them as a helpless baby in the desert, who was not yet ready to make a marriage covenant with Himself (see Eze. 16:4-8). He saw them as grapes in the desert, early fruit on the fig tree (see Hos. 9:10)

Israel's Marriage Covenant with the Lord

After the Passover of their exodus from Egypt, the Lord brought them through the wilderness to arrive at Mt. Sinai, about 50 days later. There, He entered into a type of marriage covenant with this new fledgling nation, even though they were not mature enough to honor this covenant. Still, **the Bridegroom Heart of God is evident in the Sinai covenant. He requires loyal love, voluntary obedience, and singular devotion to Him alone.** In return, He will provide all that they need, and He will be their God in a cruel desert, and will bring them into the Land flowing with milk and honey. Below, you can see in the Torah the Bridegroom's requirements in this marriage vow: Loyalty (no other gods) and Love (with all your heart, soul and strength.)

> *"I am the Lord your God, who brought you out of the land of Egypt, out of the house of bondage.* ***You shall have no other gods before Me.***
>
> *"Hear, O Israel: The Lord our God, the Lord* is one! ***You shall love the Lord your God with all your heart, with all your soul, and with all your strength.*** (Ex. 20:2, Deut. 6:4-5).

This is a covenant of jealous love, provision, inheritance and obedience. Within the framework of this marriage covenant, the Lord would cause them to subdue and have dominion over the Land of Promise. Had they fully followed the covenant, Israel would have been the earliest prototype of ruling and reigning with the Lord. They would drive out armies and nations larger and more powerful than they.

They would impose righteous government, based on *Yehovah's* laws, on the Land and would strongly influence the surrounding Canaanite nations, with the excellence of *Yehovah* as the only true God. This is a picture of marriage and governmental authority. As the Lord's Bride, Israel was meant to rule the nations with His righteous laws and precepts. Israel was called to be "a light to the nations."

However, before the reigns of David and Solomon, Israel proved too immature and backsliding to be a reliable marriage partner to the Lord. In the marriage covenant of Mt. Sinai, the new nation of Israel was divorcing not only the gods of Egypt, but she was divorcing all the Canaanite gods which would surround and seduce her when she entered the Land. The Sinai covenant is a divorcing of Baal worship, in every form. But Israel did not remain true to her Husband, tragically.

Israel reached a level of "readiness for love" (Eze. 16:4-8) under the 40-year reign of David, followed by the 40-year reign of Solomon. David's love and righteous reign paved the way for Solomon's ceremonial marriage covenant between the Lord and Israel. Solomon was thinking of this when he wrote Song of Songs, where the key elements are Loyalty ("dove's eyes") and Relentless Love ("Love is as strong as death and jealous love unyielding as the grave").

The climax of Israel's covenantal love occurred when Solomon had completed building the magnificent Temple, according to all the preparations and unimaginable wealth that David had invested. The account found in 2 Chronicles 5, 6 and 7 is unparalleled in Israel's history, and even in the history of the New Covenant church. Nothing like this permanent habitation of the Lord's manifest glory has yet been seen before or after the reign of Solomon. The Lord's tangible glory came down to dwell in the Temple. But His permanence was conditional on Israel continuing in obedience to His Torah, His ways, and His jealous heart.

But we will see this covenantal love again, before the return of the Lord. He will have a mature Bride who will stand in covenant, with priestly purity, unity and loyalty that will exceed the covenant sworn in Solomon's Temple. He will have a people who will love Him with all our heart, soul and strength. **And He will tabernacle in His Bride on earth,** before He comes to take them into the Ark of Safety (the Rapture) and before He returns to reign from Jerusalem in His glorified body, as King over the earth.

The New Covenant Bride will rule and reign over the nations of the earth during the Millennial reign of Yeshua. We will dash the rebellious nations like pottery, ruling with an iron scepter (see Rev. 2:26-27, Ps. 2:8-9).

The Bridal Paradigm

The reigns of David and Solomon were the closest (yet imperfect) fulfillments of this "Marriage-Government-Partnership" principle, among all of Israel's difficult history. In the Song of Songs, Solomon expresses the Lord's desire for a loyal bride, who will partner with Him in sowing Kingdom seed and reaping a harvest in the earth.

There are a great number of Scriptures that depict our relationship with the Lord as a marriage covenant between a righteous husband and a loyal bride (see Rev. 19:6-6, Isa. 54:4-7, John 3:29, Matt. 22:2, 2 Cor. 11:2-3, Eph. 5:30-32, Ps. 45, Isa. 62:4-5, Eze. 16:4-8). The Song is also a beautiful parable of this bridal view or metaphor. Here are two examples of this bridal paradigm in the New Testament.

> *For no one ever hated his own flesh, but nourishes and cherishes it, just as the Lord does the church. For* **we are members of His body, of His flesh and of His bones.** *"For this reason a man shall leave his father and mother and be joined to his wife, and the two shall become one flesh." This is a great mystery, but* **I speak concerning Christ and the church.** (Eph. 5:29-32).

> *For I am jealous for you with godly jealousy. For* **I have betrothed you to one husband,** *that I may present you as a chaste virgin to Christ.* (2 Cor. 11:2).

A Biblical Case for the Allegorical Interpretation

Because the Song contains a number of references to intimacy and our bodies, some conclude that it cannot be talking about our relationship with the Lord. They feel that the Lord would never use images like this, in describing His love relationship with His corporate Bride, both male and female. But the fact is that the Lord does use these physical and even sexual terms, without apology, many times in Scripture. One example of this is Ezekiel 16:4-8. If you read this passage you will see how the Lord looked at Jerusalem: first as one too immature for marriage, and then, as a sexually mature young woman, "ready for love."

Song of Songs also speaks about protecting the immature, until they are ready to become a bride. He symbolizes their immaturity by the fact that their breasts have not yet developed, just as the Lord said to Ezekiel about Israel (see SOS 8:8-10).

In periods of idolatry in Israel's history, the Lord has compared His people to a harlot, and he uses quite strong and physically descriptive language to chastise her adulterous ways (see Jer. 2:24, 3:9, 5:7, Eze. 23:20-21, Hos. 2:2, 3:1, 8:9). In the New Testament, James also rebukes the church, calling them "adulterers and adulteresses" (see James 4:4-5).

We have now seen the biblical pattern, where the Lord describes His relationship with His people as that of a bridegroom and his bride. Therefore, we will approach the Song in this manner. We will emphasize our individual and corporate relationship with the Lord Yeshua, in this bridal paradigm. He is an equal opportunity Lover, and so the Song belongs to the male and female bride of Messiah alike. This book will help to open up this intimate dimension of our journey with the Lord to His sons and daughters.

In focusing on the spiritual applications, we will not negate the natural meanings, where the natural meaning also makes sense. But as we look carefully, we will see that it cannot be merely the story of a man and woman in love. There are passages where it would just make no sense to apply these words to a normal, earthly betrothal or marriage.

Throughout the chapters, the bridegroom (or lover) is described as a shepherd, as well as King Solomon. This has unfortunately led some commentators to wonder if the maiden is speaking about two different men, competing for her affections throughout the story line. But if it is truly about the Lord Yeshua and the way He beckons His bride into ever deepening maturity and intimacy, it is suddenly so easy to understand that He carries both identities to His people: Both Bridegroom King and humble shepherd, the tender of His Father's flocks. The Lord Yeshua the Messiah is the Good Shepherd and the King of Israel, the greater Solomon.

Love versus Death

The Lord presents a covenant to us, which requires a mutual exchange of love and loyalty, even unto death. The writers of Scripture have spoken much about the inevitability of the grave, and the natural fear of death. The issue of overcoming death is one of the strongest themes in Scripture. The Lord has emphasized the power of His love being strong enough to overcome death itself.

The incarnation of the Creator God as a Jewish man, Messiah Yeshua, brings the battle between LOVE and DEATH to the big screen of human history. It is the great Tug-of-War. How could Just One Man take on the power of death, and conquer the terrible pull of the grave? All flesh dies, withers, decays. **But the Lord God reserved a secret weapon in the blueprints of Heaven, one that His enemy, the prince of death, disease and decay, could never anticipate or understand.**

For the wages of sin are death. This is a legal principle that satan understands and has gleefully exploited for 6,000 years, since our original parents gave away their immortality. The Lord God set the terms of this covenant, when He told Adam and Eve: *"On the day that you eat of the fruit of the knowledge of good and evil, you will surely die."* Disobedience is sin, and the fruit of sin is death. Who among us, of those born into this earth, have not sinned? All have sinned, and thus, all have been subjected to the realities of death that the Lord warned Adam and Eve about.

But God's love, the demand and force of His love, is as strong as death. His burning heart of jealousy for us is more consuming than the grave. And that LOVE became a MAN. And His love took Him to the mocking, the spitting, the pulling out of His beard, the scourging of being flayed alive. His passion took Him to the hill of sacrifice, where He carried the wood of His own sacrifice on His back, as had His father Isaac before Him. The fire of His love took Him to the mountain of myrrh, the impaling spikes, and the curse of being hanged on a tree, covered in the leprosy of our filth. His furious, relentless love impelled Him forward to pay the price of being pulled into the jaws of the grave. *This love took Him to the grave.*

In the final section of the Song, the Bride has come to maturity, through many trials. And she sees the price that LOVE is willing to pay, which will enable the lovers to run on the mountains of eternity together, where nothing and no one will ever separate them again. And she declares, *"For Your love is as strong as death, and Your jealousy is as unyielding as the grave."* No power of hell can separate this love, and no floods spewed out from the mouth of the enemy can sweep away our future together.

YOU, our Bridegroom King, have overcome death by the power of Your love, and Your jealous flames have conquered the power of the grave. We will rejoice and be glad in You. Rightly do we love You!

The Apostle Paul puts it this way:

> *For I am convinced that neither death nor life, neither angels nor demons, neither the present nor the future, nor any powers, neither height nor depth, nor anything else in all creation will be able to separate us from the love of God that is in Christ Jesus our Lord* (Rom. 8:38-39 NIV).

Who is the Bride?

Theologically (positionally), all sincerely "born-again" believers are betrothed (engaged) to the Lord Yeshua. This means that when He returns, He will take for Himself a pure and spotless Bride, both male and female. These are those beloved and chosen ones, whom the Father has foreknown, called, chosen, and justified before the foundation of the world (see Rom 8:29-30, 2 Tim 1:9). The Father has given them as a bride to His Son, as the joy and reward of His suffering and sacrifice.

This means that our salvation is the first step in preparation for a real Wedding Day to come. Thus, we have entered the betrothal covenant at the time of our salvation. However, if we choose not to conduct ourselves as one who is engaged to the Lord Yeshua, we will not be marriage-worthy on that day.

In Hebrew and biblical understanding, an engaged couple were legally married, and if either party broke the engagement, the Lord viewed it as divorce. We see this in the case of the conception of the Lord Yeshua in His mother, Miriam (Mary.) She was already engaged to Joseph before the supernatural conception took place. When Joseph learned of her pregnancy, he first assumed it was a natural pregnancy, and the Bible says, "He had in mind to divorce her privately, so as not to put her to public disgrace" (Matt. 1:19). We see that even though they were merely engaged, the Bible views the breaking of the betrothal as a "divorce."

Similarly, the Lord looks at our "engagement" to His Son to be a binding covenant, and one which is not to be taken or forsaken lightly. And so we are already in a marital covenant with our Lord.

But practically speaking, many believers do not behave or think as those engaged to the King of Heaven. They live a lifestyle, whether in thought, word or deed, that contradicts the biblical commitments of a betrothed couple. This creates some hindrances to the fulfilment of the destinies that the Lord dreamed for them. It will also severely impact their ultimate status before the Lord. In the natural standards of this earth, a bridegroom would not wish to marry someone who had behaved like an unfaithful wife, even before they were married. Likewise, the bride would not wish to marry a man who played around before their marriage. **Neither will the Lord Yeshua marry one who has not cherished Him in the covenant loyalty of a bride in love.**

> *For I have betrothed you to one husband, that I may present you as a chaste virgin to Christ.* (2 Cor. 11:2)

The consummation of the marriage relationship occurs at the time of the Lord's return to earth, as King, Judge and Bridegroom.

> *Let us rejoice and be glad and give Him glory, for the wedding of the Lamb has come, and His bride has made herself ready.* (Rev. 19:7, NIV)

We could define the term, "the Bride," as a company that includes all those born-again believers who walk in intentional, daily, covenantal relationship with the Lord Yeshua. They are not yet perfected, as none of us are, but they take their covenant with the Lord very seriously, and they are quick to repent when a sinful pattern, thought, or behavior is exposed. It includes those who have matured in their love for Yeshua, and those who intentionally live each day as one waiting earnestly for their Lord to return. You could say that the Lord is their magnificent obsession. At the very end of human history, many of the "bridal company" will be newly saved believers, who will not have had time to mature. But the Lord will accelerate their maturing process dramatically, as the days grow shorter, so that all will have equal opportunity to walk equally, as a bride in love with her Maker (see Matt. 20:1-16).

We will explore more deeply the biblical theology of the bride, as a subset of the larger body of Christ, in chapters 9 and 12.

A Unique Revelation of the Lord's Heart

The "First and Greatest Commandment" is to love the Lord our God with all our heart, all our soul and all our strength (Deut. 6:5, Matt. 22:37-38). The Lord commanded this because He made us for this very purpose: to be in this intense love relationship with Him. The Lord desires that we reciprocate His feelings for us, as equally committed, equally-yoked lovers. As He loves us with all His heart, in the same manner, we are to love Him with all of our being.

We were given a great capacity to love God, and to love each other. Looking at this sorry world, you wouldn't know it, but we were made in the image of the One who loved first, and loved best. So it is part of our design and purpose, to be fierce and faithful lovers of this personal, intimate Creator.

The Song of Songs reveals the depth of the Lord's emotions towards His betrothed bride, the people in covenant with Him. We see His extravagant expressions of affection and attraction for the heart that is fully committed to Him. We see that He delights in His bride, and finds her uniquely beautiful and irresistible. The Lord's heart is actually overwhelmed as He experiences the way we feel about Him.

One of the most comforting truths in the Song is that despite our weaknesses and failures, He finds us beautiful, He will never give up on us, and He will perfect us in love, until the day of our Union. We also see the evolving story of the bride's maturation, and her spiritual failures and victories, as the narrative unfolds. She overcomes hardships, pain, sacrifice and separations, to reach the consummation of the ages.

Getting an experiential revelation of the Lord's commitment to us, and His emotions towards us, will bring healing and wholeness to so many broken hearts and wounded souls. The cruelties and falseness of this world have left a multitude of bitter and broken people, who cannot believe that a good and loving God could "let all this happen." The Song of Songs is for this moment in history, and it will bring intimacy and fulfillment to the last and most broken generation, which will see the return of the Bridegroom King.

The Song ends with these words: *"Come quickly, Beloved. Be like a swift and graceful young stag, and come for us quickly, leaping upon the mountains of our incense* (AP)."

The Bible ends with these words:

> *The Spirit and the bride say, "Come!" And let the one who hears say, "Come!" Let the one who is thirsty come* (Rev. 22:17a, NIV).

> *Even so, come quickly Lord Yeshua.* (Rev. 22:20). AMEN.

Chapter 2

INTIMACY (SOS 1:1-8)

SOS 1:2-4 Let him kiss me with the kisses of his mouth. For your love is better than wine. Because of the fragrance of your good ointments, Your name is ointment poured forth; therefore the virgins love you.

Draw me away! We will run after you. The king has brought me into his chambers. We will be glad and rejoice in you. We will remember your love more than wine. Rightly do they love you.

Throughout the Scriptures, the Lord's mouth is the instrument of His Word, and thus, His communication and impartation to His people. Man cannot even live by earthly food alone, but "by every Word that proceeds from the Lord's mouth" (Deut. 8:3). The Word that comes from God's mouth accomplishes creation, restoration, healings, deliverances, and prophetic impartation (Gen. 1, John 6:63, Isa.55:11, Matt. 4:4, Rev. 19:13).

The psalmist writes that His Word is sweet to the taste, and sweeter than honey to experience. Yeshua is the living mouthpiece and Word of His Father in Heaven. John writes, *"In the beginning, the Word was with God and the Word was God."* And John tells us that at the end of this age, He will still be the Word of God. *He was clothed in a robe dipped in blood, and His name is The Word of God (John 1:1, Rev. 19:13).*

In the rabbinic writings, to be kissed by the Lord is a picture of the Torah being given on Mt. Sinai, touching the hearts of Israel with His righteous ways. After the Lord Yeshua's resurrection, He breathed upon His disciples, and they received His very Spirit from His mouth. In the Bible, our worship is compared to a kiss.

> *Yet I reserve seven thousand in Israel – all whose knees have not bowed down to Baal and all whose mouths have not kissed him* (1 Kings 18:18, NIV).

> *Kiss the Son, so that He will not be angry with you, and you will not be destroyed along the way, for His anger can flare up in a moment* (Ps. 2:12, AP).

> *A woman in that town who lived a sinful life learned that Jesus was eating at the Pharisee's house, so she came there with an alabaster jar of perfume. As she stood behind him at his feet weeping, she began to wet his feet with her tears. Then she wiped them with her hair, **kissed them and poured perfume on them**.* (Luke 7:37-38, NIV).

What would it be like, to receive kisses from the One who made you? Would it be like an earthly or sensual kiss? No, for the earthly kiss is far too limited, temporary and superficial, to impart the depth of heaven's love for His own ones.

Or would it be like a sudden river of affection flowing over you, overwhelming and bypassing your logic, at the speed of thought? Surely, a kiss from our Beloved Yeshua would impart to our soul the knowledge in the deepest place of our soul, that we are unconditionally loved, deeply cherished, and secure in His commitment to us. We are wholly LOVED, just as we are. A kiss from this One, our brother and our friend, instantly erases a lifetime of shame, self-hatred and unworthiness. Worthy or not, we have been embraced and kissed by the Lover and Maker of our lives. We are not ashamed to say, *"Let Him kiss me with the kisses of His mouth."*

The Fragrance of Lord Yeshua

Because of the fragrance of your good ointments, Your name is ointment poured forth.

The Lord Yeshua carries the priestly fragrance of the anointing oils and spices. The Lord was anointed with the fullness of the Spirit of God, when He was immersed by *Yochanan* (John the Baptist) in the Jordan River. In His eternal role as the highest High Priest in Heaven and on earth, the fragrance of priestly anointing oil is fresh upon Him eternally, and exudes from His person. This anointing oil was used in the Tabernacle, and with it, Moses anointed the priests (see Ex. 30:22-29). Paul spoke of the fragrance of Yeshua, and Psalm 45 describes the scents of the oils and spices that adorn the King's robes on His Wedding Day (see 2 Cor. 2:15, Ps. 45:8).

His fragrance is also an expression of the beauty of His character and His thought life. In heaven, a priestly fragrance is poured out at the very mention of Yeshua's Name, like costly perfume. On special occasions, His Bride on earth is permitted to smell this fragrance with our earthly senses. This is not always the case, but like a special "reward," which encourages us to remember how real and alive our King really is.

I actually experienced this very verse, when I was in a major airport in Germany. I was en route to the US, and had been flying all night from India and arrived in Germany the next morning. I never wear perfume, even when I am in a formal setting. Needless to say, I was travelling in my oldest clothes, and had not cleaned up for quite a while. I stood in a long line at Passport Control, and made my way forward to the young, Middle-Eastern looking clerk at the Passport station. I approached, set my passport down before him, and simply smiled. His eyes grew wide with what was either shock or fear, and he took a big step backwards. He asked, "WHAT is that perfume you are wearing? I've never smelled anything like it!"

Though I smelled nothing, I instantly understood that this was not my own scent, but that the Lord was surprising both of us with this priestly manifestation of His own signature fragrance. I immediately answered, "It's the fragrance of Jesus. I am not wearing any perfume, but He has His own sweet smell, when He is present. Do you believe me, that you are smelling the presence of Jesus?"

He nodded that he did believe me. To my surprise, I asked him his name, and if I could pray for him, and to my greater surprise, he agreed. And so, with a long line of passengers waiting for their passports to be stamped, this young Arabic man allowed me to put my hand on his and pray for him.

At the next carry-on security station, the waiting officer had overheard a bit, and began asking me challenging questions about Jesus and about the Jewish people. He said, "Yeah, Jesus is cool, but the Jews killed Him."

I answered in a surprisingly loud voice, "I'm a Jew, and I LOVE Jesus!" That broke his anti-Semitic mold and blew his circuits real fast. I could see the shock on his face. He said, "That's impossible." That led to some interesting conversation, before I went on to my gate for my next flight.

And so, the reality of His Name being like perfume poured out, was manifested in a European airport, and more than one of the staff and surrounding passengers heard my testimony that day. Praise the Lord for His mysterious fragrance, manifested to a stranger in an airport!

What if We Can't Feel This Love?

We need to experience the love of the Lord for ourselves, not merely read about it in our Bibles. His love is like a download of intense appreciation and affection for us, where in a split second, we grasp intuitively the way He feels about us. It is good and right to desire this manifestation, and to ask Him for it. This is a prayer He will delight to answer.

Sometimes, we feel nothing, and we might come to a number of wrong conclusions about why we feel nothing:

1) Maybe the Lord does not intend for people to share with Him the kinds of love-feelings and desires that only earthly, human love and marriage were meant to satisfy.

2) Maybe the Lord does not have deep emotions for His people, but loves them in a way that transcends all human emotion or experience, and we should not desire or expect this passion to be experienced from His heart to ours.

3) Maybe people or the enemy will turn His love into a counterfeit sensual experience, and so we should avoid that area altogether, to avoid the sensual dangers of such an experience.

4) Maybe the Lord is ignoring such experience-based desires and prayers, and is too busy with important matters of the earth and the salvation of the nations.

This thinking is not accurate, for the Scriptures tell us otherwise. The Song of Solomon is a revelation of the Lord's emotions, passion and desire for us to experience His love, which will carry us through the darkest hour of human history. There are times we will feel His love, and there are other times when we will feel nothing, and we will walk in sheer faith, trust and obedience to His Word. It will always please Him when we believe the truth of His love, whether we feel it or not, in a given moment or season of our lives.

The truth of the matter is that when we feel nothing, He feels everything. His love for us cannot be measured or judged by what we feel.

However, our emotional makeup and feelings are given to us by God Himself, who is a deeply emotional Person, as we see all through the Scriptures. We were made in His image and in His likeness. Therefore, our emotions are not to be crucified, disdained or ignored. They are precious to Him, more than we realize. Even our negative emotions are precious to Him, in the sense that He values our honest and transparent baring of our feelings before His Face.

While we cannot base our faith or obedience on what we *feel*, it is right and pleasing to Him to seek the beautiful refreshment of His touch. And it *will* come, like a cascading river of His pleasure and love, seemingly "out of nowhere," like a kiss from heaven itself. Truly, this is the love that satisfies. It is the love that heals and delivers us of our broken past. The Lord desires to fulfill all of the family relational needs that He has placed within us.

Love Heals the Broken Ones

I recently met a dear Christian brother, who was raised in a third-world, tiny island in Asia-Pacific. He was the eighth of ten children in his poverty-stricken family, and his father was a cruel and abusive man. This brother told me that often he was beaten severely, and left bleeding and broken on the ground. His mother and other siblings were also harmed physically by this father. He grew bitter and hard inside, and put up a wall of anger around his heart, understandably. He was from a tribal/aboriginal background.

One day, as a young adult, he saw a vision of a Man coming to him, and this Man touched him with a flooding download of pure love, that just overwhelmed his mind and emotions. This flood of love overcame his fossilized heart. The man said, "I AM your Father." This Man was radically different in heart and character from his earthly father, and it blew his defenses wide open. The Man then showed this brother his whole previous life's history, and replayed for him many cruel incidents he had endured. The Man was the Lord, and He showed him that in each incident, He was weeping and suffering with him as a child and youth, enduring this terrible abuse.

This brother told me that wave after wave of sobbing and weeping deluged his soul, and over a period of time, his heart was softened, healed, and he was finally able to forgive his father. Later, he witnessed to his father about the Lord and His salvation, and they wept together, and his father accepted the salvation of the Lord Jesus.

His father died as a believer, and before he died, he lovingly blessed his son and family, as a patriarch of a tribal group would do. This brother is now one of the most tender and kindest men you could meet, all because of the LOVE of our Creator, Father, Lover, Brother and Friend, and His Son, Yeshua the Messiah, the Prince of Forgiveness and Reconciliation. Halleluiah!

And once we have tasted this Love, we will no longer derive any pleasure in seeking lesser things from the world, the flesh, or the evil one. We will be ruined forever, by His precious Kiss. He will give us special feelings of His Presence from time to time, sometimes when we least expect it, nor are we asking for it at that moment.

But He also expects us to walk in steady faith and trust, even when we feel nothing. We must know that nothing in Him has changed or left us, just because our senses are dull, or He has withdrawn His manifest Presence for a season, or we happen to feel nothing. He is with us, He is the same and never changes. He is faithful and will never abandon us. It is good to be vulnerable, like a child, and to ask the Lord to let you feel more of His love, because this request pleases the Lord, and He will do it in a way that will astonish us. We will be ruined forever, for the lesser pleasures of this broken world.

Draw me after You, and we will run together.

We need the Holy Spirit to tug on our hearts, to cause us to hunger for His companionship. He told us, *"No one can come to Me unless the Father draws him."* It is right to ask the Lord to pull our hearts nearer to Him, since we get caught up in the stress, demands and exhaustion of each day. However, when we ask for Him to draw us away, we must be prepared for whatever method He might choose.

The Lord can use the kindness and sweetness of His love to draw us away. He can also use wounding, illness, pain or troublesome times to draw us away. I am currently in a season where He has drawn me away from almost all the normal ministry responsibilities and even some of the usual intense email communications. In this case, He used a prolonged illness, and a lengthy season of painful wounding at the hands of people, to draw me away. I would not have chosen these woundings, and I was in much distress, but I know that He is drawing me away as Esther, even while writing this book. I would not be intensely pressing into His Person in this way without the pain of the season I am just coming out of.

As He draws us away, we can run together into the destiny and purposes, which the Lord ordained for our lives before time began (2 Tim 1:9). Our spirit responds to this tug by deliberately closing down the many distractions that clutter our minds. *"We will run"* speaks of a lifetime of ministry partnership with the Lord, both in fulfilling our specific life assignments from Him, and in regular, intentional, intimate communion with the Lord.

We will remember Your love more than wine.

The pleasure of drinking fine wines has been a feature of "the good life" in many cultures, for thousands of years. It always seems to go with parties, weddings, social recreation, romantic dinners,

Shabbat dinners, and enjoyment of life. Wine can also symbolize the larger variety of pleasures of this world.

But what will we remember as we near the end of our lives, or when we stand before the Throne? What will be worthy to bear the stamp of eternal remembrance? On that day, we will not be thinking about the temporal pleasures that seemed so important at the time. One thing remains in the realm of the human soul and spirit. Yeshua's love and faithfulness will be the enduring memory upon our transient sojourn through this corrupted world. And every drop of love we poured out upon His heart like the best wine, He will surely remember.

Rightly do they love You.

The virgins represent all those believers who are vulnerable of heart, childlike in their simple devotion to the Lord. There are some believers who would prefer to engage in theological dialog, analysis or even heated arguments **about the Lord**, rather than clinging **to the Lord** with loyal and extravagant love.

Lord, we are drawn to Your love, since there is nothing that compares to experiencing Your kindness towards us. *Your love is my reward, my source, and my prize. You Yourself are the "One Thing" I have sought after (see Ps. 27:4).*

Running with Him into our Destiny

When the Lord shows us an assignment that He is commissioning us to do, we can approach it two ways. We can just buckle down and begin to do it, knowing our assignment and desiring to obey. This is not a bad approach, but the Lord has spoken to me quite a bit about *how* we run into our tasks.

A few years ago, I had composed some music that had a romantic sound, and I knew that the Lord wanted me to write lyrics from Song of Solomon to this lovely music. At the time, I barely understood or appreciated Song of Solomon, and began to labor to find the poetry and verses that would fit the music. (Little did I know of my in-depth future works, which would be drawn from this very book!) It was hard and frustrating work as I began to write lyrics.

The next day, I was having my early morning time of waiting on the Lord. My mind was distracted with the "task" awaiting me when I finished my time with the Lord. My mind was thinking, "When I'm finished my Coffee Talk with the Lord, I'll go downstairs and start working on those verses again." It was a daunting task awaiting me.

To my surprise, the Lord interrupted my thoughts and said, *"You can go down later and work on this alone, or I can just give it to you right now."* I was stunned.

I replied, "You mean while I'm waiting on You, I can just get my notebook, open my Bible, and You will help me arrange all the lyrics I need from this whole book?"

This was precisely what He meant, and He did exactly that. By the end of that Coffee Talk, the song was well underway, and easy to finish over the next couple days. For those readers who know my songs, that song became "My Garden," from my *Song of the Lamb* CD. We do not go off alone to do a job which the Lord assigned us. We must **run together** with Him, and run as a team. He is looking for a partner and friend, not an autonomous servant.

In my own life's journey, I was not able to receive my commissioning or destiny assignments until I had cultivated that "Draw Me Away" intimacy with the Lord. This period lasted about 3 years in my case. Each one's time frame will be individually tailored by the Lord. I could not have received the revelation or understanding of the destiny I am now fulfilling, apart from this intense period of bridal awakening.

The Lord, through intimacy, reveals our destinies to us, the very dreams of the Father's heart, and why we were put on this earth for such a time as this. Thus, when the commissioning comes, it is time to rise up from our honeymoon period.

> *The fig tree ripens its figs, and the vines are in blossom; they give forth fragrance. Arise, my love, my beautiful one, and come away* (SOS 2:13, ESV).

This, by the way, can be a very difficult and painful transition. Maybe some people are desperate to "be launched," to rise up and get out into the vineyards to do the Lord's work. At least in my own life, I did not want to leave the "Coffee Talks" behind, and begin the hard work of "raising His children," and preparing His Bride for His soon return. Nothing in me wanted to leave my family for weeks or months at a time, stand in long lines in airports, endure long flights in tiny seats, deal with jet lag around the globe, or to begin to pay a price for running with the Lord into the vineyards of ministry. I liked my rocking chair, my journal and my cup of coffee so very much. But when He draws you, you follow, and you learn to thank Him and not complain about the journey. It is a privilege to run with Yeshua, and I remind my soul of this quite often, when my body or my mind is struggling with hardship.

It is time for the Bride to awaken to Love, and to rise up to do the exact works the Father has ordained for us. We cannot just do whatever we want. The Lord has a precise set of assignments for us, and if we do not find out what they are, the outcome of His purposes will be irrevocably diminished.

For those dear parents who are raising their children, as I was for so many years, the natural question will arise: How can I run into the vineyards of the Lord, while I am taking care of young children or teens? The answer, as I'm sure you know, is that your precious family and your children are the vineyard where the Father has placed you. To nurture them from an early age is the greatest calling and privilege that any missionary could have. The babes in arms, the little ones, the youth, teens and young adults – these desperately need strong, holy and godly parenting. So for all you parents reading this, please do not for one moment think that you cannot "arise and come away," due to your family's needs. Put the Lord's holiness and love into all that you do with them and teach them, and you will be running with your Beloved in the highest calling of all.

It is also true that many parents are given other assignments by the Lord, which are possible to do, alongside raising the children. This includes a variety of assignments, but one is prayer, singing and intercession, which can be done while raising a family, as well as other opportunities to exhort and encourage others whom you come in contact with. When the Lord asked me to write my first book, He told me not to work more than 5-6 hours a day on the book, because it wasn't fair to my family. I wanted to work far more hours on the writing, but I obeyed the Lord, and it was better for all of us.

When Rick Joyner beheld the thrones of the overcoming saints in heaven, he said this:

"However, it seemed that faithful praying women and mothers occupied more thrones than any other single group."[2]

We will find our destiny through awakening to the strength of His love for us. Then we will run swiftly with His Son, and will accomplish dreams and destinies that we would have said were impossible. The smaller we are, the greater He can be in us. The weaker and more flawed we are, the more the Lord can put His glory and brilliance on display through us. The less likely a candidate for greatness we are, the greater His unfathomable strength to launch us into the impossible dream. (If you are anything like me, after reading those sentences, you are saying, "Oh goody! I qualify! I'm the weakest and smallest of all. I'm the least likely of anyone to be used for greatness. I'm the most broken vessel He could find.")

After He draws us to follow after Him, then we will be fully equipped to run with the vision. His dreams for us are much bigger than what we could have imagined, or even asked for. In fact, the Lord deliberately gives us dreams and assignments so big that we want to run away and hide from them, so great is our sense of inadequacy to fulfill them. And yet, somehow, our very lack of confidence to do it qualifies us to do it. We will depend on the Lord to supernaturally, against-all-odds, run together with us, and we will end up WINNING THE RACE!

Finally, brethren, pray for us, that the word of the Lord may run swiftly and be glorified, just as it is with you..." (2 Thess. 3:1).

This World has Left us Damaged

1:5-6 I am dark, but lovely, O daughters of Jerusalem, like the tents of Kedar, like the curtains of Solomon. Do not look upon me, because I am dark, because the sun has tanned me. My mother's sons were angry with me; they made me the keeper of the vineyards, but my own vineyard I have not kept.

This passage can be understood on two levels, as can much of this intricate Song. It is not merely speaking of our physical appearance. However, before we move on to the spiritual side of things, let's look at the physical issues for a moment.

Many people, both male and female, struggle with an underlying self-hatred about various aspects of their physical appearance, body type, or "imperfections." I know from a long history of personal experience, what it feels like to believe that no one, not even the Lord, could enjoy looking at me. I could only focus on my unforgivable flaws, as I perceived them. Some of the "flaws" were simple genetics, some could be my own fault, and some things that I viewed as flaws were just the way God deliberately made me (but He does not view flaws as our culture does).

Many can also relate to this idea: Some of my "flaws" were the result of not being cared for properly by those whose job it was to take care of me. They did their best, and they didn't understand the consequences I would deal with later, for uninformed decisions they made. Nevertheless, whatever the causes of my so-called "flaws," I needed a revelation of the way the Lord sees me, and through what kind of eyes He looks at me. It took me a ridiculous amount of decades to stop hating myself, to be honest.

In this case, the bride feels unattractive. She has been darkened by the sun, and damaged by the hardships of life, failures and broken relationships. Her mother's sons were angry at her, and forcibly put her to work in their vineyards. They are not called her "brothers," but "her mother's sons." This implies that they were step-brothers.

Later in the book, the bride refers to "the one who conceived me," and "the one who bore me," speaking of her birth mother. Whoever raised her did not protect "Shuli" (my nickname for the Shulamite maiden) from the abuses of her step-brothers. In the final chapter, in her hard-won maturity, she once again refers to her desire for a loving "sister-brother" relationship, and to the desired safety of "her mother's house." Both were apparently something she never had growing up, and she longs for the secure love that God created her to have.

All of us are broken in some way, by the conditions in this world. We long for someone who can know us deeply yet love us as a brother, a friend, a parent, even a lover of our soul. None of us can fully receive what our souls need from the people who surround our lives. Even in the best families, there will always be a hole in our soul for One who will unconditionally love and accept us with our flaws. Shuli represents each of us, and we can see ourselves in her early walk with the Lord and her insecurities. We all need a friend who sticks closer than a brother.

When the Bridegroom addresses His betrothed, He calls her *"My sister, My bride"* (SOS 4:9-10). For Him to address her this way is a wonderfully healing and respectful phrase. He loves her with a holy love, as a brother would watch over his sister with protective love and care.

I have a friend whose life story parallels Shuli's brokenness and family pattern in certain ways. His tenacious love for the Lord is all the greater in his maturity, due to the early loss of his mother, difficult family dynamics, and persecutions from both the church and the world. His brokenness drew him closer to his Beloved.

Where are the True Shepherds?

If indeed step-brothers, they would be more likely to take advantage of the little step-sister, than a full brother from both parents. She feels dark and ugly, possibly like a withered vine herself. The Israeli sun can really age or spot a person's skin, or cause undesired or exaggerated tanning, as this young bride complains about. She might see other girls who were pampered in the shade, and their complexions were of a fairer tone. This whiter skin was more prized by the Middle Eastern people, as we even observe this tendency to this day in eastern cultures.

Shuli (representing a large company of God's wounded warriors,) has been exploited by those who should have cared for her. It could have been that she was physically, sexually or spiritually abused by those in the religious structure of her community, who used her for their own goals. There are Christians in leadership who abuse believers under them. They work them hard, but for the purposes of building up their own ministry, and not caring for the souls (personal growth and spiritual health) of those who labor under them. If the person complains about their treatment or working conditions, they receive some form of rebuke, as if they should be grateful for the privilege of working for these elevated leaders.

My own vineyard I have not kept.

At times, the Lord's people feel that they have worked hard for others, yet have been unappreciated, or that their spiritual wellbeing was not taken into account. Also, they have not had the motivation or the time to make their hearts and lives (their own vineyard) a beautiful offering for the Lord to enjoy. It takes time and effort to cultivate the "garden of our own heart," which represents our own intimate and private devotional relationship with the Lord, apart from our works of service. The garden of our heart requires effort to cultivate, and our own vine cannot be neglected for the needs of others.

Biblically, I realize that the Lord asks us to be humble, and not to complain when people use us, or do not appreciate our efforts, as He will surely reward us later. It is true humility not to seek appreciation and recognition. However, just because we are not allowed to demand or expect that appreciation, doesn't mean that the ones we serve should not lovingly express honor and appreciation. I am not at all saying that we should be bitter, unforgiving or rebellious when we are mistreated by leaders of various sorts. However, the Lord has shown great displeasure with human "spiritual shepherds" who abuse the tender flocks under their care. He will not deal lightly with those who lord it over the willing workers, or who exercise guilt, coercion, or belittling to keep these servants "in line." While we need to forgive the abusers, the Lord may either remove the abusive shepherd, or move the abused sheep into another flock for safety and restoration.

Shepherds should love their flocks. They must not use them for their own egos and aggrandizement, until the sheep are just a shadow of who they were created to be, like numb and empty shells.

This is the biblical reality of the Lord's heart towards spiritual abuse (see Eze. 34, Jer. 23:1-4, Mk. 6:34, Jn. 10, Zech. 11:17).

Dark, Yet Lovely

I am dark, but lovely, O daughters of Jerusalem, like the tents of Kedar, like the curtains of Solomon.

Moving to the spiritual issue of "darkness of heart," the bride is expressing that even though her heart is dark (stained with sin, failures, or shame,) the Shepherd-King still finds her beautiful. This testimony of "dark, yet lovely," is a strong theological theme of the Song. Our hearts are still darkened by sinful thoughts, and are not the fully purified hearts that our Beloved desires and deserves. Yet in His gracious and generous love, He already finds us beautiful, and He does not criticize us, nor stare at our faults.

I am always amazed at the Lord's gracious personality. I stare at my faults with great unworthiness. But His eyes do not stare, or even pay attention to the things that upset me so much. The Lord sees the beautiful person in my spirit, the one His own hands formed in the womb. His eyes see "the real us," as we were designed to be. He sees our very near future together, when we will soon be running together over the mountains of adversity and tribulation. Soon, we will be adorned in the robes of a royal and priestly Bride. **This gift of His gracious acceptance of us, allows us to receive the Lord's strong love, despite our discomfort with our own imperfections.**

You desire me, Lord, even in my failures, weakness, brokenness and shame. You still see me through Your eyes of love and appreciation, and find my devotion to You lovely, despite the darkness in my heart and neglect of my own vine.

To those immature believers, (referred to as the "Daughters of Jerusalem" throughout the Song,) who might be looking at the lovesick bride through critical eyes, she says, *"Don't stare at how dark I am… don't focus on my flaws…I am trying to find the One I love, and when I find Him, I will be so lovely in His eyes, that no other opinion will matter to me."*

The Fields of the Kinsman Redeemer

1:7 Tell me, you whom I love, where you graze your flock, where you rest your sheep at midday. Why should I be like a veiled woman beside the flocks of your friends? (NIV)

The Lord's children are asking where they can find His grazing place, His resting place. Where does this Good Shepherd give rest and food to His weary and thirsty flock?

"I need to sit at Your table. I desire to glean in Your fields, to work alongside You. I desire to take my noonday rest with You, and to eat grain at Your table. Why should I have to veil my face from unfamiliar field hands who are strangers to me, or to work alongside those who neither know me, nor care about my welfare? I only feel safe and cared for if I can work alongside of You, and rest with Your loving and trustworthy under-shepherds. You know what is best for me. You will lead me to the safe fields, among kindred spirits."

This is so reminiscent of the story of Ruth. The Shulamite was a betrothed Israelite maiden, and Ruth was a widowed Moabite, who lived four generations before the Shulamite, but their stories are not so different, after all. Both were vulnerable women, needing to be provided for, loved, and protected in a world of untrustworthy field hands and herdsmen. Ruth might have ended up gleaning grain in a number of potential fields, managed by strangers of questionable integrity. As a poor foreigner and a young widow without protection, she would be easy prey for dishonorable field hands or corrupt foremen, who would not be afraid to take advantage of her. As

Naomi warned her, "Be careful, so that no one harms you or takes advantage of you in a stranger's field."

Naomi was overjoyed when she learned that the field where Ruth was gleaning belonged to a righteous close relative from Naomi's husband's own family lineage. In fact, according to the Law of Moses, this "brother" figure was also a kinsman redeemer, and thus, a future husband. Naomi expressed great relief that Ruth would not have to be among strangers who did not care for her welfare. Ruth was not yet engaged, but in God's eyes, the engagement party was just about to begin. The Lord led her to find the fields of Boaz, so that she could work alongside his companions, eat at his table, and to "rest in the shade" of her late husband's relative, her kinsman redeemer. Boaz spoke these words to Ruth, just as Messiah speaks these words to His last days' Bride: *"May your full reward be from the Lord, under whose wings you have taken refuge."*

In the same way, the Lord has ordained certain places of work and rest for each of His own. He has chosen the places and people from whom we will get our spiritual nourishment and be edified. There are people and ministries, through which the Lord has chosen to give us choice food for our hearts and spirits. I thank Him for these Kingdom-minded ministries, where I can participate in worship and intercession, or hear the Word of God taught with living truth. This kind of teaching satisfies me like a spring, bubbling up from inside my own heart. Through these feeding places, and through our own private time sitting at the Lord's feet, He meets us in the Paradise of our own heart – our own garden.

The Lord knows which streams and people will truly feed our spirit. Our lives are not our own, but we belong to our Beloved. We aren't meant to go just anywhere with anyone. We can't do whatever we feel like, or even marry whoever we want. We need to be careful and discerning, in terms of the people we trust, and the activities we give ourselves to. Not every church or every activity they propose for us is for our good, whether of body, soul or spirit. Each of us must find where the Shepherd has chosen for us to feed and to rest from the heat of the battle. He knows what is best for us and what we truly need.

I delight to sit in his shade, and his fruit was sweet to my taste (SOS 2:3b, NIV).

Ruth found rest, acceptance, and food to refresh both herself (representing the Gentile Bride who loves the Jewish people) and Naomi (representing Israel's welfare). As God's purposes went to the next level of glory, Ruth ultimately found love, marriage, the full inheritance of Israel. She was granted a place of honor in the genealogy of King David and the greater King Yeshua.

He who dwells in the secret place of the Most High will find rest under the shade of the Almighty (Ps. 91:1, AP).

Boaz had blessed Ruth on the first day he saw her in his fields: *"May your full reward be from the Lord, under whose wings you have taken refuge."* Ruth never gleaned again. The fields and wealth of her Kinsman-Redeemer became her inheritance. The harvest was hers, the kingly and Messianic ancestry was hers, and she received her reward and her rest under the shade of the God of Israel.

The Betrothal Veil

Why should I be like one who veils herself beside the flocks of your companions? (ESV)

Some commentaries believe that this veil is referring to that of a prostitute, citing the account of Genesis 38:14-15. They would say that Shuli does not want to appear to be like a prostitute, looking for a certain shepherd among the flocks of his friends.

I think that there is another more valid possibility, concerning her comment about the veil. In ancient Israel, when a girl became engaged, she was required to place a veil over her face, at times when she might be in the presence of other men. The veiling indicated that outsiders were not to be drawn to her beauty, as it was reserved for one alone. We see in SOS 4:1-3 and 6:7, that the Shulamite is indeed wearing a veil, which possibly signifies her engaged status.

The Bridegroom says, *"How beautiful you are, my darling! Oh, how beautiful! Your eyes behind your veil are doves"* (4:1a, NIV).

In Genesis 24:62-66, we see Rebecca travelling a long way with her nurse, her maids and Eliezer, which comprised the bridal caravan. But when her eyes saw Isaac coming to meet her in the field, she got down from her camel and placed a veil over her face. The groom came out to meet her, and she was now legally engaged; she veiled herself, according to the engagement custom.

Before departing, Eliezer had asked Abraham a relevant question: "If the maiden is not willing to leave her parents to come to your country, should I take your son back to the bride's home for the wedding?"

In a normal situation, it would have been customary for the father of the groom and his son to travel a distance to the home of the bride's parents for a formal engagement dinner and ceremony. But because of his unique covenant with the Lord, Abraham could not return the way he had come, nor could he permit his son Isaac to travel to the bride's country, to be engaged and married there. This would have violated the covenant which the Lord had sworn to Abraham, and so he had made Eliezer swear that even if the chosen maiden was unwilling to come with him to the Land of Promise, he would still not take Abraham's son back to the country he had come from.

Abraham was a sojourner in the Land, and as he looked around at all the neighbors and daughters of the Canaanites, he realized that there was no "suitable helpmeet" for his son, Isaac. He felt compelled to find a bride for his son from among his own family, his own kind. This was because the Lord was forming a genealogy through whom His own Son, the Messiah would be born, and the Lord was zealous for the perfect bride to be obtained for Isaac, like unto him and from his own family line.

Likewise, our Father has chosen a Bride for His worthy Son, and He does not pick up just any thorn of the field for His Son. He searches for a Bride who will be voluntarily conformed into the likeness of His Son, and who will beautifully reflect His purity and spiritual DNA, by the power of the indwelling Holy Spirit.

Due to Abraham's covenant, it was not possible for Isaac and Rebecca to be engaged and later married in the bride's parents' house, as would have been customary. Therefore, in this "first Jewish wedding," Isaac and Rebecca became engaged, neither at her parents' house, nor at his father's house, but in the middle of the field, near to Isaac's dwelling. His father Abraham had arranged the engagement and his mother Sarah had passed away prior to the engagement. It is not reasonable that he would have instantly taken her into his tent that very night and consummated the union, apart from his father's presence, blessing, and covenantal marriage vows (something like the signing of the *K'tubah*).

The Bible says that Isaac took Rebecca into his mother Sarah's tent (the place where his mother bore him) and **he married her**. This implies that on the night of arrival, Isaac's servants would have refreshed the bridal company with food and would have prepared places for them to bathe and sleep, after a very long journey. Within a day or two, they would have travelled a short distance to Abraham's dwelling, where the engaged couple would be joined by a covenantal ceremony. This would have been officiated by the patriarch Abraham, whose son and sole legal heir of his wealth and God's promises would be legally joined to the bride who was taken from his own relatives. Then she became his wife, and he loved her, and he was comforted over the death of his mother.

The betrothal veil protected the Shulamite maiden from seduction, to the degree that she cooperated with the wearing of this veil of protection. The Shulamite maiden in the Song does not want to go from tent to tent, veiled as one among unfamiliar sheep herders, who might entice her to compromise her vows and her purity before the wedding day. She wants to derive her nourishment and find her resting place near the safety and protection of her beloved, her betrothed. He would guard her integrity, and would nourish and cherish her until the wedding day. *For no one ever hated his own flesh, but nourishes and cherishes it, just as the Lord cares for His church"* (Eph. 5:29).

> *1:8 If you do not know, O fairest among women, follow in the footsteps of the flock, and feed your little goats beside the shepherds' tents.*

The Shulamite is aware that her labors "under the sun," (a phrase Solomon also used in Ecclesiastes to describe the activities of this world,) have left her with dark areas of her heart. Hurting people tend to look for leadership, someone to help them navigate their spiritual journey. Here, the Lord counsels us to observe where the flock is finding nourishment, and seek the true shepherds.

When vulnerable, it is important not to find spiritual food, security, or counsel among unsanctified sources of leadership, doctrine or comfort. It is good that we are "veiled" from the prying and seducing eyes of this world. Still, we long for transparency, and for a place to feel safe with trustworthy human shepherds (spiritual leadership). Not all leaders will wisely or selflessly oversee our fragile souls.

There are worthy shepherds, tireless and generous tenders of their flocks; may the Lord help us to find them. These true shepherds are a gift to us from our Beloved. We may try some unfruitful paths for a while, but His Spirit will lead us to the true shepherds' tents, those who follow the Good Shepherd.

Running With Horses

> *1:9-10 I compare you, my love, to a mare among Pharaoh's chariots. Your cheeks are lovely with ornaments, your neck with strings of jewels* (ESV).

To the kings of the Ancient Near East, horses were a symbol of wealth, majesty, beauty and military strength (see Ps. 20:7, Rev. 19:11-14, Joel 2:4-5, Job 39:19, Jer. 12:5). Pharaoh's horses were prized in King Solomon's period, and he had acquired a vast stable of the finest horses in the known world, bred for beauty, speed and valor in battle. To compare his earthly bride to one of these is a great statement of her worth, in the context of his culture. Moreover, to compare Israel or the last days' Bride of Messiah to one of these magnificent horses is a picture of the people of God, viewed as majestic and terrible, swift and beautiful.

In Revelation 19, not only does our Judge and King ride into Jerusalem on a white horse of great size, beauty and strength, but

His armies of resurrected saints who follow are also riding on these white, bridal war-horses, terrible as an army with banners. We will later see this image of the warrior-bride used in a number of descriptive passages of the Song.

The adornment of our cheeks, earrings and neck with jewels and gold speak of the Lord's adornment of His Bride with spiritual power, equipping gifts and anointings. They are compared to treasures and precious gems, adorning a bride. These will allow us to overcome and be victorious in the last days' battles and temptations. We will face the hardest trials in the final battle for men's allegiance, and we must be ready to "compete with horses."

> *If you have run with the footmen, and they have wearied you, then how can you contend with horses?* (Jer. 12:5).

Chapter 3

THE AROMA OF LOVE (SOS 1:9-17)

1:12 While the king is at his table, my spikenard sends forth its fragrance. A bundle of myrrh is my beloved to me that lies all night between my breasts. My beloved is to me a cluster of henna blooms in the vineyards of Ein Gedi. Behold, you are fair, my love! Behold, you are fair! You have dove's eyes.

In the royal cultures of the Ancient Near East, the use of costly spices, oils and perfumes were an important part of the beautification process for women, and especially, those who were to be in the King's Presence.

In the Israelite culture, there were different purposes for these scents, spices and oils. The broader purpose for perfumes and powders was the cosmetic and fragrance needs of women and of men as well. There were many available plants, oils, resins and exotic spices, which were used for perfuming and cosmetics. Even in modern times, male colognes are becoming as popular as those promoted for women.

However, in the context of the Israelite worship system, which was mandated by the Lord, we find two exact perfume recipes given to Moses in Exodus 30:22-38; these were for priestly acts of worship and consecration only. These two priestly recipes were given for the consecrating and anointing oil of the priests, and for the finely ground fragrant incense that was placed before the altar of the Lord and also burned by the priest before the curtain of the Holy of Holies. It was forbidden for any Israelite to use these recipes for common use. We will study them in more detail in chapter 7.

The Aroma of Brokenness

For now, let us examine the three fragrances mentioned in this passage. Spikenard was an exotic and costly perfume, which may have been part of the Tabernacle incense recipe (some rabbis and scholars believe that Spikenard was one of the unidentified "sweet spices" listed in the recipe.) This fragrance was greatly valued in ancient Israel. It is also called "Nard." This aromatic oil is extracted from the roots of a perennial herb that grows in India.[3] It is found growing "in the cleft of the rock crevices" of the Himalayan Mountains.

Nard was one of the most expensive perfumes in the time of Yeshua, and a pound was said to cost a year's wages. This fragrance comes from the roots, which speaks of the deepest place of our heart; thus, it was associated with acts of love and devotion.[4] The aroma from the roots lingered long after other scents had faded.

Here, the Bride begins to speak of her own fragrance, which is released into the atmosphere by the love she expresses for her Beloved. The aroma of her spikenard fills the banqueting hall, and all the guests recognize both her privileged position at the table and the intensity and costliness of her love for Him. Heaven can recognize a true bride of Yeshua on the earth, by the spiritual fragrance we emit.

Most of the ingredients found in both the sacred anointing oil and the incense are some form of plant resin, gum, sap, or distilled product which exudes or "drips" from the **heartwood** of trees or shrubs. Others are extracted or ground from reeds, bark, flowers, or roots.

The idea is that the Lord is looking for a particular fragrance which is released from our deepest "heartwood" when we have been pierced to the heart, or gashed open, like the plant which contains these aromatic gums. In other cases, it is the "stripped" bark of an aromatic spice tree or shrub, again signifying the stripping of our "self," which produces a sweet fragrance and acceptable offering to the Lord.

Once I was in Alabama, attending a conference where I didn't know anyone. I felt a bit shy, so I kept to myself the whole time. There was a man attending who asked if he could have a word with me during one of the breaks. He was hesitant to share what he had seen, since he didn't know me, and felt it might be presumptuous to say such a thing. But he felt the Lord wanted him to share with me. So I gave him permission to speak freely. He said that as he watched me walking across the lobby, he had a vision of my physical heart inside of me. He said it was gashed and torn in many places, and it looked badly wounded, scarred and it was painful to behold these injuries. But then he saw that shafts of light were coming out from all the gashed and torn areas. Each broken place of my heart was sending out light to others, like a lighthouse, and that others were drawn to this light and were comforted by it. This is my closest memory of what he shared.

In those days, I knew little of Song of Solomon, and I had never heard of the piercing and gashing of the "heartwood" of trees to extract the most precious and aromatic oils and perfumes. I now realize that some of the most costly fragrances that our lives emit come from the painful tearing of the heart, which we have experienced. We didn't ask for these wounds, and we would have avoided them if it were possible. But the fact is that the Lord allowed them, though it caused Him terrible pain to see our hearts torn and shattered like this. But He knew that He would be the Master Perfumer, and would bring forth a sweet aroma that only suffering can produce, and that it would bring comfort, love and acceptance to so many broken ones.

I have seen this principle in operation, over and over. The very areas where I've been hurt the deepest have been the areas where the Lord has given me strong and comforting authority to bring others out of similar wounds or offenses.

So many hearts are broken by verbal, physical or sexual abuse in their youth. The damage to their young lives and souls is incalculable, and the Father's heart is broken with them, as these cruel and evil deeds are done. But His heart is redemption, healing and overcoming victory. To those who will run to Him in their brokenness, He is a faithful Father, and He will bring good, even out of these evil and horrific acts, which He never dreamed or intended for our lives.

The Lord God is not the author of these grievous evil acts, but He will bring us out of it with His goodness, if we will open up our pain to Him. Thus, our precious and costly aroma of suffering will be a balm to others who are suffering. Our love and compassion will heal many, if we will bring these torn hearts to the Healer. He is faithful.

Nevertheless, the Lord desires us to pray regularly for the victims of abuse and human trafficking, that the Lord will break in and rescue them and expose the perpetrators. He hates this evil, and wants us to partner with Him, so that it will be broken open, exposed, closed down and eradicated from the nations.

This scene in SOS 1:12 is a prophetic picture of the Lord's intimate covenant relationship with His people throughout history, and of the ministry of the Lord Yeshua. His fragrance of sacrifice filled the Throne room, as His Father breathed in the offering of His perfect Son. Such is the fragrance that Heaven smells in the presence of intense devotion, brokenness and sacrificial commitment that the Bride and Bridegroom express for one another. *"My fingers dripped with liquid myrrh."* (SOS 5:5)

This banquet symbolizes several threads of God's redemptive plans in history: the giving of the Torah at Mt. Sinai; the Passover "last supper," and the Lord's sacrificial death; the costly perfume of each believer's devotion; the perpetual "Harp and Bowl" incense of prayer and worship; and the Wedding Feast of the Lamb.

> *Let the incense and the fragrance arise!* (see Mal. 1:11, Rev. 5:8, 8:3-5).

We will now examine these patterns and their prophetic fulfillments, past, present and future.

The King was at His Table

And Mary took about a pint of pure nard, an expensive perfume; she poured it on Jesus' feet and wiped His feet with her hair. And the house was filled with the fragrance of the perfume (Jn. 12:3, NIV).

The righteous, humble King is seated at His table, a dinner in His honor. Those who are privileged to dine with Him are overflowing with love for Him, and want to find a way to express how they feel about Him. But one heart overflows with costly love. The fragrance of Miriam's (Mary's) valuable nard is a symbol of extravagant love, wasteful devotion, as the greater King Solomon is honored and anointed with perfume by a Daughter of Jerusalem. This is one significant fulfillment of SOS 1:12.

This dinner took place in Bethany, six days before the Lord's death, at the house of Lazarus, Mary and Martha. The perfume was poured upon His feet, feet that were about to be twisted, pierced and impaled to the wood in a manner designed by Rome to cause the victim the maximum pain. Miriam (Mary of Bethany) is pouring out thankfulness and adoration upon Yeshua, in the language of what was valuable in her culture. He was about to be broken open, bruised, striped with lashes and pierced. All of His costly fragrance was about to be poured out for everyone in that room. His very life was about to be poured out, even for every soul who ever lived on this earth.

Perhaps this jar of perfume had been left to her by her parents as her inheritance, and it would be needed for her future. It may have been her most valuable possession. In one fleeting moment, the whole jar was poured out. It was spent on feet that would be in the grave within one week. By biblical reckoning, it was worth about 300 denarii, which Judas complained was a year's wages. So in modern western terms, this jar might have been worth between 40,000 and 70,000 US dollars.

Four days later, the Lord Yeshua was at another dinner, at the home of Simon the Leper, whom we must assume the Lord had healed of his leprosy, or he probably wouldn't be hosting a dinner for the Teacher and many other guests, in a contagious and unclean condition. An unidentified woman entered the room during the meal, with an alabaster jar of nard. She broke the jar and poured it onto the Lord's head.

From this we see that the Father desired for His Son's head and His feet to be anointed before His death. His Spirit impelled two different women to perform these very similar acts of adoration, so that these two witnesses testified that the Son was anointed with nard for His burial. This anointing took place only two days before His death. There were again complaints from some at the dinner about the wasted money, just as Judas had complained about the waste of money at Lazarus' house. But the Lord considered it a precious anointing to prepare His body for burial, which was fitting and honorable. He even gave the "unknown" woman a lasting memorial among the heavenly and earthly records of those who loved and honored Him (Mk 14:3-9).

In an earlier time, before He set out for Jerusalem for the last time, the Lord was anointed for the first time by a different woman, only identified as a sinful woman, who came into a dinner held in the region of Galilee (see Luke 7:36). She anointed Him as would a sinner, worshiping her Savior, as the Spirit caused her to understand the gift of forgiveness which He had come to offer. And so, it pleased the Father that out of the testimony of two or three witnesses, His Son would be anointed with costly perfume, as a King and as a Priest.

Some people think that the incident in Mark 14 was the same incident as that in John 12. However, they were on two different nights, and took place in two different homes, and had other differences as well. If we read the gospel accounts carefully, we see that the unnamed woman in Mark 14 was not Mary of Bethany, and her anointing was given only "two days before Passover."

In contrast, Mary had anointed the Lord in her own home, "six days before Passover." The earlier Galilean woman in Luke 7 is still a third and different woman, but all three were led by the Spirit of God to honor the Son in this way. For serious Bible students, the account of the anointing in Matthew 26 is the identical event as that of Mark 14. So there were three separate anointings, but four gospel accounts, as Matthew and Mark shared the same story.

The Heavenly Feast of Mt. Sinai

A "past rehearsal" of SOS 1:12 is found in the heavenly banquet that the God of Heaven gave for 74 Israelite leaders on Mount Sinai.

> *Then Moses went up, also Aaron, Nadab, and Abihu, and seventy of the elders of Israel, and they saw the God of Israel. And there was under His feet as it were a paved work of sapphire stone, and it was like the very heavens in its clarity. But on the nobles of the children of Israel He did not lay His hand. **So they saw God, and they ate and drank.*** (Ex. 24:9-11).

This is a unique Throne-room visitation, set in the context of the giving of the Torah at Mt. Sinai. They went up as a group! Those Israeli tour packages started 3,500 years ago! Obviously, for those readers who have bravely climbed or ridden a camel up Mt. Sinai, you will agree that when you reach the top, you find no crystal clear sapphire pavement, nor will you find an array of banqueting tables laid with the choicest foods and wines. Yet this is exactly what the Lord God granted to be experienced by the priests and elders of Israel when they ascended to the top of the mountain. Seventy-four Israelites were shown the Throne of the Lord and dined with Him!

Ezekiel's heavenly vision describes an expanse, sparkling like ice, and a throne of sapphire (Eze. 1:22-26). John describes a vast sea of crystal before the throne of the Lord (Rev. 4:6). Isaiah saw the Throne and the One seated upon it (Isa. 6:1-8). Micaiah, Daniel and Zechariah also experienced Throne room visions/experiences (1 Kings 22:19, Dan. 7:13-14, Zech. 3:1-7). The Apostle Paul was also taken to heaven, but for reasons of the Lord's choosing, he was not allowed to write out the visions, as these many others were permitted to do (2 Cor. 12:2-4). Why do some people have such a hard time believing that modern believers can also be taken to Heaven and experience these same types of awesome things? The Lord has never changed, and these witnesses who have gone before us had a nature just like ours, and by His grace, **they were permitted to testify of these heavenly encounters, so that we would believe** (see James 5:17-18, 2 Pet. 1:18, 1 John 1:1-3, John 19:35).

Although Israel would not prove faithful in the long run, in that heavenly moment, the King of Israel was seated at His banqueting table, and the fragrance of Israel's youthful devotion was a satisfying aroma to the Lord (Jer. 2:1-3). I believe that this was an early rehearsal of the Wedding Supper of the Lamb. It was a prophetic pattern set quite early in Israel's history, so that we would recognize its successive fulfillments as the Lord's redemptive plans would unfold.

The Betrothal ("The Last") Supper

> *I have eagerly desired to eat this Passover with you before I suffer. For I tell you, I will not eat it again **until it finds fulfillment** in the kingdom of God. After taking the cup, he gave thanks and said, "Take this and divide it among you. For I tell you I will not drink again from the fruit of the vine **until the kingdom of God comes**." (Luke 22:15-18, NIV).*

The Passover had come, and the King was seated at His table. The fragrance of His commitment filled the upper room. The Israeli disciples were enacting a betrothal to the Bridegroom King of Israel, though they could not fully grasp this reality at that moment.

Ancient Israel's betrothal customs included a formal dinner and ceremony at the bride's parents' house. This meeting was a legal procedure, sealing the betrothal. It contained four ceremonial cups of wine, which symbolized the stages of commitment. The fourth cup would only be drunk later, at the time of the wedding and the consummation of all things.

Part of this meal included the signing of a formal covenant, called a *"K'tubah,"* which took place after the meal, when the third cup was raised. The *K'tubah* was a written pledge from the Bridegroom, stating: *"Everything I own is yours, My Bride."* It was the "cup of inheritance." The bride was required to keep this document with her at all times, as it was the future guarantee of the covenant and the legality of their union.

Yeshua's final Passover supper took on a new meaning, beyond the Exodus from Egypt. Since that night, 2,000 years ago, Passover will never be the same. It is still the eternal Feast of the Lord, but we are no longer rehearsing only the past deliverance from the Israelite's slavery in Egypt. We are celebrating our release from the cruel bondage of our sin nature. We are pouring out our costly perfume, as we remember what the Lamb has done for our lives and our future glory at His wedding table.

Passover is the bridal covenant with the Bridegroom Himself, who pledged His commitment to His betrothed by signing the *K'tubah* in His own blood. We are rehearsing for the future banquet, when He will eat the Passover and drink the fruit of the vine with His Bride in the Kingdom of His Father. And like a true Jewish Bridegroom, He will smash the fragile glass under His foot, to signify that it is our cup and ours alone. No one will ever drink from it again. What our Heavenly Father has put together let NO ONE PUT ASUNDER. No one can ever pluck us out of His hands, and His commitment is legally binding, and so we can rest secure and safe in the legality of this betrothal. Can He trust in our commitment as we trust in His?

The "Last Supper" will become the "First Supper." We will drink the cup together, at the unimaginably joyful Wedding Supper of the Lamb. Amen.

A Banquet for All Nations

On this mountain the Lord Almighty will prepare a feast of rich food for all peoples, a banquet of aged wine; the best of meats and the finest of wines. On this mountain he will destroy the shroud that enfolds all peoples, the sheet that covers all nations; He will swallow up death forever. The Sovereign Lord will wipe away the tears from all faces; He will remove his people's disgrace from all the earth. The Lord has spoken (Isa. 25:6-8, NIV).

This feast will break off the fog, the darkness and deception that has blinded the nations. Death itself will be destroyed by the power of this Bridal Feast. As the King is finally seated with His faithful bridal company, He is now able to drink the cup anew in the Kingdom of His Father, with His "*Ezer*-Bride" (a suitable helper and military assistant)[5]. His satisfaction will be complete, as the day He has longed for becomes reality. His fragrance will fill the mountain, and our love will be as cloud of incense across the vast Millennial wedding garden.

A river will flow from His throne, cascading down through the center of our garden, and a shimmering rainbow will overarch the Bridegroom in His seat of preeminence. We will dance, dine and worship under the exquisite, bejeweled *chuppah*, the bridal canopy that stretches over our garden wedding feast for miles under Jerusalem's peaceful skies. His banner over us is love.

The Lord has prepared a table before us in the presence of our enemies. We are seated in places that were assigned to us before the foundations of the world. Our names are engraved on special "cards," personally chosen for our assigned place among the Lord's tables. The Lord has found rest, as He finally has His family around His table, like olive shoots that have borne fruit.

And now, what adoring perfumes will mingle as one, and fill that banqueting hall? What will the Son of David breathe in, as all nations, tribes, tongues and peoples pour out their combined jars of costly nard upon His head, running down His beard, and spilling over the robes of His glowing wedding garments? Will He weep tears of joy? Will He lock eyes on each and every one of us? He will be our God and we will be His people, ruling and reigning with Him over the renewed and restored earth. And every tear will be wiped away.

Bitter and Sweet Myrrh

> *1:13 A bundle of myrrh is my beloved to me, that lies all night between my breasts. My beloved is to me a cluster of henna blooms in the vineyards of Ein Gedi.*

Behold, you are fair, my love! Behold, you are fair! You have dove's eyes.

In Song of Songs, we find myrrh spoken of in seven places (1:13; 3:6; 4:6, 14; 5:1, 5, 13). We see the scent of myrrh on both the bride and bridegroom in the Song.

In the book of Esther, we see that before she could qualify to go before the King, she had to undergo six months of applying oil of myrrh to her body, and another six months of other perfumes and cosmetics.

Myrrh is an aromatic gum resin, which exudes from the inner wood of the balsam or myrrh tree, grown in India, Arabia, and Ethiopia.[6] It was very costly, and we see it many times in the Bible, both in the realm of commercial perfumes, as well as in the holy oil used to anoint the priests and to consecrate items in the Tabernacle. Additionally, in the holy incense recipe, the "gum resin" mentioned is thought by many to be liquid myrrh.

Myrrh was used in the treatment of dead bodies before burial, as we see in John 19:39-40. The Hebrew word for myrrh is *"mor,"* which comes from the root word for "bitter," and myrrh indeed is bitter to the taste, but sweet to the smell. We remember in the book of Ruth, when Naomi has been dealt many terrible blows, she laments, *"Do not call me, 'Naomi,' meaning 'pleasant,' but call me 'Mara,' meaning 'bitter.'"*

Myrrh is also mentioned in joyful biblical occasions, such as the marriage of the King in Psalm 45 and in the wedding procession in SOS 3:6. The King's garments are scented with myrrh in Psalm 45:8, which speaks of the Lord Yeshua, who is the King of kings and also the Highest Priest of Heaven. Myrrh is the primary ingredient of the priestly anointing oil. On His wedding day, He will be King and a Priest forever, according to the order of Melchizedek (see Ps. 110:4). Thus, we find the priestly myrrh on His garments.

But myrrh is primarily connected to sacrifice and suffering. It is interesting to note that both at the Lord Yeshua's birth and at His death, myrrh was given to Him.[7] The wise men from the east brought myrrh to Yeshua soon after His birth, as a prophetic symbol of His future sacrifice and sorrow (Mt. 2:11). And moments before He was crucified, He was offered wine mixed with myrrh, which is very bitter (Mk.15:23). Because of the cost of myrrh, it is impossible to picture the Roman army giving it to a convicted Jew, about to be executed, whose pain they wish to intensify, not to diminish. Therefore, it was certainly the loving daughters of Jerusalem, or those from among His closest disciples and relations, who would have prepared this mixture for Him, to possibly alleviate some of His pain (see Luke 23:27-28).

Nevertheless, He did not accept this bitter drink. One possible reason for His refusal was that wine had been mixed with the myrrh. A high priest was not permitted to drink wine or fermented drink when about to enter the Tent of Meeting or bring offerings. Since the Lord Yeshua was about to offer His own blood before the Altar in Heaven as a higher priest than Aaron, He could not defile Himself by drinking the wine offered to Him just before His crucifixion (see Lev. 10:8-9).

However, at that moment, even His disciples and relatives did not realize that He was being offered as a sacrificial lamb, but was also serving as the High Priest Himself, so they would not have thought about the issue of drinking wine at such a horrific moment.

Tears on the Tree

The time consuming process of producing myrrh is as follows: A skilled gardener cuts deep into the wood of the myrrh tree, and causes the resin to ooze out to the surface. He waits about two weeks until it hardens into a bitter, reddish drop. These hardened forms are called "tears." Then he takes a special tool, and slices off the tears from the tree. These tears can be treated and mixed with olive oil or distillates, to create "liquid myrrh," or "oil of myrrh."[8]

As the Lord Yeshua wrestled with the Father's will in the Garden of *Gethsemane* (in Hebrew, *"Gat Shemen,"* meaning "the olive press"), great drops of sweat, mixed with blood came out of His forehead. Some medical experts say that the pressure and agony of His soul caused the capillaries in his head to burst and be released as "tears" of blood oozing through His pores. He was like the myrrh trees, exuding great and bitter drops of pain, under the deep gashing they endured in the garden. These drops of blood were the first of seven losses of blood our Lord would suffer, before the remaining six wounds would be inflicted to draw out His blood (the beatings, the scourging, the crown of thorns, His hands, His feet, and His opened side.)

The sins and filth of all the 12 billion souls who have ever lived, including this last generation (about 6 billion currently,) were being laid upon this innocent Man. Their weight crushed Him in the fury of God's winepress of judgment. Isaiah tells us that the weight of sin is so heavy, that even the earth reels and staggers like a drunkard under the weight of its sin (Isa. 24:20). How much more would Just One Man stagger under such an unbearable load? (See Isa. 53:6, Mt. 20:28, Heb. 9:26-28).

Romans 8:17 also tells us that we will inherit all that belongs to Yeshua the Messiah, if we will also share in the fellowship of His sufferings. The Lord told disciples James and John that they would indeed drink from His cup of bitterness, the cup of suffering. This cup was the myrrh that gave off the most beautiful fragrance of a life laid down voluntarily, to save many lives for all eternity. We must also taste the bitterness, as well as the sweetness of Yeshua's submission. It is painful to die to our own will and rights, but the fragrance of our yieldedness is breathed in by the Father with satisfaction. The aroma of a yielded heart means more to Him than the smoke rising up from all the burnt offerings of Lebanon.

Hebrews tells us that the Lord "learned obedience through what He suffered" (Heb. 5:8). We must learn obedience too, even when it is to our own hurt. It will not always feel good or comfortable to obey the Lord. It might be the hardest thing we ever had to do, and it will go against everything in our personal desires to obey. This is costly obedience, and it is MOST valuable to our Lord.

Single-Minded Devotion

1:13 A bundle of myrrh is my beloved to me, that lies all night between my breasts.

Just as Esther had to apply myrrh for six months before appearing before the king, it was common in the wealthier segments of society for women to wear a necklace with a sachet of perfumed powders against their chest at night, while they slept. The scent would remain with them throughout the next day. Perhaps King Solomon had actually given his betrothed this expensive gift of myrrh. But it is more likely that the betrothed bride is comparing her sweet memories of her Beloved with a sachet of myrrh, which is unforgettable. She thinks of Him through the night, and she holds Him in her heart like a perfumed necklace, ever giving off the fragrance of their shared love. *"She is asleep, but her heart is awake,"* (5:2) with the memories of who He is to her, and how she longs to be with Him.

My nights are difficult, and I am awake so often during the night. I think about the Lord during those long hours. I try to hold Him close to my heart. Still, He feels every loving thought that flies up to Him from our waking words, and even from our sleeping lips, murmuring our love without even our conscious knowledge. This is real love to Him, and He catches every word, every thought, every tear, and it is all recorded in Heaven. We may forget these "little" gestures, but He will remember your love more than wine, and you will see the happiness on your Master's Face on that day, for all those nights of myrrh.

The Lord Yeshua has given us an even more expensive gift than costly powders. He has given us His own life, His own blood, as the **bridal price** to secure our love and our future together. The bride price was a demonstration of the value which the prospective bridegroom places on the bride, and which he pays her parents, so that she will belong to him. The price that Yeshua paid reveals how high a Bride Price He was willing to pay for us. It demonstrates the value He places on having us with Him forever. Can you meditate on this staggering truth? We are valued that highly, that He would pay such a price. We must hold this close to our hearts, night and day, and remember His love more than wine, more than myrrh.

1:14 My beloved is to me a cluster of henna blooms in the vineyards of Ein Gedi.

Ein Gedi is a fertile oasis and nature reserve, located on the westerns slopes of the Dead Sea in Israel. It is one of only two fresh water springs in the region of the Dead Sea, and it is fed by an Artesian well. The aromatic white, pink or red henna flowers grow on a shrub, in clusters. In ancient cultures, henna was known for its healing properties of skin conditions, including leprosy and boils.[9] These blossoms are known for their desirable fragrance, and are used in the making of perfume, along with a long tradition of making red dyes from the leaves of the plant.

The Shulamite compares her Beloved to these sweet-smelling, intricate clusters of flowers, perhaps because the beauty and fertility of this oasis stands in stark contrast to the Salt Sea and the surrounding brown, dry and rocky slopes. Once again, His love is a treasure to her, in a dry and thirsty land.

The Hebrew word for henna is *"kopher,"* which is the same root word as, *"kapar." Kapar* means to cover or make atonement, from where we get the name, *"Yom Kippur,"* as the Day of Atonement. Therefore, henna speaks of redemption, and the red dye reminds us of Yeshua's precious blood.

> *1:15 Behold, you are fair, my love! Behold, you are fair!*
> *You have dove's eyes.*

The King speaks doubly of His love's beauty, noticing that she has "dove's eyes." This attribute is very important to the Lord, and His bride must cultivate this beauty and single-minded devotion. The Hebrew word for "beautiful" carries more than mere physical beauty, but speaks of an inward beauty that His eyes can perceive. This is not about comparing ourselves to the artificial standards of perfection found in this world's media and glamour industries. It is about the pure and gentle loveliness of a heart that is wholly devoted to Him. The dove is loyal, and mates only once in its lifetime. This speaks of the need for bridal loyalty to One alone. The dove's eye focuses on one object, and does not see through peripheral vision. Thus, she is not distracted, but is of singular focus.

Brother Wade E. Taylor explained it so beautifully:

"In the first chapter of the Song of Solomon, the Lord compliments His Bride, for He sees within her a quality, which He intensely desires to cultivate and use.

When a dove fixes its gaze upon its mate, it is not distracted by any activities around it. Therefore, it is often referred to as being a 'love bird.'

Our having this "dove's eye" indicates that we are becoming increasingly aware of the Lord's person and presence, and that we possess a spiritual awareness that will lift us above the pulls of the earthly. This 'single eye' will enable us to become sensitive to the Lord's presence, and obedient to His desire and purpose.

The Lord's favor rests upon those who have cultivated a "single eye" toward Him. These can be easily led by Him, for they are close enough to see which way His eye is looking.

> *'I will instruct you and teach you in the way you should go; I will guide you with My eye' (Ps. 32:8).*

A horse, on the other hand is distracted by side-vision. Therefore, it must have "blinders" placed beside each eye, and a 'bit' set within its mouth. Only then, can it be kept on the path.

Therefore, we are admonished:

> *'Do not be like the horse or like the mule, which have no understanding; which must be harnessed with bit and bridle, else they will not come near you' (Ps.32:9).*

Once we have developed this 'single eye' toward the Lord, we will no longer respond as a horse or mule – according to our desires. We will have become responsive to Him alone.

Now the Lord can further instruct us, in order to prepare us to be brought into His chambers, a special prepared place where we can share with Him in the outworking of His redemptive purposes."[10] [end excerpt from Brother Taylor].

Meditation

Give me dove's eyes for You, Lord. Let all my distractions fade in importance. I want to fix my gaze on You, whether I'm working, praying, emailing, or resting. I want to see what You see, and be responsive to Your every thought. Amen.

Chapter 4

FINDING OUR IDENTITY UNDER HIS ARMS (SOS 2:1-7)

We are a Unique Work of Art

2:1-3 I am the rose of Sharon, and the lily of the valleys. Like a lily among thorns, so is My love among the daughters. Like an apple tree among the trees of the woods, so is my Beloved among the sons. I sat down in His shade with great delight, and His fruit was sweet to my taste.

The early portions of the Song revealed the betrothed bride's expressions of:
- Her feelings about herself ("I am dark but lovely")
- Her upbringing ("My mother's sons were angry at me")
- Her desire to find her Beloved ("Where do you feed your sheep?")
- How much His affections mean to her ("Your love is better than wine.")

The early stages of the bride's development are sincere, but somewhat self-centered. She saw the relationship as her dearest possession, but had not walked out the deeper levels of partnership, commitment and sacrifice. It was mainly about what she derived from this love relationship, which is understandable, but it is not the whole picture of discipleship. We see our own development in the Lord, as the Song progresses, in an amazing parallel to our journeys into our Beloved's maturity.

We also saw the Lord's affirmations. He knows that her love is genuine, even though she is young in her feelings for Him. ("You are fair, my love! You have dove's eyes.")

But now we see a progression, where the betrothed is more secure in her position in His heart. She knows that her heart is a special treasure to Him, among all the cold and cynical hearts in this world. He responds that she is like a fragrant white lily in a field of thorn bushes.

When man fell, the earth was cursed with thistles and thorns. The Lord is looking for the beauty and innocence of creation restored in the lives of those who love Him. To walk as Adam and Eve walked before they tasted disobedience and hid from Him. How He loves the pure in heart! It is possible to cultivate or recapture this childlike purity, no matter how much this world has broken and corrupted us. His Spirit can restore what years of human therapy could never do! We really can walk in relative purity and cleanness.

I am the rose of Sharon, and the lily of the valleys.

According to botanical experts, the biblical flower which is commonly translated as the "rose of Sharon" is not actually a rose. In Hebrew it is a *"chavatzelet,"* a bulb of some sort. There are various views on which biblical flower was the one Solomon wrote about, when he compared the Bride to the "Rose of Sharon" (in English). Some believe it is a Tulip that grows in the Sharon coastal plain. Others believe it is a species of Hibiscus, a magnificent Asian flower, in white, pink or purple with a deep, blood-red center. Other candidates are the crocus, the rock rose, or the white water lily, growing in the sandy soil along the coast of Israel.

One day we will know which Israeli flower was compared to the Lord's bridal company. But we know that in His eyes, each of us is like a work of art, a sculpted flower, beautifying creation in the midst of many common plants, weeds and thistles. **We are His**

treasured one. If we can believe this, it will change our confidence and increase our desire to approach the Lord more often and more easily.

The lily of the valley is a lovingly cupped small white flower, which hangs down its perfectly crowned head, drooping over in clusters, from a tall, bent stem, framed by broad green leaves. They look like dozens of tiny, white wedding bells, or white wedding dresses, hung up for their wedding day. They are the most fragrant flowers, and their sweet aroma can be detected from a long distance away. They are magnificent, yet humble, as they bow so low, facing the ground, and they appear as a bridal company before the King. They are wildflowers, and yet each one is a work of art, without a doubt.

Beauty Among the Thorns

Consider the lilies of the field, how they grow: they neither toil nor spin; and yet I say to you that even Solomon in all his glory was not arrayed like one of these. Now if God so clothes the grass of the field, which today is, and tomorrow is thrown into the oven, will He not much more clothe you, O you of little faith? (Matt. 6:28-30).

The Lord was thinking of King Solomon, when He spoke these awesome words. He knew that Solomon had considered the lilies, and had also thought about the splendor of their adornment.

When individual believers (comprising the male and female Bride of Yeshua) say, *"I am the rose of Sharon, I am the lily of the valleys,"* we are stating that our primary identity is as Yeshua's handiwork, His skillful creation, His inheritance, His lovely one. We realize that we are the prize of all the ages that Yeshua longs for. We are the joy for which He was willing to die.

The Beloved responds and affirms this truth: *Like a lily among thorns is My love among the others.* He finds each of us as a lily among a hedge of thorns. He sees so many who purport to love Him, but he sees their motives and shallow love. He finds them unsafe for His trust, as if they were thorns, too painful to get close to. He delights in the simplicity of the heart who is wholly devoted to Him. We bow our head like a beloved bride, despite our struggles and low self-image.

The lilies of the valley are a picture of the purified bridal company, in a world of unsafe hearts. Without understanding our bridal identity to Yeshua, it is hard to grasp the bigger context of why we are here on this earth, and where this is all going. It's all about a Wedding Day, and our eternal governmental partnership with the Lamb.

We are the first fruits of the restored creation. The curse will be reversed, and the earth transformed to its pristine beauty upon His return. And likewise, the hearts of men are being transformed, even now.

Under the Shadow of His Tallit

> **2:3-5** *Like an apple tree among the trees of the woods, so is my Beloved among the sons. I sat down in His shade with great delight, and His fruit was sweet to my taste.*

The apple tree can grow so large, and spread out so far, as to provide a massive canopy of shade. It is covered with hundreds of apples, some very high indeed, and is such a picture of boundless generosity, rest and sweetness.

Out of all the trees in the woods, our Beloved is like an apple tree with His branches spread wide, and His fruit free for the asking. He has opened His arms of love so wide, even on the cross, and has produced sweet fruits for us to enjoy, out of the tree of His suffering. He offers refreshment, rest, security and transformation. This is where we rest in the heat of the battle, under His shade, and under His work on the cross, the tree of suffering.

> *2:4 He brought me into His house of wine, and His banner over me is Love (AP).*

In the original Hebrew, the words that are usually translated "banqueting hall" are *"beit yayin,"* meaning, "house of wine." Wine is a picture of a marriage celebration. It denotes joy, love and feasting.

Notice that it is the Lord who brings us into His house of wine; it is not a place we walk in, uninvited, just like we can't go into a wedding uninvited. When He brings us in, the first thing He does is to cover us with His banner of love. I have experienced this a number of times, in my times of waiting on the Lord.

We are so broken that we don't even feel worthy to enter His house of wine, nor to take our place at the King's table. We are not in the mood for feasting, and we are not joyful over our circumstances. This world has broken us, and we lack grace, peace and confidence to take our rightful place, dining beside our Beloved.

Perhaps this is why the Apostle Paul so often greets the Bride with, "Grace and Peace to you, in our Lord Yeshua." He realizes that we are burned out and worn down by our labors "under the sun." We need grace and peace to receive the banquet of truths, which Paul pours out in his love letters to the Bride, scattered across the globe and the generations. Although we are already "seated in heavenly places with our Messiah," we have a hard time perceiving this reality. But the King leads us in, takes us by the hand and places us at His table. In one beautiful worship song, Leeland sings:

> *"I was carried to the table*
> *Seated where I don't belong*
> *Carried to the table*
> *Swept away by His love*
> *And I don't see my brokenness anymore*
> *When I'm seated at the table of the Lord*
> *I'm carried to the table*
> *The table of the Lord."*[11]

I always feel that His "banner over me" is His prayer shawl, which the Lord wraps around me or spreads over me, as with the wing of His garment. Perhaps you remember in the Book of Ruth where she uncovers Boaz's feet, lies down next to him, and says,

"Spread the corner of your garment over me, for you are my kinsman redeemer" (see Ruth 3:9). Or the bleeding woman who knew that the corner of Yeshua's garment carried her healing.

> *And suddenly, a woman who had a flow of blood for twelve years came from behind and touched the **hem of His garment**. For she said to herself, "If only I may touch His garment, I shall be made well."* (Matt. 9:20-21).

In Hebrew, the word for "the hem of His garment," is *"canaf,"* which means corner or wing. If she could only touch the corner, the fringe, the wing of His covering, she would be healed of an incurable disease. There is healing in His wings! (see Mal. 4:2).

Before my life and ministry got "too busy," I used to literally do this with the Lord near the end of our "coffee talks," which I've written about in my other books. These intimate times included a *tallit*—a Jewish prayer shawl—which I would spread lengthwise on the side of the bed, representing the Lord's seat of honor. Opposite the bed was my rocking chair, where I sat and had my devotions. These sessions always ended with a resting period of time where I'd get up from the chair and come over to lay on my side under the Lord's tallit.

I would gently lift up the corner of the outspread tallit and lie down along the side of the bed and cover myself with the tallit. It gave me physical rest, and also allowed me to feel that I was under His banner of love and protection. He is my Kinsman Redeemer.

The Lord spreads His banner of covering and healing love over our lives, shielding and overshadowing us with His kindness. We are seated at His table, and are under His shade. He brings us into His house of wine, though we feel that we are not worthy to be seated there. It is all about His kindness and covering love.

> *He who dwells in the secret place of the Most High shall abide under the shadow of the Almighty* (Ps. 91:1).

Meditation

I came under Your arms of love, and was covered with Your Presence. Being with You early brings a sweetness to my day, and peace to my thoughts. You invite me to a spiritual place of feasting. It is like we are rehearsing for the Marriage Supper of the Lamb. Your Lordship over my life feels like protective love. Love is the motivation for all that You do in my life, even the very hard things. You work in my life to deepen my trust. You show me Your love, as an example of how I am to love You, and love others. You work all things together to increase my trust in You.

2:5 Sustain me with raisins, refresh me with apples, for I am lovesick.

Sometimes we feel desperate to find the Lord, to hear His voice, to feel a touch from Him. In my walk with the Lord, this can be a major difficulty, causing depression and frustration. I want to find Him, yet lack the patience to wait "long enough" for Him to come, if in case He was planning to come that day! At times, I lack motivation to wait and to keep trusting that His Presence will come. I want to give up and just go back to my emails, my work, my distractions, my physical comforts. I need Him to sustain me, as I am often falling apart. I am lovesick, but I am too weak to wait for Him at times.

Lord, please sustain and refresh me, because the waiting and hoping to find You can just be so hard and even frustrating at times. You do not come on my terms, or based on my demands, pleading or neediness. But in wisdom and kindness, You respond. Your answers will come, according to what is truly best for me. Help me to be patient and wait for Your timing, knowing that You will answer me. You will satisfy my desperate lovesickness for You.

Do Not Awaken Love

2:6 His left hand is under my head, and his right hand embraces me.

This unusual statement is found twice in the Song (2:6 and 8:3). Some have interpreted it in a physical (marital) way, but I truly believe this is a profound statement about the Lord's relationship with us. I never really understood it until I had an experience in my sleep, about four years ago. I've never met anyone else that this has happened to, but I testify that it happened to me.

I was sleeping during a certain night, fully asleep and unaware of anything happening around me or to me. Suddenly and abruptly, I was awakened by the sensation of a hand rapidly being withdrawn from under my head. I had been sleeping on my right side, facing the edge of the bed. I was awakened instantly as this hand whipped out from under my head. While asleep, I had not felt the hand under my head, for however many minutes or hours it had been there, but I very distinctly felt it being removed at high speed.

At that point, I was fully awake, and I noticed it was early morning. This verse from the Song immediately came into my mind. I began to ponder, as anyone would: Whose hand was that? Was it the Lord's hand? How long was it there? Was He there for hours? If He were kneeling by the left side of my bed, where I was facing the edge, it would make sense that it was His left hand that had been under my head, without my knowing it. Was His other arm wrapped around me as I slept?

I have never forgotten this incident, and I now believe that He was preparing me for the writing of this very book. **I believe He wanted me to know, experientially, that this is a picture of His unseen protection, tenderness and attentiveness to our every moment, waking or sleeping.** His left hand under our head represents all of His unseen deeds and thoughts of love and kindness that we are not aware of. His right hand embracing us represents all of the affection and protection, with which He holds us close to His heart, whether we know it or not.

We might never know how many unseen things the Lord has done to save us from death, accidents, diseases, or demonic onslaughts that satan was demanding permission to do to us. We should thank the Lord for His acts that we don't even know about, in which He lovingly protected us. He awakened me to His Presence at the moment of HIS choosing, not mine. I was sleeping and oblivious. He chose the moment to awaken me to His love. **Now look at the very next verse!**

> 2:7 *Daughters of Jerusalem, I solemnly charge you, by the gazelles and the does of the field: Do not arouse, disturb or awaken love until it so desires (AP).*

The Bride is sleeping, and we are unaware of the love that is being ministered to us. We are unaware of the Lord's smile of appreciation, His hand under our head, His tears of empathy, His desire to touch us. We might feel timid, like a vulnerable gazelle, if we knew the full measure of affection and passion that burns in His heart towards us. Sometimes the intensity of His intimacy makes us feel uncomfortable.

Several years ago, I had a dream that revealed that we are uncomfortable with the intensity of the adoration that the Lord feels for us. We pull back from His strong love. I recorded this dream in my book, "A Prophetic Calendar," and am inserting the excerpt of this dream here:

In this dream, I was sitting at a table in a restaurant, having lunch with someone. For the first part of this dream, I had no idea who I was dining with, because I never saw the person. I was turned to my right, observing a long line of people and activities passing by our table. I saw so many interesting people of all varieties, each one doing or saying fascinating things. Many, many people and activities passed by, and I was so captivated that I could not take my eyes off of them. Because of this, I was completely unaware of anyone else at the lunch table with me.

Suddenly, I heard a man's voice from the other side of our round table – pleading, urgent, calling me to attention: "He-y-y-y, we're having lunch here!" This caused me to turn to look at my companion, instantly feeling sheepish for having ignored him thoroughly for so long, without even realizing he was sitting there with me. I could feel his hurt that although we were on a lunch date, I was looking at everyone and everything but him.

For the first time, I looked at my companion. He was a gentle, middle-aged, balding man with sweet brown eyes, and he was looking at me with an expression I had never seen before. He was smiling at me with an expression of immense tenderness, joy, admiration, sweet affection, adoration, and a sense that he was consumed with the wonder of being with me. Since no one has ever looked at me that way, I felt a bit uncomfortable. I realized that his face was very close to mine, and his relentless, joyful gaze never left my eyes. I felt he had invaded my personal boundaries and I said, "Don't get so close."

The moment I spoke these words, he was instantly "transported" to a new location at the table, about two or three feet further away from me. However, his expression never flickered or altered. His face didn't reflect hurt or anger at my saying that he was too close, but without physically getting up, he was just suddenly in a new location, a bit further away. Still, he gazed at me with the same radiant smile of concentrated adoration.

Then I woke up and realized it was the Lord, even though he had been disguised as a normal person. If I had known it was the Lord while I was dreaming, I would not have told Him that He was too close to me; this is probably why the Lord disguised Himself, so that I would reveal my true heart on the matter. I am afraid of intimacy. [End excerpt here.]

This dream was very significant to my understanding of my difficulty with being loved. I have thought about it often, since it revealed that I was very awkward with that gaze of His. The Lord wanted to not only feed me lunch, but to cherish me and gaze at me with deep affection, but I felt very timid and I even felt like my personal boundaries were being violated. This taught me that He has guarded us, and even kept His respectful distance, as one would with a shy deer. He waits until we are ready for Him to awaken this ability to both give and receive intimate love. That is why He warns others not to disturb or arouse this love until He, who is Love Itself, so desires.

The Lord's left hand is under our head, and His right arm is pulled protectively around our shoulder, but we remain asleep, undisturbed, unaware, unawakened to all that is being poured into us from His heart of love. The very next verse advises, *"Look at the gentle and sensitive gazelles and deer in the field. The slightest movement will startle them. You can watch and admire them from afar. You can photograph them in great fascination. But do not startle them and make them aware of your presence until the right moment. You might frighten them away with your nearness."*

It takes sensitivity to allow each believer, at whatever season they might be in, to come to an awakening of the Lord's passion for them. This love cannot be stimulated artificially with guilt or pressure. They might be at the earliest stages of intimacy, and it cannot be disturbed, manipulated, pumped up or thrown off the path.

This is a matter of respecting the delicate times and seasons of every believer's journey. Only the Lord knows each one intimately, and what issues need to be dealt with before they can enter this bridal love. It takes healing and maturity, and He must cultivate our readiness in an individually-tailored plan for each of our lives.

Until that time, the "little ones" must be protected. If the wounded, immature or "sleeping" believer is confronted at the moment which was not of the Lord's timing, they will be frightened away like a skittish doe. Learning to eat out of His hand and depend on Him alone does not come naturally. There is healing and cleansing necessary for this level of vulnerability to be reached. This season will change and prepare us for our destiny assignments.

The daughters of Jerusalem represent believers who don't understand the ways of the Lord with His people, or the different seasons He has ordained for each one. The Holy Spirit solemnly charges others not to judge, disturb, or meddle with someone else's delicate relationship with the Lord, whose heart is known only by Him.

On the other hand, there are definitely times when intervention is required. If we see someone in serious depression or crisis because they do not know the Lord's help or compassion, it is right to offer wise and loving counsel. I went through severe depression after my second child, and no one intervened. The consequences of my not receiving help were lasting, and damaged others as well.

It is right for us to ask the Lord to awaken this bridal passion for Him in our own hearts. Whatever level of love we are able to give Him right now is pleasing and acceptable to Him. The Lord does not need our love to be perfected before He will receive what we are able to give Him now. Our love is real and precious in His eyes, and knowing this will encourage us to keep pressing in for more. We have not yet reached the bottom of our God-given capacity to love the Lord with all our heart, all our soul and all our strength.

Seasons of Promotion

Song of Songs reveals the wisdom of knowing the times and seasons in our pursuit of the Lord. It emphasizes His passionate desire for of us and our relationship with this elusive King, who is seemingly "lost and found" at various times in our lives.

Solomon has crafted the message as a love story of a shepherd girl (1:8) and her fiancé, who is at times revealed as a humble shepherd (1:7), but who is also King Solomon Himself (1:4, 12, 3:6-11). The two male roles (Shepherd/King) move in and out throughout the story line. But the shepherd girl also turns into nobility (7:1), whether because of the Lover's adoration, or because she too, has a double identity: Shepherdess and Princess, similar to the male identities being fluid.

Could this be about our identity before the Lord? A humble servant, yet of noble spiritual birth, and seated with Princes at His heavenly banqueting table? Is it a Cinderella story? The King is giving a royal dinner-dance, searching for a bride for His Son. She is a humble servant, abused by her step-sisters and step-mother, and she is elevated by His love into nobility and royalty. Song of Songs is indeed a kind of Cinderella story, with much prophetic significance for the bride of Christ.

Indeed, the Lord is showing us seasons of spiritual promotion, as we lay aside every hindrance and begin to love and obey Him implicitly. He will take this abused child, this broken beggar, and this condemned harlot, and will elevate us to exalted royalty, purely by the force of His love and generosity.

A Composer like David

Like David, Solomon viewed himself as a Shepherd-King, leading the flock of Israel (see Ecc.12:11). Solomon knew that his father had spent his youth in the fields with Jesse's flocks. David had fought wild predators and won. He had built stringed instruments and composed countless love songs and poems about the Lord during these long, lonely years in the hills and pasturelands of Judea. The Lord was David's shepherd, his friend, and the love of his life. He had no one on earth or in heaven but the Lord Himself for comfort, protection and companionship.

Solomon knew David's testimony of how the Lord had taken him from Bethlehem's sheepfolds and had made him a shepherd over the Lord's people, Israel. David's relationship with the Lord did not change when he was elevated from shepherd to king. His love was unwavering. David taught his children about the greatest and most worthy quest on earth: to know and love the God of Israel.

With David as his example, Solomon grew up with musical training. The palace was full of the sounds of home-made harps, lyres, tambourines, drums and flutes, and David's sweet voice singing his love songs to Adonai. But Solomon also watched his father struggle through unjust accusations, periods of fasting and prayer, long nights of weeping, wars, betrayals from his colleagues, generals and even priests, as well as rebellions from Solomon's own older brothers.

Solomon had six older half-brothers from David's other wives (1 Chr. 3:1-9). Like his father David, who was the eighth son, and the most disdained among them, Solomon also knew what it felt like to be mistreated by arrogant older half-brothers. They cared nothing for Solomon's inheritance and destiny as a future king of Israel. In fact, at least two of them schemed to take the throne away from David themselves! Had either of them succeeded, both Solomon and his mother Bathsheba would have been executed as potential contenders for the throne (1 Kings 1:17-23).

He reveals these themes in the Song, including the damage caused by unkind treatment among step-brothers and sisters, as well as those "watchmen" who are abusing their positions of authority. The Song explores our stages of maturity, as we grow in the Lord, and prepares us for hardship. Understanding the bigger picture of the bride's journey prepares us for the joys, the tests, the aching hearts and the criticisms we must face, in our pursuit of the One who loved us first.

Solomon considered the Song of Songs to be the ultimate love song about the Lord and His bridal people. He was called, "the Teacher," just as the Lord Yeshua was often called by this title during His earthly ministry (see Ecc. 1:1-2; 12:9-10; Mt. 10:24, John 3:2, 13:14). The Song is more than a song: it is a poetic teaching about the Lord's affection and yearning for His people, and for the future Bride from all nations who would later be born out of Israel's roots. It is a teaching about the burning flame of the Bridegroom's jealous love for us, presented as the Song of all songs.

Who is the Shulamite?

Let us examine the identity of "the Shulamite." In Hebrew, her name is pronounced "Shulah-MEET," with the emphasis on the last syllable. It is derived from the same root as *"Shalom,"* meaning peace.

Solomon's name in Hebrew is *"Shlomo,"* coming from the same root word and meaning "his peace." The emphasis is on the first syllable, and is pronounced, "SH'LOH-moh." The Lord had told David that he was a man of war, who had shed blood on the earth. But his son, Solomon, would be a **man of peace**. He would build the temple for the Lord, because he was *"Shlomo,"* a man of peace.

The Shulamite's name and Solomon's name seem like male and female versions of the same name. Bible commentaries cannot identify a town called *"Shulem,"* where she might have come from. Some scholars suggest that she was from *"Shunem,"* a town near the Jezreel Valley in northern Israel. They theorize that the letter "n" in *Shunem* was changed to the letter "l," in the only verse where her name appears (see SOS 6:13). This would create the name "the Shulamite," rather than "the Shunamite." However, I believe that this letter-switch is unlikely. In Hebrew, the two letters do not resemble each other, nor are there any known biblical cases that I can find where these letters were switched.

It is more likely that the Shulamite's name simply comes from Solomon's name. The NIV commentary suggests that her name might mean "Solomon's Girl," meaning that her name is the feminine version of his name. Solomon was expressing his wisdom through both the male and the female character, representing the manifold wisdom of God.

We have seen that both of their names are taken from the Hebrew word for peace, *"Shalom."* One of the last words the bride speaks in this Song is, *"Then I became in His eyes as one who found peace"* (8:10b). This might confirm that her name is about the peace that we find when we understand what the Lord desires of us and how to walk that out.

Shuli's background reflects Solomon's own journey of living in a family of unsympathetic step-mothers and ambitious older half-brothers. Shuli's step-brothers put her to field work. Solomon's mother, Bathsheba was not able to help or defend him from his half-brother Adonijah's treachery until the most critical, life-or-death moment, when King David was on his deathbed. Then the Lord intervened, and all that had been stolen was gloriously restored (see 1 Kings 1).

Solomon's Weakness

The Lord never withdrew His love or destiny from Solomon, for the sake of a solemn vow He had made to David (2 Sam. 7:4-16).

However, as you study Solomon's life, you see that he did not ultimately find the intimacy with the Lord that his father David had attained. He built the temple, offered uncountable sacrifices, and walked in favor with the Lord more than any other king, apart from David. Despite this, Solomon must have had some gaps between his superlative wisdom and his experiential/emotional satisfaction.

He acquired seven hundred wives and three hundred concubines, most of the wives being foreigners. Many were from the very nations that the Lord had commanded the Israelites not to marry into (see 1 Kings 11). Possibly, he acquired women like someone who was dissatisfied, and desperate to fill the void of his heart and spirit. Or else he viewed the acquisition of beautiful women as he would view his thousands of prize horses from Egypt and other lands. Unlike David, it would seem that his need to intimately connect with the Lover of his soul was never met, **or else it was lost with the acquisition of great wealth and power.**

The enemy used his weakness for women to lure Solomon into participating in pagan idolatry. He built pagan altars to demonic gods, in order to please his many foreign wives, and he was led astray by their false worship. The Lord did not punish Solomon in the fullest measure, as He had permanently punished and removed Saul. However, the dividing of Israel into civil war and the enmity between the northern and southern kingdoms was a direct judgment on Solomon for his unfaithfulness and idolatry (1 Kings 11:9-12:33).

Solomon never truly found his identity under the Lord's arms of love.

Chapter 5

THE VOICE (SOS 2:8-17)

2:8-13 The voice of my beloved! Behold, he comes, leaping over the mountains, bounding over the hills. My beloved is like a gazelle or a young stag. Behold, there he stands behind our wall, gazing through the windows, looking through the lattice. My beloved speaks and says to me:

"Arise, my love, my beautiful one, and come away, for behold, the winter is past; the rain is over and gone. The flowers appear on the earth, the time of singing has come, and the voice of the turtledove is heard in our land. The fig tree ripens its figs, and the vines are in blossom; they give forth fragrance. Arise, my love, my beautiful one, and come away" (ESV).

Here we see the Lord initiating an encounter to "get up and go," with the clarion sound of His voice. In the Hebrew text, He calls His bride with the exact same words with which He called Abraham to go out of his country, to come to a new land (see Gen. 12:1). What sound could ever awaken a spiritually sleeping believer more than the voice of our Beloved? Even when He is still at a great distance, we hear this soul-arresting Voice ringing through our spirit. His voice makes the distance between heaven and earth as nothing more than a flimsy veil. No separation. Someone is calling.

Our Beloved effortlessly flings away the veil that separates us with a tiny wave of His hand, and His voice invades our loneliness, busyness, complacency, distractions, routines, depression, disappointment, and disillusionment. It also cuts through everything that made us feel overlooked! The order of His revelation is important here:

First, we HEAR the Voice of our Beloved.

Second, we BEHOLD Him at a distance, in our spirit, leaping over mighty mountains, bounding even over the stars to draw near, to reveal and initiate something from His Father's plans for us.

Third, we SEE Him a little closer, running and skipping over the nearer hills, like a young stag on a spring day. His heart is glad to be bringing us a message from heaven. He is coming on an assignment that makes Him happy. Encountering us makes Him glad.

Fourth, we REALIZE (revelation) that He is standing right behind the wall – the wall with which we protect ourselves from complete vulnerability.

Fifth, we LOCK EYES on the One who is right there, gazing at us through our window. His face is so close, we could touch Him, just on the other side of the window. There is nowhere to go. He went from being millions of light years away to one thin pane of glass away, in one split second, at the speed of thought!

This is the "SUDDENLY" of God, the surprise invasion of our Lord.

> *And the Lord whom you seek will suddenly come to his temple; and the messenger of the covenant in whom you delight, behold, he is coming, says the Lord of hosts. But who can endure the day of his coming, and who can stand when he appears? (Mal.3:1-2).*

The Urgent Request

In many cases, the Lord is calling us into unknown territory, to a Kingdom assignment that will stretch our trust levels to the breaking point. Some of us have not yet received the call, or have only received the first of many installments. This has happened to me in progressive stages of being sent into the Lord's vineyards, with increasing challenges. After I passed one test, the next one would come at a harder level.

> *"Behold, there He stands, gazing through the windows...*
> *My Beloved speaks to me and says, 'Arise, My love, and*
> *come away.'"*

Once, this verse was fulfilled in a kind of half-waking dream. I saw the Lord through a window pane, and our faces were so close, we could have touched. I put my hand up to the pane of glass, stretching out my fingers, and His hand and fingers aligned with mine on the other side of the window. The Lord has reduced the separation between us to one thin piece of glass. Soon, Beloved – soon, there will be not even a thin wall of glass between us.

He is calling me to a level of ministry that would seem to push me beyond the limits of my physical and emotional endurance. There is no middle ground. I either quit, or I move forward into the "too hard," in sheer obedience, mingled with my weak faith that He WILL see me through, somehow.

Perhaps your heart is seeking the Lord for His invitation. The Lord will suddenly be right there, even if we thought this moment would never come. But He has come. He now extends the invitation, the assignment, the beckoning, the authoritative and personal Word. In an instant, we are both honored and yet fearful, due to our instant accountability and responsibility to respond rightly. *Arise, My love, and come away.* Once it has been spoken, we are accountable for our response. Oh beloved bride of Yeshua, make your decision now to say "yes," no matter what He will ask of you. It will almost never be what you are expecting!

Yeshua looks at His bride through the window, desiring to draw us into a deeper trust relationship with Himself, which will include leaving our nest (usual routine) to accept some form of ministry assignment, in whatever harvest fields He has chosen just for us.

The Signs of Fruit Appear

For behold, the winter is past; the rain is over and gone.
The flowers appear on the earth, the time of singing has
come, and the voice of the turtledove is heard in our land.
The fig tree ripens its figs, and the vines are in blossom;
they give forth fragrance.

In Israel, winter is the season for the rains. In a good year, the rainy season would begin right after *Succot* (Tabernacles) and it would continue through November, December and January, though there will be dry days from time to time. In a bad year, very little rain would fall, even in winter time, which would leave the Land unprepared for the long, dry season ahead. Much of the harvest could fail in years like this.

This wet season gives way to the success of the early spring trees and crops. It also prepares the earth for the summer and the final crops: the wheat, the ripening fruit, the olives and the vines. The rains are a sign that harvest is coming. The flowers and buds are a sign that the fruit is not far behind.

A Page has Turned in Heaven – Are We Ready?

So it is with the harvest of souls and the awakening of individuals and nations (the Bride of Yeshua) into their purpose, their calling, and their destiny. If we miss the signs, the integrity of the harvest is endangered, and it is the sleeping church, the hibernating bride, who will give an account to the Lord Himself. The very thought should fill us with the Fear of the Lord.

There are markers and signs when a page has been turned in heaven. These markers usually align with the Feasts of the Lord, which fall on His own calendar of prophetic markers. These moments are ordained by Heaven, and they occur when a longstanding season that seemed "permanent and normal," has unexpectedly given way to a new, very different season.

Can you feel this, even at this time on the earth? It affects governments, nations, everyday life, finances, schedules, weather patterns, and infrastructure. Nothing will ever be as it was, as time will delay no longer (Rev. 10:6-7). In this critical, transitional hour, the true bride must be ready to arise and move quickly to the sound of the Lord's voice, having prepared herself by already being familiar with His voice.

If we are slow to obey and respond to His voice, it will be hard to catch up, when that page has turned, and a frightening acceleration of last days' events begins to unfold before us.

The Time of Singing Precedes the Harvest

The great revivals of history have always been preceded by a season of intense prayer, worship, and intercession, by a small core of intercessors in a given region, city, island or nation.

> *The time of singing has come, and the voice of the turtle-dove is heard in our land.*

New songs that express the Bridegroom-Bridal intimacy are being released like wedding jewels, from Asia-Pacific to the Arctic Circle. The fallen Tabernacle of David is being restored across the earth (Amos 9:11-2, Acts 15:16-18). As the incense of day and night prayer and worship rise up from across the globe, touching the heart of the Lord, the flooding latter rains of the Holy Spirit will prepare the earth for the final harvest.

> *Be glad then, you children of Zion, and rejoice in the Lord your God; for He has given you the former rain faithfully, and He will cause the rain to come down for you— **the former rain, and the latter rain in the first** month. The threshing floors shall be full of wheat, and the vats shall overflow with new wine and oil.* (Joel 2:23-24).

As the Lamb of God takes the Scroll from His Father, and breaks the seals that release His redemptive end-times stripping of the earth, these prophesied events will increase on the earth (see Rev. 5-6). The fuel of worship and intercession will cause the atmosphere to shift in the hearts of the complacent, the fearful and the distracted. The Holy Spirit will cultivate a great urgency and hunger to know the Lord, in those who were previously too busy to care. But now, they will be desperate to receive a word of help, healing, salvation or deliverance from Him.

> *Do you not say, 'There are yet four months, then comes the harvest'? Look, I tell you, lift up your eyes, and see that the fields are white for harvest. Already the one who reaps is receiving wages and gathering fruit for eternal life, so that sower and reaper may rejoice together* (Jn.4:35-36, ESV).

Time is running out. Be sensitive to the call of the Lord's voice. He needs laborers in the harvest fields, a vast company to reap the final harvest, and to prepare the Bride for the final battles. Winning souls and preparing the Bride are the two major assignments left to us. The Lord knows which fields are best for the way He designed each of us.

> *I must work the works of Him who sent Me while it is day; the night is coming when no one can work* (John 9:4).

The Lord will leap over many obstacles and much resistance to come to you, and He desires for you to move quickly into the purposes that were laid aside for you before the foundations of the world (see 2 Tim.1:9). It may come when you are seeking hard after Him, or He may surprise you at an unexpected moment. Be ready, in season and out of season, to answer quickly. He is calling you: *"Arise, My love, My beautiful one, and come away with me."* No one is excluded from the Lord's assignments, dreamed just for them by the Father Himself.

Let Me See Your Face

> *My dove in the clefts of the rock, in the hiding places on the mountainside, show me your face, let me hear your*

voice; for your voice is sweet, and your face is lovely
(2:14, NIV).

The Lord Yeshua is a real Man with a relational, intimate heart. He truly desires face to face encounters with His people, where their eyes are open, transparent, vulnerable and honest. Someone might say, "But I can't see Him, so what is the point of looking into His invisible face with my eyes open? That is a great question. The basic answer is this:

When we see nothing, He sees everything.

When we feel nothing, He feels everything.

Whether we see, hear or feel Him, the Lord is drinking in every gesture, word, thought, tear, hope, hug and kiss that we are, **in faith alone**, willing to fling out to Him. He'll catch it, and in many cases, we'll **know** that He caught it. That is called "faith." Without faith, how can we make Him happy?

> *And without faith it is impossible to please God, because anyone who comes to him must believe that he exists and that **he rewards** those who earnestly seek him* (Heb. 11:6, NIV).

I've walked this path, and there have been long seasons where I was hiding behind my bent, wretched, ashamed head, with my eyes closed. I could even feel the fact that I was hiding from the Lord, but I couldn't bring myself to look up into His face, the face I could not see. It comes naturally for fallen man to hide from the One who sees everything anyway. This is the precise result of the fall. We know that we are naked, we feel shame and we hide, and want to "crawl under a cleft in the rock."[12]

If we were merely left here to grope through life in our "natural" state, we would surely revert to hiding, one way or another. Aren't you glad He's too good to leave us in our hiding place?

The redeemed, obedient, trusting believer will "boldly approach His Throne of Grace," without shame, and without our pitiful fig leaf to shield the Lord from how awful we really would be, apart from His Blood (see Heb. 4:16).

The Lord Yeshua took our shame and our sin, our nakedness and our wretchedness upon His own soul, and bore the consequences in His own body. If He paid so horrific a price to carry away our shame and nakedness, then WHY ARE WE STILL HIDING? Does this not negate the very reason He came? To reverse the curse? To pick us up from being FALLEN? To give us boldness to meet with Him face to face, as a man would meet with a friend? **Yes, this is expressly why He came to earth.**

The Lord is now asking for transparency, intimacy, and an end to hiding. He does not want His bride to hide anything from Him. Whether the good, the bad or the ugly. The Lord wants to see our face and to hear our voice. He finds our voice, our prayers and our conversation sweet to His ears and our face lovely to gaze at. **Whether we like ourselves or not, this is who He is, and this is how He feels.**

The betrothed wore a veil over her face. The Lord Yeshua is asking us to let Him see our face, unveiled. He can be trusted to protect our integrity if we will remove the final veil for Him alone, even now.

> *But we all, with unveiled face, beholding as in a mirror the glory of the Lord, are being transformed into the same image from glory to glory, just as by the Spirit of the Lord* (2 Cor. 3:18).

Perhaps Solomon was thinking of Moses, when he described the bride, hidden in the cleft of the rock like a dove. This was a picture of the Lord dwelling in "unapproachable light," His glory unable to be seen by sinful man.

But under the shade of the cross, under the Blood of the Lamb, under His *tallit*, in the Bridal paradigm, we have an invitation to *"Come closer, come closer still."*[13] It was right for the Lord to cover Moses at that time, as we need to learn to reverence the holiness of Adonai (see Ex.33:21-23). We still must fear the Lord; but the veil has been torn, and the way has been opened to come, with unveiled faces before the Lord, and to dare to come closer still.

*O my dove, that art in the clefts of the rock, **in the secret places of the stairs**, let me see thy countenance, let me hear thy voice; for sweet is thy voice, and thy countenance is comely (KJV).*

In Hebrew, it literally says, "in the secret of the stairway (or ascending place)." This means that we are in a process of seeking and finding His secret place, and we are beckoned to ascend the Mountain of the Lord's Presence. It is as if He has hidden a stairway, a portal into the realm of the Spirit, and we are invited to come.

Coming up to Jerusalem was always called "ascending" in Scripture, because it was a geological ascent to reach there. But to come up to the Mountain of the Lord is more than just the physical city of Jerusalem, although Jerusalem will always be the "city of the Great King." There is the spiritual Mount Zion, also called the heavenly Jerusalem, which is in the realm of the Spirit, where we can ascend and come up higher, in our spirits, and commune with the Lord.

*Then the Lord said, **"There is a place near Me where you may stand on a rock.** When My glory passes by, I will put you in a cleft in the rock and cover you with My hand until I have passed by."* (Ex. 33:21-22, NIV).

This is an invitation from the Lord, to encounter Him: *"There is a place near Me."* This is not a physical rock, this place near His Person. This place is still available, this place near to His bosom. It is the place of intimate communion, the Secret Place of the Most High. Hebrews tell us that we have access to this heavenly meeting place, even that we have already "come to Mount Zion." This is where the saints on earth and the saints and angels of heaven come together as **one family under the Father** (see Eph.3:14-15).

But you have come to Mount Zion, to the city of the living God, the heavenly Jerusalem. You have come to thousands upon thousands of angels in joyful assembly, to the church of the firstborn, whose names are written in heaven. You have come to God, the Judge of all, to the spirits of the righteous made perfect, to Jesus the mediator of a new covenant, and to the sprinkled blood that speaks a better word than the blood of Abel. (Heb. 12:22-24).

It says **"you have come,"** meaning that this is meant to be a present reality, not a future hope only. I have not arrived, but have slightly tasted this place in encounters, dreams, visions and hearing music, in very small measure. I know that this is available to each and every believer who knows that there is more of Yeshua to intimately know, than what we were taught. There is more to grow into, as we diligently seek and ask. We will feel so safe in this place, because it is what we were made for. The love and acceptance in this place erases our misery, shame, and insecurity. It is in the secret place of the ascent to our Father's house that we will come into the "rest" that the Lord promises us (Heb. 4:9).

When we let the Lord see us as we are, like a trusting child, we finally come into REST, and the Lord will receive joy and satisfaction in this love that we share with Him. No one else will drink of this cup of intimacy. **It is in this place of supernatural rest amidst the storms in this world, that we will prevail against the darkest onslaughts yet to be seen.**

The Integrity of the Harvest

Catch the foxes for us, the little foxes that spoil the vineyards, for our vineyards are in blossom (ESV).

This is one of those slightly difficult sentences to explain, in terms of the Hebrew grammar. Someone is speaking to a plural audience in this command, based on the plural Hebrew verb for "catch" that is used, i.e., "You guys catch them." And he says, "Catch them for **us**..."

Since there are plural "little foxes" that relentlessly try to ruin the vine just when the fruit is almost formed, there must be a need for many (plural) laborers, who can keep up with these little marauders.

Logically, it cannot be the bride telling the Shepherd to do this, for He is only one person. It seems that it is the Shepherd, telling the plural bride to catch the foxes. The "us" makes sense here. The damage to the harvest will hurt the Lord and will also harm His people. He needs us to agree and partner with Him to catch these little things that destroy the harvest before it is fully mature. The Lord means that His beloved (thus including all believers in this admonition) must catch the foxes. It will help all of heaven's purposes and earth's destiny if we will do so. If the foxes are left to endanger the integrity of the harvest, we will all suffer. Catch for us the little foxes, so that He may enjoy the fruit of His labors, and we may drink the fruit of the vine with Him on our wedding day.

Internal and External Foxes

There are at least two ways to define these "little foxes" in the life of a believer (maybe you can think of others that I missed).

One way is to consider the little foxes to be errors in our understanding, distorted thinking patterns, wounds or offenses in our individual hearts, which keep tripping us up in our walk with the Lord. It might be envy, fear, rejection, or resentment. It could be wounds from the past, which have emotionally crippled us, and continually rob from us our beautiful moments. At an enjoyable event where we should be so happy, we find ourselves oddly subdued, glum, depressed, angry, or self-pitying. It robs us of the fruits of peace, joy, and selfless love. It also hinders wisdom, as we misinterpret situations.

The old wounds and offenses keep nipping at our good fruit, just as it is ripening before the Lord. I've seen this play out many times in my own heart and in the bizarre mood swings of even those closest to me. I cannot figure out how everything seemed fine, and suddenly, they are in a dark and foul mood, and are closed off from even explaining themselves. Something ruined the fruit of the entire conference or fellowship, and it is a little fox in their past or in their wounded soul, that pops out at unexpected moments, for no seeming reason.

In the case of these "internal foxes," we alone are responsible to catch these little foxes. (When I say "alone," I don't mean that we can do this apart from the Holy Spirit's help – I only mean that our friends can't do it for us.) It would be hard for others to help us catch them, unless we are in counseling, or under some type of accountability. This is a job we must mostly do with the Lord, but others can help us if we are transparent and serious about rooting out these little foxes. We need inner healing, and when the wounds are bandaged with oil and wine, the foxes will have no power over the vineyard of our heart.

The other possible meaning is that these foxes can be people, perhaps close to our lives, or on the periphery of our lives. We all know them. They are the ones who are always coming up with criticisms, doubts, arguments, or pessimism; they attempt to pull us away from our passion for the Lord or our work in His vineyards. They are "*provocateurs*." They can turn a lovely evening into an exhausting argument, and you don't even know how they did it! They can take your best intentions in what you thought was a loving conversation, and turn it into an ugly and frustrating battle, and you want to leave the room, but you are trapped for one reason or another.

Sometimes, they are in our own family, and this is a hard and wearing-down situation. When these foxes are part of our own household, we are usually not in a position to "catch them," if they are of an age to have free will. Nor can we avoid or change them. I can only say, from personal experience, that the only little foxes we have the power to "catch" are the attitudes that form in our hearts, in response to the painful provocations that come at us from these other ones, who are close to us, or in our very home.

In other words, we must not let their provocations rob us of our inner fruit of the Spirit. We can't let them separate us from our intimacy with the Lord, due to the pain, anger, resentment and other destructive emotions that come up in our hearts, in response to the provocations. We have to pour out our pain to the Lord, but to let Him give us His love, in what would normally be "impossible to love" situations. We can walk away from the tug of war, but we cannot change the other person.

Apart from family issues, these people will often be professing Christians, or even self-righteous Christians. And yet their whole job description seems to be "to wear down, debate, discredit, discourage, cause doubt, disgrace, draw into a lengthy argument, or defame the servants of God," who are trying, to the best of their conscience and abilities, to do the very works the Lord has sent them to do. I think the devil applied for that job about 10,000 years ago, and was hired! But he seems to have some assistants in the earth who fit that job description, doing his dirty work of discouragement.

When Nehemiah arrived in Jerusalem to rebuild its walls and its gates, there were three little foxes, just waiting to ruin the work. It seems that no matter what your assignment, there will always be a Sanballat, a Tobiah and a Geshem, who will discourage, despise and mock you, just as they did to Nehemiah (see Ne. 2:19).

Nehemiah strengthened the builders with the commitment and love of the Lord, but he also took practical steps to protect them from harm. With one hand they built, and with the other hand, they held defensive weapons against attackers. I suppose this is a good model for our lives as soldiers in the Lord's army.

There are little foxes and then there are savage wolves. Sometimes it is hard for me to know the difference.

We are to be loving and to pray for our enemies, but not to stand by carelessly, while they damage the tender ones on the vine, who are being prepared for the greater works that the Lord promised we would do (see John 14:12). Paul did not take these "destroyers" lightly, but warned against them and refuted them forcefully, as a father who guards the integrity of the harvest he was sowing into with his tears.

I know that after I leave, savage wolves will come in among you and will not spare the flock. Even from your own number men will arise and distort the truth in order to draw away disciples after them. So be on your guard! Remember that for three years I never stopped warning each of you night and day with tears (Acts 20:29, NIV).

Turn, My Beloved

2:16-17 My Beloved is mine, and I am his. He feeds his flock among the lilies. Until the day breaks and the

*shadows flee away, turn, my beloved, and be like a gazelle
or a young stag upon the mountains of Bether.* (2:17).

Each section of the Song represents a new stage of the bride's
maturity, intimacy, and obedience. And at this point in her journey,
the maiden now feels confident in knowing where the Shepherd
feeds his flock – in green pastures, among the lilies. He feeds us with
the choicest food. This speaks of the bridal garments, spiritual gifts
and adornments. We see these adornments all through the Song, as
well as in Genesis 24:22, Isaiah 25:6-9, 61:3,7,10, and 62:1-5, Luke
12:35-37, Ephesians 4:7-8, and Rev. 19:8. **These speak of the superior provisions and pleasures of the Lord Yeshua for His bride.**
Shuli reasons that He belongs to her ("My Beloved is mine,")
and she knows where He feeds His flock. Perhaps this familiarity
and her "ownership" of Him lead her to conclude that she doesn't
have to follow Him into the harvest fields at this moment. This line
of thinking is a little fox in her heart, which is about to cause her
pain and hardship. She then gives Him her answer: *Until the day
breaks and the shadows flee away, turn, my beloved, and be like a
gazelle or a young stag upon the mountains of Bether.*

The maiden is telling her Beloved to **turn** to the mountains,
saying, "It is still night time. Until morning light, go your way,
Beloved, and run on the mountains without me." In Hebrew, the
word *"Bether"* literally means "separation," or "dividing." Bether
is not a physical location that is mentioned in the Bible, so we do
not know if she is referring to separation itself. Does this mountain
represent a period of separation, because she was not able or willing
to leave her "nest," or her comfort zone?

We are not told why she would not come away with Him. It
seems that the full measure of yieldedness to His leadership has not
yet developed in her heart. Perhaps she wants Him to stay on her
terms: familiarity, convenience, and close to home. He is disrupting
her world of safety and security and asking her step out, **using the
same vocabulary with which He called Abraham to step out.**
The bride doesn't realize that this decision not to leave will prove
difficult and costly for her.

Meditation

I have you by the hand. I lead you through the fires, battles, and floods. I preserve, protect and perfect that which I have ordained for you. Trust Me, as I AM with you in every step of the journey, even when you make costly mistakes. I will turn it all for your good in due season. I have your best at heart, always, My beloved.

Chapter 6

NOT FINDING HIM–PART 1 (SOS 3:1-11)

3:1-2 All night long on my bed I looked for the one my heart loves; I looked for him but did not find him. I will get up now and go about the city, through its streets and squares; I will search for the one my heart loves. So I looked for him but did not find him (NIV).

It's not a matter of love. Or is it? The betrothed clearly loved Him, and kept the thought of Him close to her heart all night long. Her fragrance and devotion were real to Him, and He saw her as a lily among the prickly, unsafe hearts in this world. But it's about the cost of discipleship, the cost of obedience. The Lord Himself defines love in terms of obedience, even though our emotions and commitments are very important to Him (see Jn. 14:15, 21, 23-24).

For anyone with a heart, it would be hard not to love the man Messiah Yeshua. Just to consider the height from which He came to rescue us, and the depth to which He stooped to save us. To think about the suffering and scorn it cost Him, the humiliation and betrayal that He endured, just to purchase us with the highest Bridal price. As we reflect on His patience, kindness and endurance, all for our sakes, who wouldn't love Him? It's a no-brainer.

The problem is that He is Lord and Master. And as Lord, He rightly asks us to do things that are the Father's predetermined plans and good purposes for our lives. These things are not always what we wish to do, or what we feel qualified to do. At times, we don't even fully understand what He is asking, yet He expects us to obey Him. Sometimes, what He asks us to do is embarrassing, humbling, inconvenient, physically uncomfortable, or it goes completely against our soulish desires.

Sometimes, we will get a warning that a test of obedience is coming up. Sometimes, there is no warning for us, when one of these difficult "challenges" is about to invade our comfort zone. We may be caught unaware, and yet He will still hold us accountable for how we handle the test, even if it came out of the blue. The fact of the matter is that the Lord deliberately tests our hearts, to see what is really inside there (see 2 Chr. 32:31, Deut. 8:2).

> *Remember how the Lord your God led you all the way in the wilderness these forty years, to humble and test you in order to know what was in your heart, whether or not you would keep his commands* (Deut. 8:2, NIV).

The Testing of our Hearts

The Lord does not define love solely on the basis of our fervency or our emotions, though nothing is lost on Him. He defines it in terms of trust and obedience, where the rubber meets the road. In SOS 2:8-13, the bride heard His voice in advance, and she knew He was coming. Suddenly, He was right there, traversing huge distances at the speed of thought. And He instantly presented her with a challenge, an invitation, and an announcement of the harvest awaiting.

The Lord wants a partner, and the choice is immediately before us. He desires to see our face and to hear our voice. In other words, He wants us to be transparent, so that He can know how our heart is responding, upon hearing this invitation. He even warns us to catch the little foxes, those doubts and fears that will ruin the harvest by hindering the laborers.

After her Beloved departed, she was alone all night with her thoughts, possibly her regrets. She misses Him so much, it hurts, and no matter what she tries to say or do, she cannot find His Presence. It would be natural to think that the Lord is punishing the bride, or is displeased with her decision not to come away. Thus, He has withdrawn in this way.

The Lord has many lessons He needs to teach us, but that is not the same as punishment. A good father disciplines the child, for their own good, though it does not feel pleasant at the time. He is a good Father, so even His hard disciplines are lessons that will help us in the final assessment of our lives, as we stand before His throne to be evaluated. **They will end up for our good**, though we cannot perceive it in the moment of discomfort.

Rick Joyner has said, "Don't waste your trials." If we embrace them, they will produce the necessary fruit in our lives. Let's pass our tests the first time, so that we don't have to keep taking the same test again and again, because it gets harder each time.

ATTENTION: WISDOM ALERT!

Let's pray for wisdom that we will **recognize** when the Lord is testing us, which will help us to pass the test, knowing it is from the Lord, and ultimately for our good. I've started to learn to recognize the "fingerprints" of being tested by the Lord. It's almost an adventure, (even though painful), because I can actually make decisions differently, realizing I'm being watched and my responses are either going get me a passing grade, or I'll have to be presented later with the same test in a harder and more disguised form. Knowing this is a huge help to our success, don't you think? It works for me – maybe not every time, but many times it helps me pass the test.

Solomon wrote these words about the Lord's discipline in Proverbs, and he incorporated this same message into the bride's difficulties and disciplines in Song of Solomon as well.

My son, do not despise the Lord's discipline, and do not resent his rebuke, because the Lord disciplines those he loves, as a father the son he delights in. (Prov. 3:11-12, NIV)

He Never Really Leaves

We know that He has promised never to leave or forsake us. Therefore, the Lord has never withdrawn from us in the true sense of abandonment. However, as far as our perceptions are concerned, He seems nowhere to be found.

Almost all believers can testify to having gone through a "dark night of the soul," some of us multiple times. I'm in a particularly long one right now, as I write this book. I can cry and press in, when I find the strength to do so. But no one can manipulate the Lord's hand, so as to hurry Him in His deliberately calculated process to bring out the best in us. Who can find fault with the Lord, or complain that He is slow to come, slow to answer, or slow to respond to our desperate need? Isaiah tells us why He waits.

> *Therefore the Lord will wait, that He may be gracious to you; and therefore He will be exalted, that He may have mercy on you. For the Lord is a God of justice;* **blessed** **are** *all those who wait for Him* (Isaiah 30:18).

> *And again, No one who hopes in You will ever be put to shame* (Ps. 25:3, NIV).

Sometimes my need for Him feels so huge and desperate, and I cannot imagine why He would not rush to comfort me. But He is producing in me patience and perseverance, so that I will press in consistently, over a long period of time, and not give up. He is building my stamina, and my desire to find Him.

> *Not only so, but we also glory in our sufferings, because we know that suffering produces perseverance; perseverance, character; and character, hope. And hope does not put us to shame, because God's love has been poured out into our hearts through the Holy Spirit, who has been given to us.* (Rom. 5:3-5, NIV).

However, I have the kind of personality that is easily discouraged and quickly gives up. So maybe I need to fight longer, so that my perseverance will yield the character of Messiah that the Father is looking for.

> *Be patient, then, brothers and sisters, until the Lord's coming. See how the farmer waits for the land to yield its valuable crop, patiently waiting for the autumn and spring rains. You too, be patient and stand firm, because the Lord's coming is near* (James 5:7-8).

On the other hand, what we perceive to be the lack of the Lord's Presence is actually very distorted and inaccurate. To us, it feels like He has left us. **But the truth is that if He truly left us, we would be plunged into hellish, bewildering blackness of soul and hopelessness. This experience would have a hideous and inescapable quality that only the damned will know.** This is the truth, and we should be careful to even complain that His Presence has left us, because if He ever let us feel the reality of that statement, we would give *anything* to get back what we thought was abandonment five minutes before! Even at our worst moments, those who are saved live with a level of His love and Presence that is qualitatively different from what an abandoned soul feels. Now, back to our story...

Have You Found the One I Love?

Shuli goes into the city streets to search for him. She cannot find him for quite a while, but she does find "the watchmen." These are the guardians of the peace and orderliness of Jerusalem's city streets. This will not be her last encounter with the watchmen, who may represent a segment of religious or spiritual leadership in the church or in other religious or spiritual congregations or entities.

She asks them, *"Have you seen the one my heart loves?"*

First, we must notice that she seeks out their help in finding him. This might be a clue to us about *how* we go about searching for the Presence of the Lord. Perhaps the Lord is warning us not to try to find Him through those who we assume can help us, based on their authoritative position.

In asking them this question, the implication is that they know who she is talking about, but they are unable or unwilling to help her in any way. They seem not to be particularly sympathetic to the bride's lovesick heart. Her desperation is not their concern. Keeping things neat, orderly and *controlled* is their concern. In fact, they probably disapprove of her chasing after this person. Whether he is a beloved public figure or an unknown shepherd is not clear in this story. (This is one of those many elements that make the Song not a normal love story of a regular couple.)

The watchmen think she should be at home, sleeping, or doing what others expect of her. It looks undignified for her to be wandering the streets, asking if anyone has seen the one she loves. However, she does find him after her encounter with the watchmen, **but not through their help.** This shows that he was willing to be found by her, apart from the watchmen's help. It also shows us that she never really lost him, but that she didn't know how to regain the awareness of his presence. This is something we can all relate to.

> *3:4 Scarcely had I passed them when I found the one my heart loves. I held him and would not let him go till I had brought him to my mother's house, to the room of the one who conceived me* (NIV).

Having lost him was a great shock to her soul, and very distressing. Once she finds him, she clings desperately to him, holding on for dear life. She wants to be in control, and tries to "keep" him at home, where she'll never lose him again. The Lord will sometimes permit this childlike, "self-centered, possessive love for Him," for a season. But in the bigger picture, He will not be manipulated, and He will come to us on His terms, in His perfect timing for our good, and the maturity we will need for our future with Him.

> *But Mary stood weeping outside the tomb, and as she wept she stooped to look into the tomb. And she saw two angels in white, sitting where the body of Jesus had lain, one at the head and one at the feet. They said to her, "Woman, why are you weeping?" She said to them, "They have*

taken away my Lord, and I do not know where they have laid him."

"Have you seen the One I love?"

Having said this, she turned around and saw Jesus standing, but she did not know that it was Jesus. Jesus said to her, "Woman, why are you weeping? Whom are you seeking?" *Supposing him to be the gardener, she said to him, "Sir, if you have carried him away, tell me where you have laid him, and I will take him away."*

"Have you seen the One I love?"

Jesus said to her, "Mary." She turned and said to him in Aramaic, "Rabboni!" (which means Teacher). Jesus said to her, "Do not cling to me, for I have not yet ascended to the Father...(John 20:11-17a, ESV).

"I held him and would not let him go..."

Miriam (Mary Magdalene) had the privilege of being the first person to find the One she loved, and when she found Him, she would not let Him go. Yeshua loved Miriam and understood her desperation to hold onto Him. However, in this case, the Lord had heaven's business to complete, and she couldn't keep Him all to herself at that moment of joy.

However, there was a higher way for her to "not let Him go." Not by physically holding onto the Lord's body, but by carrying the message of His resurrection back to the base camp (home). Figuratively, Mary Magdalene took the Lord back to her mother's house, to the room of the one who conceived her. Her salvation was born among the Lord and His spiritual family. His disciples were "His mother, His brothers, His sisters," and Mary was bringing the resurrected Lord back to them, through her testimony.

The hope of the New Covenant was being birthed at that very moment. The Lord's resurrection was a new birth, a new and eternal life for all the families of the earth. Mary was the lovesick Shulamite, carrying the Beloved back to her mother's house, the place where His earthly ministry was conceived, and where her new life was born.

*... **Go to My brethren** and say to them, 'I am ascending to My Father and your Father, and to My God and your God* (John 20:17b).

*And **go quickly and tell His disciples that He is risen from the dead,** and indeed He is going before you into Galilee; **there you will see Him**...and as they went to tell His disciples, behold, **Jesus met them**, saying..."Do not be afraid. **Go and tell My brethren to go to Galilee, and there they will see Me**." (Matt. 28:7-10).*

The timing of this first encounter between Mary Magdalene and the risen Lord was chosen by the Lord, and no one else was permitted to interfere with that relationship. It was an extremely sensitive event and the testimony that would follow would be pivotal.

In our lives, bringing the Lord to our "mother's house" speaks of bringing the Lord with us, into our normal routines, families, work-places. The lovesick bride must also bring Him to a sleepwalking and lukewarm church environment, as well. We do not just meet with Him secretly in the night. We are not ashamed to bring the Lord into situations where others are not aware of the intense love and commitments that exist between the Lord and us.

In the storyline, for Shuli to bring him to her mother's house can signify two things: her desire to secure his permanence; or a formal engagement, which would normally take place at the bride's parents' home.

Losing and Finding Each Other

One striking aspect of the Song is that we see Shuli losing and finding her Beloved a number of times. This is one of the aspects that makes this an unusual love story. She asks Him where He grazes in 1:7, and is found dining with Him during 1:12-2:5. She loses Him in 3:1 and 5:2-6, and finds Him in 3:4 and 6:2-3. They lose each other in 2:17, but He knows that she will pursue and find Him after her "dark night of the soul" (3:1-3).

At the end of the story, when they should be living happily ever after, she still says, *"If only you were like my brother...if **I found** *you outside, I would kiss you and no one would shame me"* (8:1, AP). Why is she still talking about **finding Him** at this point in the story? This is just another clue that the Song is our love story with our Beloved Yeshua.

Can you relate to this problem of both finding and losing the One you love? I can deeply and painfully relate to finding and losing Him again, many times over, as it were.

Even in the epic, "Gone with the Wind," Rhett Butler and Scarlett O'Hara don't lose and find each other as many times as Shuli and her Beloved!

It almost seems that He loses her in 2:14. In a sense, the Lord has actually lost me several times as well. He says that she is hiding from Him.

> *"My dove in the clefts of the rock, **in the hiding places** on the mountainside, show me your face, let me hear your voice; or your voice is sweet, and your face is lovely* (2:14, NIV).

I experienced this very verse at one period in my life. In fact, when the Lord had asked me to write this book in early 2013, I had protested that I did not understand Song of Solomon well enough to write anything intelligent about it. First, He had sent me His Word through a trusted prophet, who said to me, "The Lord wants you to write a new book – a commentary on the Song of Solomon. You are already living out this book. You merely need to write it down."

I had a hard time believing that word. The prophet who spoke it knew almost nothing about my life, past or present. I couldn't see how I was living out this confusing and highly romanticized love story.

Then about a month later, when I began to obediently write this book, I found the same old confusions intimidating me. Again, I couldn't understand the story line, and so many things made no sense to me. I wanted to tell the Lord that He got the wrong person to write this book. I probably did tell Him exactly that.

Then the Lord spoke to my spirit, and said, *"Actually, you have lived out the journey of the Shulamite in your relationship with Me.*

Everything that she experiences, even in the order they appear in the Song, you have run in a parallel track with her experiences, losses, struggles and her overcoming stages into maturity. You may think that you don't understand it, but you are living it out, and I will help you to connect the pieces to your own life."

And so in faith and obedience to His Word, I am now including some of my personal experiences, to supplement my teachings and interpretations of this book of the Bible. In this way, the reader can connect the phases of their own lives and ministries to this journey through Song of Solomon. I know that each individual life will take different twists and turns, and God designed each of our paths very uniquely.

However, one of the most stunning proofs that Song of Songs is truly about our journey with the Lord, is the fact that almost all of us can relate to the phases of the Shulamite's struggles, successes and failures in her relationship with the elusive Shepherd-King.

The Good Servant who Broke His Heart

In telling this story, I will use this term: "my ministry." I just want to clarify that I don't truly view it as "mine," but rather, I see it as "the ministry the Lord has entrusted to me for a season." But to make things simple, I'll call it, "my ministry."

My ministry began with a call to intimacy directly from the Lord. This was after having walked with Him for many years. I loved the Lord and had some special, rare encounters. But much was lacking in my zeal and passion for Him, just for Himself. I was searching hard for more of the Lord, but did not know how to go to the next level.

The call was intense, and it began with a growing hunger in me to know the Lord personally. It culminated in an urgent invitation to spend three days and three nights shut up in my room with Him, allowing no contact with others for that period.[14] It was literally springtime, and the winter was over and gone.

From this point onward, I experienced about three years of intense growth, intimacy, revelatory encounters, and new assignments. The Lord gave me books to write, new songs, and the teachings flowed out. The Fear of the Lord came with fearful glory. It was an adventure in encountering the Lord Yeshua. He became to me an intimate Savior.

The new assignments were similar to: *"Arise, My love, and come away with Me."* By the Lord's support, the ministry grew, and so did the stress, travel, demands, and the business-related problems that I had never asked for. These increased to a point where there was no peace or intimacy in my life. It became harder to hear the Lord's voice and to find Him in a personal way. I was too busy to even notice that I had lost Him, except for those rare moments of quietness. But it never, ever occurred to me that **He had lost me!** I felt I was being an obedient servant, and was trying to prepare His Bride, and to raise up His children to maturity quickly, for these perilous times.

I knew that the Lord saw everything I did "for Him," and I imagined that He understood why I didn't have time for long sessions of journaling and intimate gazing. It's true that He understood, but it's not true that this didn't hurt His heart. This situation extended for about four years of increasing demands on my life and time. I was on a relentless treadmill, but had no way to say "no" to most of the situations, so I just kept going on strength I did not have.

On one particular ministry trip, I was ministering in a long series of meetings in Canadian Bible schools and churches. The meetings and people were wonderful, and as always, I poured myself out to the last drop for the precious Bride who came for teachings, worship, and at times, even personal prayer. I truly loved all the people and churches where I ministered. But I was worn out, and I just ignored it, since the needs were so great.

At one small church, I had just finished my teaching and musical ministry, and it was late in the evening. One woman asked me for personal prayer, and I sat down next to her on the pew, as I was too tired to stand any more. While I was praying for her, I noticed that a different woman sat down at my feet, weeping. I assumed she was waiting for prayer, and was hurting badly. When I finished my prayers for the first woman, I looked down at this lovely young woman at my feet, and asked her, "What can I do for you?"

She took my right hand, and held the back of my hand against her right cheek, and started stroking my hand across her cheek over and over, weeping so hard. I was stunned and mystified.

She then said, "I see the Lord sitting here where I am. This is what the Lord is doing to you, right now." (She meant that He was holding my hand against His cheek, and stroking His cheek with the back of my hand.) I was puzzled. She continued, through desperate weeping, "He misses you. It's been a long time. He feels hunger.... thirst. He is...I don't know the English word...it's like He is envious for you." A giant "Oh NO!" flooded my heart upon hearing this.

I realized she meant that the Lord was jealous of all that I give to everyone else, but not to Him. I knew it was accurate. This sweet girl, who didn't know me, and who I had thought needed my help, was prophesying over me in a most stunning, accurate and grievous rebuke of sorts.

That just pierced my heart instantly. I was in shock, as this started to sink in. My heart sank in grief and shame. I knew beyond any doubt that she was speaking the Lord's heart to me. He had lost me. He missed me. He hungered and thirsted for my companionship. He was jealous of the endless streams of love I was pouring out on everyone but Him.

The pastor and a few others, including this young lady's husband, gathered around us, me on the front pew and she on the floor. They hesitantly offered to remove her from bothering me. I said, "No, let her do this. She is a prophet. She spoke what is true." The pastor replied, "Yes, she is a prophet."

I went back to my host home that night in stunned repentance. I sat on my bed and told the Lord, "You shouldn't have to miss me. You deserve better. I am so sorry that I have neglected You and poured myself on everyone but You. You don't have to miss me anymore. I'm here."

Just like in the Song, it was not a quick or easy path to "get Him back," or to find His Presence again. I can't say how long, because the blur of my life just clouds my ability to reckon time accurately. I can only say that it was a long journey of trying to assess my life and reconnect with the One I love. He was not holding out on me, but He needed to know if I meant it.

After that word, there were still some seasons where I remained too busy for serious, consistent time with Him, and honestly, they were not my fault. The Lord Yeshua, who is most kind, was not blaming me, but His heart hurt to see me under such impossible stress, to the point of breakdown. Nevertheless, I had to make some hard decisions, and I still need to seriously reconsider my priorities, even to this day.

I am determined not to break Yeshua's heart again, even if it means radically changing my schedule and commitments. I'm being more careful to only go where He sends me, and will not always be able to respond to the call from other ministers who believe I am needed in a given location or series of meetings. I will need to hear more clearly from the Lord where He is sending me.

We cannot coast for too long on our past times of intimacy. The Lord Yeshua is a living Person, and relationships need time and commitment, in the NOW. We won't always have extra time to spare, but we can still maintain a lifestyle of intimacy with the Bridegroom we love, by using every spare moment or hour to grab time with Him. Sometimes it will need to be in the middle of the night, and He is worth it.

Who is This: The King's Procession

Immediately after Shuli has found the one she loves, the Song bursts into a glorious chorus about the sudden appearance of King Solomon's bridal carriage and royal entourage, coming up from the wilderness into Jerusalem.

3:6-11 Who is this coming out of the wilderness, like pillars of smoke, perfumed with myrrh and frankincense, with all the merchant's fragrant powders? Behold, it is Solomon's couch, with sixty valiant men around it, of the valiant of Israel. They all hold swords, being expert in war. Every man has his sword on his thigh because of fear in the night. Of the wood of Lebanon Solomon the King made himself a palanquin: He made its pillars of silver, its support of gold, its seat of purple, its interior paved with love by the daughters of Jerusalem. Go forth, O daughters of Zion, and see King Solomon with the crown with which his mother crowned him on the day of his wedding, the day of the gladness of his heart.

As we try to understand why this passage appears here in the story, we could conclude that this Song does not seem to be completely chronological. **It is laying out wisdom about the seasons in our lives, seasons on His prophetic calendar, and seasons in our growth in the Lord, but not something we can always pin down to a timeline.**
The big question is: Who is riding in the carriage: the Bridegroom or the bride? Since the verse says, "It is Solomon's couch," and "Solomon made himself a palanquin," it appears to be the entry of the Bridegroom King, ascending into Jerusalem in His glory. There, He will be crowned on His wedding day, which is also the day when He destroys all His enemies. But some believe that this carriage is carrying the bride into Jerusalem for her wedding with the King. We could look at it both ways, so let's examine it.
There are three prophetic passages in the Song that begin with the question: "Who is this?" (SOS 3:6-8, 6:10, 8:5). This is the first one. All three passages have prophetic meaning, as they point back to Israel's history, and forward to the resurrection and ascension of the Lamb, as well as to the Lord Yeshua's return to earth and the Marriage of the Lamb. That's what is so awesome about the prophetic word. It can reflect the past, the present and the future, all at the same time, with parallel meanings and layers of fulfillment. Just amazing and awesome, God's Word!
In Hebrew, the word *"this"* has gender, either masculine or feminine, depending on what it is referring to. There is a different phrase for "Who is this [man]" versus, "Who is this [woman]." But in English, *"this"* is a neutral word, without gender.
The Hebrew phrase used in all three of these passages is the feminine phrase, *"Mi zoht?"* *Zoht* is feminine, so the answer to the question should be a female person. Therefore, it could seem that the passenger is not the Bridegroom, but the bride. However, the answer to the question is "Behold, it is Solomon's couch." In Hebrew, the word translated "couch" is a feminine noun, and so it is likely that

Solomon is riding in his royal carriage, and the feminine question is answered by the feminine word, "couch." Meaning, "It is Solomon, reclining on his royal couch."

We see a regal procession. Surrounding the exquisite carriage are sixty of Solomon's bravest soldiers, to protect the king from harm. They are riding into Jerusalem from the Judean, Egyptian or Edom wilderness, depending on which prophetic moment in history it is pointing to.

It is likely that the Daughters of Jerusalem ask the question in vs. 6. Then the bride answers them (vs. 7-11), and speaks about this unique royal carriage, and what loving care was put into its design. It was designed by Solomon and decorated by the Daughters of Jerusalem. It would be like the King building a *Succah* (Tabernacle) and His children decorating it with their loving artwork.

The bride is encouraging them to come and see the wedding of the King, where His mother will crown Him with the wedding crown. This is different than the other crowns which Yeshua has received, each one representing a different aspect of His title (rank), His authority, His victories and conquests, and His worthiness. The wedding crown is very special, and it fills Yeshua with the greatest joy. It speaks of His fulfillment and satisfaction in His bride's equally-yoked passion, desire and loyalty to Him. It is the consummation of all things, in heaven and on earth. She is His joy and His inheritance. She is the joy that was set before Him. This is the day of His overflowing joy.

The descriptions of this portable throne remind us of the construction of Solomon's Temple. The carriage is made from the finest scented and enduring cedar wood from Lebanon. The cedars were used in building Solomon's temple, where the glory of the Lord dwelt. This wood was the sturdiest and most fragrant wood in Israel, and it never corrupted.

The pillars and supports were made of gold and silver, which speak of royalty and redemption. The fabrics of purple were reminiscent of the curtain of the Holy Place. The interior (floor) of the carriage was "inlaid with **love** by the Daughters of Jerusalem." The word for "inlaid" in Hebrew is *"ratzuf,"* which means the laying down of tiles, paving or flooring material, inside another material.

But the floor of this carriage was inlaid with LOVE. Inlaid with adornments of our love. This speaks of the place where the King rests His feet, the floor under His throne. They placed their love at His feet, like breaking open their costly perfume.

When Lord Yeshua rode into Jerusalem, the Israelite crowds spread palm branches and their cloaks under His feet, even the feet of His colt. They were laying the ground with LOVE, welcoming their King into Jerusalem. This was truly a picture of the Daughters of Jerusalem loving their King, even though His reign would be rejected by the "watchmen" of the city, the spiritual leadership.

Later, who was it that wailed in mourning and love for Yeshua, as He staggered up the hill to the cross? **It was the Daughters of Jerusalem**, who wept and mourned, as their King was bearing the weight of our sins upon His back. The Lord Yeshua called them by this very title, as He prophesied of the destruction of the city He loved.

The carriage appears as pillars of smoke, perfumed with exotic powders, myrrh and frankincense. The smoke and incense speak of the priestly ministry in the Temple and the fire that fell from Heaven, during Solomon's dedication of the Temple. The myrrh speaks of the anointing oils used by the priests, as well as the oils and perfumes that anointed the robes of the king on his wedding day (see Psalm 45). The warriors surrounding the carriage would be his highly trained personal military guards in ceremonial regalia, yet alert for danger. They represent the guardian angels around the Throne of God in heaven, and the angelic presence with the bride on earth, in all of her holy worship, warfare and intercessory work. Let's look at the prophetic view of this scene, both its past and future interpretations.

A Rehearsal of Israel Coming up from the Wilderness of Sinai

As a "rehearsal of the past," all three passages can symbolize Israel's coming out of the wilderness after 40 years of wandering. Solomon was the greatest of Israel's kings, and to the Israelites, the greatest love story of all was the love story between the God of Israel and His people. The Lord considered Himself to be Israel's husband, and Israel to be His Bride. It was their Song of Songs!

Our Beloved carried us out of the wilderness on wings of eagles. He gave us bread from heaven and water from the rock. He adorned us with the wealth of Egypt, and kissed us with His Torah. Then He consecrated us and took us across the Jordan, and gave us the land of our enemies.

> *Who is this coming out of the wilderness, like pillars of smoke, perfumed with myrrh and frankincense, with all the merchant's fragrant powders?*

We see the God of Israel as the invisible Bridegroom, who carried His people "on eagles' wings" across the cruel wilderness and into the Promised Land. His Glory, fire and cloud had been manifested in the desert for 40 years, and He was now carrying His bride to the Land flowing with milk and honey, a picture of the Kingdom of God on earth. In this view, *"Honey and milk are under your tongue"* speaks of Israel's Land of Promise, abundance and fertility.

Solomon's valiant warriors are likened to the young army (except for the aged and faithful Joshua and Caleb) of consecrated, newly circumcised Israelite men, who would defeat the Canaanite armies. The portable throne is likened to the Ark of God's Glory. The Ark was carried by Levites (worshipers), and it preceded the fighting men (warriors) and the bridal company (the children of Israel) across the Jordan. The Ark was carried by her priests and Levites on their shoulders, just as Solomon's portable throne was carried by his men on their shoulders. Davidic worship was established before Solomon's reign, just as Levitical worship preceded the conquest of the Land. The Levites and priests were perfumed with incense, anointing oil, and carried all the exotic powders of the spice traders, required for the Holy incense recipe.

The Lord God dried up the waters of the Jordan, and the Hebrews crossed over on dry land, just as forty years before, they had crossed the Red Sea on dry land. They came with their sword on their thigh, and the Glory of the Lord going ahead of them, like a King entering enemy territory. There was no human king enthroned in that procession, but the golden Ark of the Covenant was a glorious picture of the crowned King of Israel. He was enthroned on the praises of His people. The Lord led His bride out of the wilderness and into her new country. Their arrival struck terror in the hearts of the inhabitants of Jericho, and the other towns in Canaan, who had heard of the fame of this mighty God of the Hebrews.

A Rehearsal of the Future Triumphal Entry of King Yeshua

We also see a picture of King Yeshua on the day of His return to Jerusalem, after conquering His enemies. This is the day when He will be crowned as the rightful heir to David's throne. In Scripture, when it says "a day," or "in that day," it is often not a literal day, but rather refers to a brief but intense period of time. Therefore, the day of His literal conquest of the earth is also the day of His wedding.

The Daughters of Jerusalem now represent the fullness of the New Covenant people of God, Jew and Gentile, One New Man in Messiah. We, the bride from all nations, will crown Him with our love. The Lord will only come when He is fervently desired. This day is also described in Psalm 45, where we see the conquering King coming for both His wedding, and to destroy His enemies.

Solomon's kingdom was a prototype of the Messianic kingdom on earth. He reigned from Jerusalem at the height of Israel's international prestige and glory. It was a long, peaceful and prosperous period in Israel's history, unlike any other time before or after this unique period. Solomon's wealth, wisdom and peace were famous across the earth. The kings and queens of the nations came into Jerusalem, bringing the king their wealth and finest offerings. The gentiles honored the God of Israel for His blessings upon His people, and honored His Word for its wisdom. Israel was truly a light to the nations under Solomon's reign. It was a microcosm of what King Yeshua's reign will look like.

Isaiah wrote his prophecies about 150 years after Solomon's reign. Therefore, most of what he wrote was pointing to the greater, future Messianic Kingdom, where the whole earth would be governed from Yeshua's throne in Jerusalem.

One example is Isaiah 60. This description points to the greater fulfillment of the restored Davidic kingdom, when the Lord Yeshua returns in power and glory, and restores the kingdom to Israel (see Acts 1:6-7).

> *"Foreigners will rebuild your walls, and their kings will serve you. Though in anger I struck you, in favor I will show you compassion. Your gates will always stand open, they will never be shut, day or night, so that people may bring you the wealth of the nations— their kings led in triumphal procession.*

> *"For the nation or kingdom that will not serve you will perish; it will be utterly ruined. The glory of Lebanon will come to you, the juniper, the fir and the cypress together, to adorn my sanctuary; and I will glorify the place for my feet.*

> *"The children of your oppressors will come bowing before you; all who despise you will bow down at your feet and will call you the City of the Lord, Zion of the Holy One of Israel"* (Isa. 60:10-14, NIV).

Before this Messianic Kingdom will be inaugurated, the final fulfillment of SOS 3:6-11 will be the Bridegroom-King's glorious coming to judge and make war. He will ride up from the Wilderness of Edom, and will turn towards Jerusalem, surrounded by His warriors. Isaiah 63:1-4 begins with these three words: **Who is this?**

> ***Who is this*** *who comes from Edom, in crimsoned garments from Bozrah, he who is splendid in his apparel, marching in the greatness of his strength? "It is I, speaking in righteousness, mighty to save." Why is Your apparel red, and Your garments like his who treads in the winepress?*

> *"I have trodden the winepress alone, and from the peoples no one was with Me; I trod them in My anger and trampled them in My wrath; their lifeblood spattered on My garments, and stained all My apparel. For the day of*

115

vengeance was in My heart, and My year of redemption had come." (Isa. 63:1-4, ESV).

The Lord will descend with His resurrected saints and angels, and they will ride up the King's Highway, up through the desert of Edom. [15] This army is the valiant warriors from SOS 3:7. They will do physical warfare against the armies of Antichrist. They will rescue and defend those who remain of His persecuted Bride and of captive Israel. They will dispense the Lord's righteous judgments (Isa. 63: 1-4). Lightening and fire will flash from the Lord's fingers and fever and pestilence (the bowls of plagues) will follow Him, against all who hate Him. He will startle the nations and explode the mountains (Hab. 3:3-7). He will dash the rebellious armies and nations to pieces like pottery (Ps. 2:9). He will judge and make war (Rev. 19:11).

They will move up the eastern side of the Dead Sea and the Jordan, and will cross into Jerusalem to cleanse the city and the Temple, and to establish the millennial government of Yeshua. The King is returning for His coronation, and for the joy of His wedding day.

The Resurrected Lord

Another type of fulfillment of this scene is the first coming of the Messiah. After He had triumphed over death on the cross, the Father raised Him from the dead. At some point soon after His resurrection, the Lord needed to ascend to His Father (see Jn. 20:17).

The Lord needed to present Himself as High Priest of heaven and earth, after His triumph over sin and death. He needed to present His own blood on the altar before the Throne. This would have been a needful legal ceremony, as atonement needed to be made (the removal of sin), for all the souls on earth, once for all (see Heb. 9:26-28). And even the heavenly things themselves needed to be cleansed with "a better sacrifice" (see Heb.9:23).

As the perfect Lamb and the High Priest of the order of Melchizedek, the fragrance of incense, anointing oil and all the chief spices would be beautifully exuding from His Person. He had just accomplished the perfect and permanent atonement for all the sins ever committed on the earth, since Adam and Eve.

Yeshua lived without sin in this defiled world. **He came out of the wilderness of this corrupted and bent earth**, and ascended into Heaven as a victorious King, an overcomer, and as a Priest. The fragrance of myrrh would perfume His garments, to signify the suffering He endured. The Lord ascended to heaven in His glorified body, and was received **into a cloud** before many witnesses.

Who is this, coming up out of the sinful earth, entering Heaven in triumph, with pillars of incense and clouds, with myrrh (suffering) and frankincense (intercession) on His garments? It is the High Priest Yeshua, the Lamb of God, the King of Kings and the Holy One of Israel.

> 3:11 *Come out, you daughters of Zion, and look upon King Solomon wearing the crown, the crown with which his mother crowned him on his wedding day, the day of the gladness of his heart.*

Marriage and government were always meant to go together, as we saw in the Creation account, and as we saw at Mt. Sinai. This will be the culmination of the purposes of God, which were always His plan from the beginning. The King will be seated at His table, and the fragrance of our love will fill the room. As a Jewish Bridegroom, He will drink the fourth cup, the cup He did not drink at the Last Passover – but will drink it anew in the Kingdom of His Father. Amen.

> *For as a young man marries a young woman, so shall your sons marry you, and as the Bridegroom rejoices over the bride, so shall your God rejoice over you* (Isa. 62:5, ESV).

Meditation

> *Our Bridegroom-King, your Father has anointed you with the oil of joy, and your garments have the fragrance*

of the priestly incense. Listen, O Bride, for the king greatly desires your presence. Leave your people and your father's home, for you have captured your King's heart. You will be adorned with royal robes, woven with gold. Surrounded by your dearest companions, you will be led into the glorious presence of your King, with great rejoicing and gladness of heart.

The Bridegroom:

I will betroth you to Me forever. I will betroth you in righteousness and justice, in loving kindness and mercy. I will betroth you to Me in faithfulness and you shall know Me and love Me with all your heart, all your soul and all your strength. And nothing will ever separate us again, My beloved.

Chapter 7

THE BRIDE'S QUALITIES (SOS 4:1-16)

4:1-5 How beautiful you are, my darling! Oh, how beautiful! Your eyes behind your veil are doves. Your hair is like a flock of goats descending from the hills of Gilead. Your teeth are like a flock of sheep just shorn, coming up from the washing. Each has its twin; not one of them is alone. Your lips are like a scarlet ribbon; your mouth is lovely. Your temples behind your veil are like the halves of a pomegranate.

Your neck is like the tower of David, built with courses of stone; on it hang a thousand shields, all of them shields of warriors. Your breasts are like two fawns, like twin fawns of a gazelle that browse among the lilies (NIV).

"Gladdening the Bride"

Within Judaism, an early wedding tradition arose, probably based on this passage in the Song of Solomon. The groom or guests sing or speak praises of the bride's beauty, character or attributes, to "gladden the bride's heart." It became an expected part of a Jewish wedding to celebrate the beauty of the bride.[16] In some weddings, the guests would encircle the bride to dance and sing her praises.[17]

This is one of three passages where the bridegroom expresses his delight in his bride's beauty. In the same manner, the Lord wants everyone to know how He feels about us. He is truly proud to call us His own, and speaks uplifting words over our lives, so that we never doubt His love, in times of separation or trouble.

If we take these descriptions (vs.1-5) literally, it may be hard for us to connect these words to the Lord's feelings about each of us who are His bride, whether male or female. I admit that this is not an easy subject for me either.

The Lord's View

Let us take a step back from the beautiful metaphors from nature to which Solomon has compared his beloved. Culturally, we are a bit alienated from Solomon's imagery. But in the context of his culture, we can appreciate the beauty of his poetry.

Various commentaries have taken each of these physical descriptions, and attributed a spiritual quality that applies to each one. I have chosen some samples to interpret, from all three of the "praising the bride" sections in the Song. Here are some interpretations of these descriptions, as symbols of our inner beauty. There are other symbolic meanings as well, found in many commentaries.

Her temple being like a slice of pomegranate is compared to the complexity and fruitfulness of our thoughts, as so many intricate networks of seed are found in every section of this exotic fruit. The juice of the pomegranate is wrapped around each precious seed, and this juice is prized for its health benefits and unusual flavor. It even looks a little like a human brain, with all its pathways. Each tiny unit of this fruit is filled with a seed of our destiny. It speaks of the multiplicity of plans and connecting purposes for every segment of our lives.

Her mouth being a "strand of scarlet" speaks of the scarlet thread that was placed in Rahab's window, as a sign of protection when the Israelites destroyed Jericho. This phrase, "a scarlet strand," represents the redemption and atoning work of the Lord. Therefore, the bride's message in her mouth is that of covering, atonement, and mercy. When others receive the word, they will place the scarlet thread of Yeshua's blood over their lives, and they will be saved.

Her waist being like a mound of wheat speaks of the nourishment we feed on, and share with others, which is the mature bread of the Word. Wheat is the most nutritious grain, from which the finest breads were made. The poor tended to eat barley bread, which was less nutritious and cheaper.

Her breasts being like two fawns, grazing among the lilies, speak of our nurturing gifts. The Lord gives us the choicest spiritual adornments (lilies) and in return, we give wisdom, encouragement and life-giving truths to His people. Breasts speak of fruitfulness (parenting) and nurturing qualities. As a mother nurses her newborn, a bond of love is created between parent and child. As she nourishes the baby, the baby gazes up at her with contentment. As we have been fed by the Lord, He expects us to nourish and nurture others, who are young and hungry for His truths.

Her teeth being white and fresh like newly shorn sheep represents our beautiful smile, so fresh and clean, washed with His Word and made joyful by His love. A smile can open up a world of testimonies about our Beloved, as you remember from my experience in the airport in Germany. I only smiled at him, and he instantly smelled the fragrance of Jesus.

Other commentaries suggest that our teeth represent the way we "appropriate" spiritual food, and how we chew it up and add it to our base of understanding, until it becomes a part of our characters. Sometimes I will hear an excellent teaching that builds up my soul with strength and encouragement. I mentally "chew on it," and I intentionally weave it into my knowledge base and into my emotionally weak areas. I appropriate it and make it part of my "treasury house," from which I feed others.

Her neck being compared to the tower of David hung with warrior's shields, speaks of unusual inward courage, hope and strength to "lift up our head" and not crumple in times of onslaught. Much of my life, I had chronic problems with my neck. They would come and go at random intervals. The muscle spasms were so painful that my mother called me, "The bird with the broken neck." It ran in our family.

When I was a young adult, the Lord healed me supernaturally, through an anointed prayer by Messianic Rabbi Dan Juster.[18] I praise the Lord for Dan's ministry and for this healing, and have great compassion for people with neck pain. The Bride's neck is a tower of strength and it spiritually represents the redemptive hope of "lifting up our heads," knowing our redemption draws so near.

Her hair is compared to a moving flock of black goats, rippling down the mountainside. This speaks of our spiritual covering. Hair is a picture of the glory of God, and it is also a picture of Nazirite consecration and purity (see Nu. 6:2). For those who have lost their hair, take heart! The Lord still covers your head with His glory and His spiritual Nazirite consecration, if your heart is that of a Nazirite. He sees the heart beyond the weaknesses of our outward covering. We'll get all our hair back, with kingdom interest, very soon!

There are other spiritual qualities that these physical comparisons can be likened to. These understandings are important to contemplate, as no word in the Bible is merely poetry; each word truly teaches us truths about our relationship with the Lord. But apart from the specific attributes of the bride of Messiah, let's step back and look at the bigger picture of what the Lord wants us to know about His heart.

Through His Eyes of Love

The Lord wants to tell us something so important to His heart, that He placed this book in the Bible. It is not an accident that this book is part of the Scriptures. He has an urgent message, and it is my job to share it with you. Many others have shared this point as well, but now it is my turn to express His heart to you, His uniquely beloved one, a lily among the thorns in this world.

Creation was a loving and deliberate choice of the Lord's heart. He made everything in the universe, and saw that it was "good." What an understatement from such a humble God! But then, He saved His best wine for last, and He created His crowning achievement in

Creation: Human beings, male and female, both in His own image and His own likeness.

In Hebrew, the word for "image" is *"tzalem,"* which means "to photograph, to film, to photocopy." The word in Hebrew for "likeness" is *"d'mut"* which means "figure, image, personality, identity, character." [19]

The Lord God made us so much like Himself, that He compares us to a photocopy of Himself, like Him in beauty, image, personality, appearance, figure, and **identity**. When He looked at us, whom He made in His image and likeness, He saw that we were "very good." Again, an understatement, compared to the throbbing joy and adoration in His heart, as He beheld these awesomely formed creatures with forms, beauty, personality and character JUST LIKE THEIR DAD!

After the Fall

The tragic results of the fall were that men saw their nakedness, ugliness, wretchedness. Their vision was blinded from the innocence and beauty of what their Father had created. They needed to hide in shame and self-hatred. All of this, which we live with since that terrible day, is a result of the fall. The Lord even needed to kill animals to make skins that would cover our nakedness, and so animal sacrifice began, on account of our disobedience.

It was not meant to be this way. We were meant to see ourselves as the dazzling display of our Creator's beauty, image, personality, character. We were designed to flow in childlike love, innocence, beauty and obedience, each one of us delighting in the unique way He made us for His own pleasure and joy. This was how it was meant to be.

We were supposed to feel, know, experience and enjoy the way His eyes saw us. We were designed to share and agree with His view of us, His perspective on our unique, one-of-a-kind beauty and radiance, both outward and inward. Our bodies were a sculpted work of art, and our minds were a complex network of millions of pathways, carrying brilliant transmissions of understanding and communications at lightning speed. Our souls were a well of living water, pulsing emotions and depth of feeling for the Lord and knowing His heart for us.

The Lord Yeshua came to earth in the image of sinful man, yet without sin, to live unashamed in the Presence of His Father, while still interacting on this broken earth. He knew who He was, and He had no need to hide. He was beautiful in the eyes of His Father, even though Isaiah tells us that in the eyes of man, *"He had no beauty or majesty to attract us to him, nothing in his appearance that we should desire him. He was despised and rejected by mankind, a man of suffering, and familiar with pain. Like one from whom people hide their faces he was despised, and we held him in low esteem* (Isa. 53:2b-3, NIV).

The Lord Yeshua came to purchase back souls from the fall. **He came to restore the image of His Father in fallen mankind.** Ultimately, the Lord Yeshua came even to restore the entirety of Creation to its original pristine beauty, innocence and perfection.

In His first coming, not all of this lofty assignment would be fulfilled. He would pay for our broken souls with His life and His blood. This would restore us to unbroken fellowship and relationship with our Creator. This would allow our eyes to see ourselves as the Father sees us, since He sees His own beautiful Son when He looks at us.

We who are saved and walking in the Lord, are clothed in His image, robed in the beauty of perfection and holiness with which Yeshua's righteousness has fully covered us. He has removed the stain, the sin, the shame, the self-hatred, and the need to hide. He has done so much more than we can recount, even if this whole book were only on the subject of what He has done for us.

Stop Condemning Yourself

Know for certain that when the Lord looks at us, He is moved with our beauty, and He desires to proclaim to us (His bride) and to all the "guests at the wedding," how lovely and unique we are in His eyes. He desires to describe our faithful traits and attributes to all who will listen to His voice. He would say these kinds of things about us, like a proud Bridegroom gladdening His bride. Consider these cases, for they were written for your great encouragement, even if they don't fit your exact scenario:

"Look at My beloved son! His heart is so fiercely committed to Me. He has just suffered such a great injustice, yet he is not pointing an accusing finger at Me, but is choosing to love Me through this trial. His wife has wrongfully left him, and he has been cheated out of a significant amount of money, which he cannot recover. Others are assuming the worst about him, and it is not true, but he is weeping to Me, and bringing his sorrow to Me, but is not blaming Me for this injustice. I will defend him in due season, if he will hang on to this trusting faith."

"Look at My steadfast daughter. Her eyes are focused only on My opinion, and she does not worry about what others think about her. Some believers, who should know better, are misjudging her badly, and she feels shame. But she is pushing past this feeling, and seeing her beauty through My eyes only. She is intentionally loving and forgiving those who are speaking against her. She knows how I see her heart and her life, and I am overcome with the strength of her exceptional resolve, forgiveness and tenderhearted devotion to Me."

"Look at this precious 11-year old child, who loves Me. He is bullied in school, and no one thinks he is worthy to be part of the "cool group." He eats lunches alone, with no one to care for his well-being, and he cannot wait for each unkind school day to be over. In gym class, he is ostracized by the athletic youth around him. But my son is not blaming Me for the cruelty of the other children. He knows this is NOT how I see him, and he realizes that when they behave badly, I am still a good God. He knows I will come and rescue him at the right moment in his life. He knows it will not always be this way. Bless My

beloved son, for he shall be exalted before those who abuse him now."

"Look at My brave daughter. She was severely burned in a car accident, and her face looks deformed and ravaged, by this world's standards. People stare at her when she enters the market. They avert their eyes from her. She holds up her head, knowing that I find her dazzling and radiant. I see her as she is eternally, as her spirit already looks in heaven, and as she will be with Me forever: a perfect dove, a lovely princess, whose form and features are captivating to Me and to all who can see with the eyes of My Spirit. She is whole in heaven, and this is her eternal identity. I AM so proud of her for overcoming this handicap without bitterness or offense. Oh, how beautiful you are, My dove! Your face is like the heavens in its brightness, and your eyes are like pools of liquid love to Me."

"Look at My dear son. He has been obese since those OCD (Obsessive-Compulsive Disorder) medications in his adolescence caused him to gain almost 100 pounds. People do not want him to sit next to them on airplanes, because his body will spill over into their private space. They look at him like a circus freak. They assume he eats like a hog, and they judge him for being so gluttonous. They do not know what he has suffered. But he is not angry and hateful towards them. He knows they cannot under-stand why he looks this way. He loves Me, and he knows with all his heart that I find him desirable, handsome, perfectly formed and made. I see his body as it was meant to be, and soon, very soon, it will indeed be restored. He knows full well that one day, very soon, I will give him relief from this shell of brokenness, and I will give him a sculpted body of resurrected beauty and strength, like the finest of statues, dressed in elegant, royal robes, and he will dance with Me on the sea of glass, as all heaven

watches my love and adoration for him, and for his over-coming spirit."

Beloved, this is the real meaning of "Gladdening the Bride," through the eyes of the only true Bridegroom. When we read Solomon's descriptions of his perfect dove, we must see ourselves through the loving, gentle, humble, adoring eyes of the One who made us. He loves us passionately and He will come and marry us, soon and very soon. Keep your eyes on the prize, as He keeps His gaze on your unique, one-of-a-kind beauty.

Remember His heart when you read these love passages in Song of Solomon, and know that this is truly the way our Lord Jesus feels about you and the way you love Him. He hears all that you tell Him, and He observes your private decisions to love and trust Him. All is captured in His eyes, and He is singing these bridal praises over you, before all of heaven. Soon it will be heard, even by our enemies. Does this "gladden your heart," O Bride of Yeshua? Oh Halleluiah, for a hope and a future with One who actually loves us!

The Mountain of Sacrifice

4:6 Until the day breaks and the shadows flee away, I will go my way to the mountain of myrrh and to the hill of frankincense.

The Bridegroom is still speaking, as we are still in the midst of a lengthy bridegroom speech (4:1-15). Is he announcing a physical or spiritual trip to the distant mountains?

This is the Lord speaking to us. He is saying, *"Before this night is over, I will go to the mountain of myrrh (suffering) and the hill of frankincense (intercession). I have work to do that you do not yet understand, and I will go my way, and spend the night wrestling with what our commitment will cost Me."*

He is deliberately using the exact words that His betrothed had used in 2:17, when she had not agreed to come into the harvest fields. She had said, ***"Until the day breaks and the shadows flee*** *away, turn, my Beloved and be like a young stag on the mountains of Bether."* This section (4:1-16) is a continuation of that same conversation (2:10-16). It is an ongoing dialogue between them, and we need to see the continuity here. So He uses her same expression, and says, ***"Until the day breaks and the shadows flee away,*** *I will go my way to the mountain of myrrh and the hill of frankincense."*

He lets her know that He is finding no fault in her (*You are all fair, my love, and there is no spot in you,* 4:7), although she had not been ready for the first challenge, due to fear or immaturity. He knows that after He has been to the mountain, she will be ready to come with Him in the second challenge. This readiness and maturing of the bride is evidenced in the lines that follow. But first, He is declaring that He must go and accomplish His purposes, through sacrifice and intercession. **The mountain of myrrh is not a romantic place**. It is a place of the perfume of sacrifice. He must go to the mountain of sacrifice for her sake, to bring the bride to the fullness of His stature and her maturity.

Abraham was promised more than he could ever imagine. A father of multitudes, and his children more numerous than the stars and the sands of the shore. The Lord promised him that he would become the father of the future bridal company from many nations, who would arise in the last days in the greatest numbers ever seen.

But Abraham had to travel to the mountain of myrrh alone, and to offer his son, before his destiny could be fulfilled. Without that three-day journey and sacrifice on the mountain, Abraham could not have brought forth the mature bride, the victorious company of millions of sons and daughters, which the Lord God had promised him.

Abraham has waited for this day with longing, to see his spiritual "daughter," the bride of the Lamb, arise into her priestly destiny. His eyes will now see her purified devotion to the Lord. He saw this day when the Angel of the Lord stayed his hand from slaying his son, Isaac. He saw the Lamb, and He saw the bride (his spiritual offspring, through the Seed that would come through Isaac).[20]

Hebrews 11 tells us that the cloud of witnesses who have run their race before us, died without receiving what was promised to them. In the final verse, it says that they will not receive their promises **apart from us** (see Heb. 11:39-40). Thus, we must run the race hard, putting aside every obstacle to our arising to maturity, even to the full stature of Messiah's character (see Heb. 12:1, Eph. 4:12).

In the same way, if the Lord Yeshua had not left us for a season, to go to the mountain of suffering alone, He would not be able to raise us up to the full stature of our partnership with Him. We could not go with Him to the cross. *"Where I am going, you cannot follow, but you will follow later"* (John 13:36). We could not be equally-yoked partners, nor run on the mountains with Him, until He had raised us up, through His forerunner journey of suffering and intercession. *"I will go my way to the mountain of myrrh."* Yeshua had to pay what we could not pay, for us to be permitted to ascend the mountain of the Lord. He knew that we would follow Him, once He had paid the price. His sacrifice would enable us to go all the way and to love not our lives unto death. Oh, Hallelujah for this selfless love!

Running on the Mountains Together

The Lord then reassures the bride that he finds her "altogether beautiful, with no flaw in her," so that we will not fall into guilt over our failure. This is the Lord's way of expressing His commitment to us, as in the signing a betrothal contract with us. He is pledging His full inheritance, and that all He has is ours, no matter the cost.

After affirming that her heart pleases Him, the Lord immediately prepares her for her next assignment, the "second challenge" (vs.8). He knows that this time, she will come and look with Him from Lebanon, and she will say "yes," to all His assignments for her.

At the Last Supper, the Lord shared His own flesh and blood with His betrothed ones at His table. *"Everything I have is yours, even My own body and blood. Until we can drink the fourth cup together in My Father's house, I pledge my commitment to you."*

At that meal, the Lord predicted that Peter would deny Him three times that very night. So Peter did not pass "the first chal- lenge." The Lord knew that Peter would fail the first challenge, but He was so committed to Peter's destiny that He added, *"But when you have turned, restore your brothers."* The Lord knew that Peter would agree to the second challenge, and would go all the way to the mountain of myrrh with the Lord. **Yeshua found Peter's love to be beautiful, despite knowing that he would fail the first test.**

When the Bridegroom returns from the mountain of myrrh, He then calls her to come with Him to Lebanon, so that she can become His partner in strategy and in government.

4:8 Come with me from Lebanon, my spouse, with me from Lebanon. Look from the top of Amana, from the top of Senir and Hermon, from the lions' dens, from the mountains of the leopards.

He says "with me" twice. Our eye is drawn to the urgent repetition of **"with me."** There is something they must do **together**!

When He says, "Come with me *from* Lebanon," it does not actually mean that they are leaving Lebanon. Let me paraphrase this sentence, to make its meaning less confusing:

"Come with Me, My bride, and from Lebanon, from the mountain peaks and dens of the lions, from the crest of Hermon, we will look together at the panorama of the Lord's Land and His purposes."

He is calling her to come with Him to Lebanon, in order to gain the Mountain View **with Him**.

Following the natural story line, they have gone to Lebanon together, possibly to Solomon's summer home in the north. Lebanon is known for its cedar forests, mountain streams of melting snow, plants and flowers, and spices and fragrance (see SOS 4:11, 15; Ps. 29:5-6, Hos. 14:6, Isa. 35:2). Lebanon's climate is as different from Judea, as Vermont's climate and ecology are from Arizona's. But this vast variety of climates and geology exist within tiny Israel!

It was also known for dangerous predators that lived in those mountains, lions and leopards. "Senir" is the Amorite name of Mt. Hermon (see Deut. 3:8-9). Mt. Hermon (pronounced hehr-MOHN) is on the eastern side of the Jordan, situated about halfway between Damascus and Tyre.

It is located in what is now called "the Golan Heights." This territory was taken by the Israelites in Deuteronomy 3, by the Lord's help and direction. Moving forward thousands of years, it is still rightfully Israel's to this day. It is desperately needed for Israel's security, and should not be negotiated away under any terms.

The Beloved must show many things to His bride; He desires to teach and train her for seasons that will come in her life and destiny. The rugged mountains and forests, the glorious flowers, the spice-bearing trees and plants, and the dangers of predatory beasts, pose a very different environment than the courts and palaces of Jerusalem. And the vantage point from these mountains, to this very day in Israel, is highly strategic in understanding the Lord's plans and purposes.

The Lord brings His bride with Him to the observation points of the mountains, where she can view a vast region with Him and see things from the Lord's perspective, to see how He views Israel's purposes and destiny. **He is now treating her as a military partner**, wanting her to see much of Israel, from these strategic heights. She is His partner in warfare, just as His ancestors partnered with the Lord to drive out the Canaanite enemies. You may remember that in chapter 3, we learned that the term *"ezer"* (helper), is what Eve was to be to Adam: a bride and military assistant.

Just as those areas north and east of Israel were known for fierce predators, so even now, there are human and demonized enemies in these very locations, seeking to destroy Israel, like ravenous beasts. As I write these very words, a group of prophetic intercessors from a number of nations are standing on these very mountains we read about in these verses. They are praying to bring the Lord's rule, reign and revival to this severely oppressed Middle East. These very mountains, as in days of old, will be vital to the Lord's Kingdom invading the Middle East. God's enemies will also attempt to use these strategic heights for evil purposes.

The Lord wants us to look at situations on this earth as His eyes see them. He wants to take us to the mountains, to the depth and height of His perspective, above all our immediate circumstances that cloud our vision. Only then can we know His plans and agree with Him in prayer, fellowship and strategic activities.

We could pray "whatever we want or feel," but this would not be effectual, and might not even be the will of Heaven. This Mountain View will allow us to speak into situations from the courts of Heaven, rather than battling on the earth, without seeing the bigger picture of what is happening in the realm of the Spirit. We will be given the Lord's perspective from the mountains. How we need to ask the Lord for that, and to wait for His vision to be granted to us.

From the lions' dens, from the mountains of the leopards.

There is one costly reality that most intercessors have learned. When the Lord calls us to walk in the realm of the Spirit, to share His "mountain view," we are going to encounter fierce, predatory beasts, who wish to devour us and destroy our work for the Lord, and our very lives, if possible.

For most of us, these are not literal animals, although in some regions of the earth, or in the future, wild animals will become a real problem for all mankind (see Rev. 6:8). We also know that our adversary is like a roaring lion, seeking to devour us (see 1 Pet. 5:8). For those who live in Israel, the wild beasts are usually terrorists, who have been taught since infancy that it is an honor to die in the act of murdering Jews, and thus, to become a martyr for their violent demonic god.

I have a dear friend in Israel, who loves the Lord and is filled with His Spirit. She told me a shocking testimony, which exactly illustrates this principle. One day, she was going about her business in a certain city, and the Holy Spirit told her to walk to a particular restaurant in the city. This instruction came unexpectedly, and she had no natural reason to go to this place. But she went there, because the Lord told her to. She prayed in the Spirit while waiting to see why the Lord had brought her there.

Soon after she got there, a ragged looking man wandered into the restaurant. He just seemed poor, or homeless. No one thought anything of it. Then, one of the security guards felt a bit suspicious, and approached this man, and asked him to show his I.D.

As the man began to reach into his clothing, the guard saw that the man was a suicide bomber, and they were all one second away from death and destruction. The guard threw himself on top of the terrorist, hoping against hope that he could prevent the man from detonating. This guard, without having time to think about it, was willing to give his life to absorb some of the explosion in his body. My friend kept praying in the Spirit. Soon, the man was overpowered by security, and against all odds, he was unable to push the detonation switch, which would have created unimaginable horror, death and injuries.

As my friend was settling down from the terror and shock of it all, the Holy Spirit told her that because she had come and prayed, this murderous assault was thwarted. This is an example of the Lord's "Mountain View" allowing us to partner with His purposes. If He had told her that He was sending her to a restaurant that was about to be targeted by a suicide bomber, it would have been so terrifying for her to obey, that her prayers might have been less effective, due to sheer terror and survival instincts. But the Lord did not tell her why she should go. So she obeyed, and her prayers saved many lives, as well as the many other lives that would be devastated by severe injuries, shock and trauma. That restaurant is there to this day. No one will ever thank her, nor know of her role in the outcome, but the Lord knows what His bride did to save those He loves.

This is an example of looking with the Lord from the tops of the mountains, from the den of lions, to see His plans, and then, partnering with Him, for the saving of many lives. He sees it all ahead of time, and we don't. So we need His eyes to see.

In addition to predators who seek to literally murder God's people, there are other kinds of predators, who can hurt the heart and soul, but not so much the physical body. One surprising factor is that in a number of cases, these types of predators are other Christians. This is hard to believe, and harder to understand, and yet the enemy definitely uses Christians to try to destroy each other, if he is permitted to do so.

The weapons of these predators are slander and accusation. In today's media, the attacks often come electronically, through email, internet or radio. They think they are doing the Lord's will by exposing and discrediting these men and women of God. The problem is that in many cases, the accusations are not true, and are based on twisted versions of the teachings and history of these ministers. These believers will face a difficult shock when they meet the Lord. They will see the ones they spoke against, being honored and defended by the Lord, and for once in their life, they will be speechless.

The attack and accusations wear ministers down, as they feel the need to write some kind of defense, over and over, and it robs their time and energy from the work they are called to do. In many cases, it is best not to write articles in defense of ourselves. It never convinces the accuser, and there will always be another accusation that bounces back. Better to let the Lord defend us, in His own good time.

Therefore, when the Lord says, *"Come with Me, My bride, from the lion's dens and the mountains of the leopards,"* He is saying this: *"You are in a place of attack, and you are receiving wounds. It is wearing you down. Come **with Me**, and I will show you how I see things. I want you **with Me,** so that you can step back from the constant attacks and accusation. I want to free you from the war zone from time to time, and to take you high above the angry airwaves **with Me**, to see how I view your purposes in this earth and in this last generation."*

If the Lord wants to remove us from the tug-of-war, then let go of the rope. He will defend us, if we will refrain from defending ourselves. Only the Lord's opinion of us will matter on that day. Be of good cheer, and know that your Defender is alive, well, and has overcome the world.

His Heart is Overwhelmed

4:9-10 You have captivated my heart, my sister, my bride; you have captivated my heart with one glance of your eyes, with one jewel of your necklace. How beautiful is your love, my sister, my bride! How much better is your love than wine, and the fragrance of your oils than any spice! Your lips drip nectar, my bride; honey and milk are under your tongue; the fragrance of your garments is like the fragrance of Lebanon (ESV).

There is something about standing with the Lord in His purposes, "keeping Him company" in His burdens, pleasures or pain. It captivates and comforts His heart that we would come with Him, and try to see things as He sees them.

One glance of our eye moves the Lord, because it takes uncommon faith to glance up at the One we cannot see. Just to know that our eyes are meeting His eyes, is an act of faith on our part. Add to that the look of love in our eyes, with which we look up into His face, though we do not see Him – the Lord cherishes these moments, and they are imprinted forever in His heart. The Lord knows it takes great faith for you to know that He is looking right back into your eyes of tender love.

I can only give a small personal testimony about this matter. There have been several times, during a time of waiting on the Lord, when I have looked upwards, toward Him, in the direction I imagine Him to be, there in the room with me. As my eyes would go to that general area where I picture His eyes, such a strong love would bounce back into me, it made me kind of crumple over. It was hard not to turn my eyes away, since it was an overwhelming feeling. Faith tells me that the One I am gazing at really sees the look in my eyes, and instantly reflects back to me His stronger version of love, so that I will know that our eyes are truly connecting. Once (and only once), I looked up and He was sitting right there in plain view! But that is not the normal encounter.

"One jewel of our necklace" represents the adornments that the Holy Spirit has deposited in us as advance preparation for the Wedding of the Lamb. It speaks of the Bride making herself ready in inward beauty, truth, humility and a heart that cries out for justice. He sees our spiritual strengths and gifts as adornments, as Eliezer adorned Rebecca, and as a Bridegroom would adorn His bride.

How much better is your love to Me than wine! Your lips drip nectar, my bride; honey and milk are under your tongue; the fragrance of your garments is like the fragrance of Lebanon.

Think for one moment of all the ugly, cruel and blasphemous words the Lord's ears have to hear every day. Think of how refreshing are our precious words to His ears, in the vast, salty sea of unkindness and profanity. His Bride's lips should drip nectar, which means that healing words should proceed from the treasures of our heart.

The loving words we whisper and speak to the Lord are like sweetness to Him, coming from our lips as nectar, milk and honey. He is moved, not only from our glance, but from the words that come from our lips. There was once when I actually felt the Lord's heart being overwhelmed by a statement I made to Him, concerning our future together. I even saw evidence that I had overwhelmed His heart, which is too precious to write down.

Are We a Locked Garden?

4:12-15 A garden locked is my sister, my bride, a spring locked, a fountain sealed. Your shoots are an orchard of pomegranates with all choicest fruits, henna with nard, nard and saffron, calamus and cinnamon, with all trees of frankincense, myrrh and aloes, with all choice spices— a garden fountain, a well of living water, and flowing streams from Lebanon (ESV).

After words of praise, the Lord makes an unexpected observation about His bride's heart, which He calls our "garden." He says, *"My bride is a locked garden, a closed up spring, and a sealed fountain."* There are two ways one could interpret this passage.

Some feel that the Lord is glad that His bride is a locked garden and a sealed fountain, as if she is undefiled by the world outside. They would say that He is pleased that we have closed ourselves in, only for Him, and no one else can get in.

Rather, it is my understanding that He is saying, *"My Bride is a locked garden and a sealed fountain. I cannot enter the garden of her heart and enjoy the fruits and spices found there. I will not force My way in, if she has locked her garden to Me.*

Prophet and teacher Neville Johnson was once taken in an experience. The Lord took him to a locked, neglected garden, with weeds, overgrowth and disrepair. Neville was appalled by the condition of this garden. Still, he felt the Lord's great love for this garden. He didn't know what this place was. The Lord told him, *"This is My church. This is the condition of most of My church. It's like Song of Solomon 4:12. I cannot get into their garden. Tell them that when I can walk in their garden, I will let them walk in My garden."*[21]

The Lord expects His bride's heart to be an open garden, where He is welcome to enjoy the plantings. This speaks of transparency and holiness, which is the opposite of hiding. From the beginning, the Lord designed us to meet with Him in the garden and to enjoy our sweet and intimate times there. **He has planted Paradise, the garden of the Lord, in our heart**, by His Spirit. Solomon wrote this also in Ecclesiastes.

He has made everything beautiful in its time. **He has also set eternity in the hearts of men** (Ecc. 3:11a, NIV).

We spoke in chapter 5 about why we feel the need to hide from the Lord. When Adam and Eve hid from the Lord, their fellowship was broken. They were afraid of Him, instead of in love with Him, like innocent children. *Oh My dove, in the cleft of the rock...let Me see your face, let Me hear your voice!*

In my first book, Coffee Talks with Messiah, the Lord gave me a stunning revelation of the way our hiding hurts Him, and how it separates us from the intimacy He desires and requires. I had spent three days of seclusion with the Lord, and had poured out everything in my heart, to a greater degree than I had ever done, in all my years of knowing the Lord. When those days were over, I took some time to thank the Lord for many things He had shown me during those three days. While I was thanking Him, His glory came over me in a powerful way. I saw Him in a vision, and He spoke to me:

"I now know that you love Me with all your heart. You have shown Me your heart, and have not withheld from Me anything that was in your heart. Even though I know

137

the thoughts of people's hearts, if they don't share them with Me, I don't really know them (He is referring to knowing the person, not the thoughts) *because I will not violate their privacy. This is part of My humble and respectful character which I was showing you yesterday.*

"You have proven that you will just enjoy being with Me, even if I don't manifest in any dramatic way you would have liked. You are truly My friend. Now I can trust you, because you proved you will be My friend and enjoy My company, without expecting anything from Me."

The Lord Jesus valued greatly the fact that I withheld nothing from Him that was in my heart. At that time, He sealed me with His own blood, in a spiritual act, assuring me that I would be with Him forever.

If we do not tell Him everything in our hearts, He warns, *"I don't really know them."* In Hebrew, the verb "to know" is a most intimate word. It is not a passing acquaintance. When Adam became intimate with his wife, Eve, it says, "And Adam *knew* his wife." I encourage every reader to be utterly transparent with the Lord. Never assume that because He knows your thoughts, you do not need to verbalize them.

I now understand that this revelation from my first book was preparation for the writing of this book. The Lord was telling me that most of His church is a garden locked up – He cannot enter our hearts by force, because He respects our free will. We have to intentionally and voluntarily open the garden of our hearts to the Lord.

He is Looking for Eden in Us

Our hearts should be a Garden of Eden in the midst of the thorns of the fallen earth. Our hearts should be a lovely and welcoming environment for the Lord to walk and abide. He desires to come into the garden of our heart, and to have free access to everything that resides in our hearts. No part of the garden should be locked from Him, and He won't open it without our permission.

In the beginning, the Lord planted a garden, and set Adam and Eve in Eden to enjoy its perfection. Eden was a well-watered garden, and it was the place where God dwelt with man, the place where the soles of His feet walked, in the cool of the day. He commanded them to be fruitful and multiply and to "subdue the earth." This meant that if we had not disobeyed, it would have been our responsibility to cultivate the earth, and make it like the garden of the Lord (see Ps. 115:15-17).

Eden was like the Tabernacle of meeting, because it was where we could meet with our Lord in face-to-face intimacy. After the fall, the garden was **locked up.** Its entrance was guarded by Cherubim with flaming swords, and we could not get into our garden sanctuary. Since we were locked out, nothing good from Eden would be able to flow into the rest of the earth. No one was there to cultivate it and to spread the fruits and blow the fragrance of its spices abroad in the world. The intimacy could not be "shed abroad" in the hearts of men.

A closed up spring, and a sealed fountain

The Lord desires that we would be a bubbling spring of water, giving refreshment to the weary. Our living water must flow out to the thirsty. The living water He has placed in us will make the desert rejoice, the fruit to abound, and will bring strength and encouragement to the weary people of God, whose labors "under the sun" have worn them down.

> *The wilderness and the wasteland shall be glad for them, and the **desert shall rejoice and blossom as the rose**; it shall blossom abundantly and rejoice, even with joy and singing... **Strengthen the weak hands, and make firm the feeble knees.** Say to those who are fearful-hearted, "Be strong, do not fear!* (Isa. 35:1-2a, 3-4a).

There was a French film many years ago about a family who inherited a lovely farm with orchards in southern France. Unbeknownst to them, two scheming neighbors got to the property before they arrived. These men plugged up the spring on the property with cement, and covered up the evidence, so that no one would find it. This was done so that the family would fail in their farming. The goal of these evil men was to force them off the land, so they could acquire it, unplug the spring, and make money growing flowers.

It was heartbreaking, watching the discouragement of this hard working man (who was a hunchback, which made it even sadder), as no matter what he did, he could not locate the spring that would have saved them. In the end, he died, trying to dynamite open part of the land to find the source of water. His wife and little flaxen-haired daughter were left with nothing, and they left the farm desolate.

This devastating film made a huge impression on me in my youth. Now, when I read the verse, "My bride is a closed spring, a sealed fountain," I think of this film. The land was rich with fruit trees and all the best produce, but with the spring sealed, nothing could grow, and no fruit could be produced for the surrounding villages.

This passage speaks of three things in the garden of our heart: Fresh, living waters, fruits and spices.

The Lord Yeshua has deposited His own Spirit in us, who is the living waters referred to in John 7:37. The life of His Spirit in us will bring forth fruit, which is His heart attitudes formed in us. **It is our fruit which is the evidence of being conformed to the image of the Lord Yeshua.**

And His Spirit, in cooperation with our own soul, will produce our unique spices (the particular flavors of our sanctified personality, natural gifts and humor). Our spices are the part of us that makes the Father look down, shake His head with affectionate amusement and say, *"That's My girl!"* Or, with longsuffering love, *"There he goes again!"* Have you ever felt that response from the Lord? It is so funny and humbling at the same time. At those moments, you see Him as an actual Father, just enjoying us, teasing us, loving us, spoiling us. These are treasured moments with the One who loves us.

Once, my best friend and I were praying and worshiping in my basement. We were just pouring out our love for the Lord, and were telling Him how much we wanted to please Him. At one point, one of us said, "Lord, even though we know You can't be surprised by anything, we want to surprise You." Like children, we wanted to give Him a happy surprise.

Then we forgot all about it, as we kept praying and worshiping. At one point, we started singing a really nice worship song, but we started in the wrong key. It was way too low for our voices, and we were stuck – it was too late to change to a higher key. So we plowed through the song, realizing it didn't sound that stellar. And I plainly saw the Father fold His arms, and heard Him interject: *"Now THAT was a surprise!"*

He meant it was so terrible-sounding that it surprised even Him. We laughed so hard at His humor and gentle teasing our unpleasant rendition of that song! We still laugh at His sense of humor to this day. That's part of our unpredictable spice garden!

Fruits are nourishing and refreshing. Spices make food interesting and aromatic. His Spirit in us will cause the spices of our unique fragrance to flow out from our lives and testimonies, into a world that smells of death and decay. We will be the aroma of Messiah, a priestly fragrance amidst the death around us. Remember that the Jews would enshroud their dead with expensive spices. They knew that the scent of spices was the opposite smell than the stench of death and decay. This is a prophetic picture. The dead smell dead. The living smell like a bed of spices, and our fragrance is perceived by those among us.

> *But thanks be to God, who always leads us as captives in Christ's triumphal procession and uses us to **spread the aroma of the knowledge of him** everywhere. For we are to God the **pleasing aroma of Christ among those who are being saved** and those who are perishing* (2 Cor. 2:14-15, NIV).

A Well of Living Waters

> *A fountain of gardens, a well of living water, and streams from Lebanon* (4:15, NIV).

The Lord now shows us what He intends for us to be. A flowing, inexhaustible source of His living love. Our fountain will water many gardens, not just our own. And again He says, "streams from

Lebanon." Within the Body of Messiah are many streams – these various groups or movements are not in competition, but all flow together into one river of life.

A well is a deep reservoir of fresh water. It does not contain stagnant water like a cistern. The water in the well is continuously being fed or seeped by an underground source. So it is living water, always being replenished. Our well contains the depth of our history and the unique themes which the Lord has impressed on our journey. Our testimony is never stagnant, but is always developing. His mercies are new every morning, and His faithfulness is renewed each night.

When we share what He has done for us, other lives are changed by the power of the Spirit, which is released by the word of our testimony. One of the three ingredients needed to be an overcomer is, "the word of our testimony" (see Rev.12:11).

I learn so much about the Lord through the testimony of others. I think, "Wow...if He would do that for them, He is the same God. He would do that for me too." And then I press in harder, because my faith was boosted by their testimony. All of us have testimonies that will heal and deliver others.

Naomi had a bitter testimony. In her brokenness, she felt that the Lord had dealt her a bitter blow, and there was nothing good in her well-water to testify. But the Lord turned her bitterness into sweetness, joy, love and grandchildren. He gave her Ruth, whose love transformed her destiny from brokenness to inheritance. He gave her a joyful testimony after her long night of bitterness, which lasted many years.

We must realize: We have not seen the end of the story. The Lord turns the bitter into sweet, to those who put their trust in Him, even in the worst of times. But we must fight the good fight, so as not to be offended with the Lord when these things seem impossible to overcome. **He turns the bitter into sweet! Keep trusting in His love, and LOVE will have the last word of your story.**

Despite the troubles, our souls will be like a well-watered garden, resting in the Lord's provisions.

Therefore they shall come and sing in the height of Zion, streaming to the goodness of the Lord— for wheat and new wine and oil, for the young of the flock and the herd; **their souls shall be like a well-watered garden, and they shall sorrow no more at all** (Jer. 31:12).

Our hearts should be an Eden, where the Lord can enjoy the atmosphere of peace, transparency, and voluntary love. We must guard the gates of our lips, so that only sweet waters will flow out. Our words are meant to sustain the weary with encouragement.

The Sovereign Lord has given me a well-instructed tongue, to know **the word that sustains the weary** (Isa. 50:4, NIV).

Our locked garden is a result of the fall – the fallen nature causes us to hide in shame and self-protection. The Lord gave His life to remove the curse of the fall from our innermost being, so that we can approach Him with "unveiled faces," with no more need to hide. Yeshua is SAFE with the depths of our hearts, the good, the bad and the ugly. He is safe and faithful to help us, when we are honest before Him.

Even before we reach the Eternal state, He has already removed the curse of shame and separation from us, if we will open up our garden, like trusting children.

The curse caused us to lose access to Paradise, and to the Tree of Life. The Lord's finished work on the cross has reversed the curse, and we have been granted access again. We do not have to wait for Eternity. The Kingdom is already planted within us, and Eternity is already set within our hearts (see Luke 17:20-21, Ecc. 3:11a).

He is Searching for Fruit

Your shoots are an orchard of pomegranates with all choicest fruits

The Paradise of God is full of fruit-bearing trees, an orchard of life and healing in the midst of His Eternal City (see Rev. 22:1-3, 2:7).

143

The Lord desires to find good fruit in our lives. His Spirit deposited good seeds of Yeshua's character at the time of our salvation. For these seeds to mature into the fullness of the stature of Yeshua's character requires time in His Presence, and feeding on His Word (see Eph. 4:12-13). Every garden has different fruits and scents, and the Lord enjoys our diversity.

However, evil thoughts and destructive emotions also have an odor. Sometimes Neville Johnson will ask the audience, "So what do you smell like?" That one question brings the room to repentance!

Yeshua is a Man on a mission. He is looking for fruit, **and expects to find it**, even in the driest seasons. The Lord once showed me a vision of Himself, padding swiftly and skillfully through a thick evergreen forest, like a Native scout. He was bent forward, ducking His head and pushing large branches aside, as He kept moving forward rapidly. He was looking intently for fruit on every branch, and pushed them aside with great force in His exploration for fruit. I noticed in a different part of that vision, that even on bare branches, He still expected fruit.

Once I was ministering in a church; while I was up front speaking, one of my ministry team had a vision; he saw the Lord walk into the church, and He walked right up to the front. The Lord seemed to be looking for fruit in this church, on a tree which could not be seen. After a short time, the Lord turned and walked out, without saying a word, nor making eye contact with the prophet who saw Him. He just left. The prophet had the distinct impression that the Lord did not find fruit in that church. It was a very disturbing picture.

This is a continuation of the recurring theme throughout the Song: His voice is echoing over the mountains; He is calling His Bride; He is knocking at her door; He is gazing through her window; He is thrusting His hand into the lock on her door, He is inviting her to come; **He is waiting to be invited to come into her garden.**

Blow upon my Garden

4:16 Awake, O north wind, and come, O south! Blow upon my garden, that its spices may flow out. Let my beloved come to his garden and eat its pleasant fruits.

This is the bride's response to His statement about the garden of her heart. Every call of the Lord requires a response from us. Every Word that goes out of His mouth is for a specific purpose. Nothing He utters should be allowed to fall to the ground, or hover aimlessly above the atmosphere. His Word requests, requires and desires a response, and our response will be recorded in heaven.

When He says, *"Arise, My love and come away,"* we have a choice. When He leaps over mountains and bounds over stars to find us, will we be ready to respond quickly, or will His appearance catch us unaware or unprepared? When He beckons us to step out of the boat, out of our comfort zone into the raging seas, will we find the strength and courage to obey?

When He dreams a destiny for us that seems too big, too impossible, will we shrink back or will we dare to believe that this is truly what He dreamed for us?

When He gently points out to us areas of our hearts that are not yet yielded, will we take the steps necessary to give Him access, no matter how painful, humbling or shattering? Be sure of this. He will surprise you, and it won't be what you were expecting. Be prepared to respond rightly, even if the Lord calls you to something you had not planned for.

When He says, *"My bride is a locked garden, a blocked spring, a sealed fountain,"* the Lord is alerting us to a heart condition that requires a response. There are very few believers who live in complete transparency and yieldedness before the Lord. We may think we do, but He is letting us know that we are not yet an open garden for Him to walk into.

We were created with a vast capacity to love the Lord and to love others. We have treasures in our hearts that have not been released, developed or even discovered. We also have wounds, pains, offenses, fears, doubts and shame in our hearts that we have not yet allowed the Lord to heal, remove, discover and uncover, mend, bend or break off. Can we allow the Lord to prune good branches and remove that which is bad seed from the garden of our heart? The enemy is the one who sows bad seed in the field of our hearts (see Matt.13:27-28).

The response of the bride is seen in 4:16. "Awake, North wind and blow, South wind, blow upon my garden, so my spices can flow out – let my Beloved come into His garden and enjoy its choice fruits."

Meditation

Whatever it takes, Lord, take me through it. Whatever winds need to blow across my life, send the winds, Lord. Blow over me, so that I can be a safe place for the Son of Man to lay His head. I want to be an Eden for You to enjoy. If this is the only way my fragrance can be released, then come, you winds of the Lord, and blow over my life.

I want You to feel welcomed here; I want You to be able to breathe the atmosphere of my heart, my thoughts, my motives, my plans, my hidden ways. If You are looking for a resting place, Son of Man, a place to lay Your head, find it here in me (see Isa. 66:1). I will open up my treasures. I will trust You with my pain, my shame and my brokenness. I will produce fruit worthy of repentance.

Come into Your Garden

After this encounter, she now says, "Let my Beloved come into **His** garden and enjoy the fruit."

It is interesting that after calling for the winds, she calls the garden "His garden," and not her own anymore. This sentence represents a major shift, a step of maturity in the Bride's heart. She is starting to realize that she belongs to Him, even more than He belongs to her.

In 2:16, she had said, *"My lover is mine, and I am His."*

In 6:3, she reverses the order and says, *"I am my Beloved's and He is mine."* In reversing the order, she is acknowledging that His ownership of her is predominant.

In 7:10, she has matured more in understanding His heart and her position with Him. At that point, she says, *"I belong to my Beloved, and His desire is for me."* She acknowledges that she belongs to Him, and she understands that her identity is defined by His desire for her. By inviting Him to come into "His" garden, the bride is giving Him preeminence in all things. Our lives are not our own, but we belong to our Beloved.

The Heavenly North Wind

When I lived in North America, it was easy to think of the North winds as those bad, cold winds of adversity. Whenever I hear Americans teach on this subject, this is how they view the North winds. Likewise, they consider the south winds to be those lovely warm breezes, when all is well with the world. I can fully relate to that understanding.

But when you live in Israel, you get a whole different perspective on the North and South winds. We still have cold winters here in Israel, and there are times where a north wind is bone-chilling and uncomfortable. Sometimes I am freezing here in Israel's wet, cold winters. But generally, since the warm season is so much longer, for those living in the Middle East, we would be so thankful for the refreshing North winds to blow.

There is one terrible wind from the southeast that is dry and destructive, with blowing, blinding sand. It feels like a plague, and it is a dreaded, hot desert windstorm. It affected Napoleon's soldiers, as well as soldiers fighting in World War II in Egypt.

I don't believe anyone in their right mind would ever call for that terrible southeast wind to come and blow on our garden! In Arabic, it is called *"Hamsin,"* meaning "fifty," because it blows on and off for about 50 days. In the story of the ten plagues, the Lord sent an "east wind" which blew across the land all day and all night, and brought the dreaded locust plague. But it didn't blow for 50 days, because Moses prayed, and the Lord sent a west wind to drive the locusts into the Red Sea.

Once I was attending an intense conference, held in an outdoor tent on the Mount of Olives, in the heat of Jerusalem's summer. As the days wore on, the heat inside the tent increased, and by afternoon, many began to suffer from weakness and heat exhaustion.

There was one afternoon where my body was so disabled from the relentless heat, that I was unable to worship, pray or even lift my hands a few inches. I was depleted to the uttermost. I said to the Lord in my heart, as I couldn't even speak, "I cannot even lift my hands, I am so weak from the heat. If You don't strengthen me supernaturally, I cannot participate in the work You sent me here to do."

Suddenly, I felt a strong cool wind begin to blow. It was so cool, it was what you would feel with air-conditioning. I was shocked, as there was no cool air outside, and nothing that could produce chilled air in that tent. It was the most refreshing feeling imaginable, and even better, knowing that it was supernaturally generated cooling. My strength totally returned to me in a huge way.

Later, we all discussed it, and everyone I talked to felt the cool winds come at the same time. Someone outside the tent saw an angelic force, whirling around on the roof of the tent, generating this cool breeze. I always remember this testimony from the Tent of Meeting in Jerusalem, when I read the words, "Awake, North Wind and blow upon my garden."

I love when the Lord makes a Scripture come alive in a super-natural way, so that we can relate to it. As soon as that cool "north wind" blew into the tent, my spices were able to flow upward and outward. I began to pour out the strength of my prayers, and to fully enter into the work needed. My garden came alive with that wind, and my fruits and spices were there for the Lord to enjoy.

We are a kingdom of priests, who minister to our God. The priesthood required incense and anointing oil, made with the per-fumer's spices. This priestly incense must burn in the garden of our heart, which represents our prayer life. Our heart is also to bear the fruits of the Spirit (in Hebrew, "Spirit" and "wind" are the same word: *Ruach*). After the winds have blown, testing and trying us, our Beloved can come into His garden and enjoy its fruits.

The Plants and Spices of the Bible

I'm including here a brief look at the plants and spices mentioned here in the Song, as well as those that pertained to the anointing oil and the priestly incense. This is a more "technical" section, and if it is not what you need right now, just skip to the next chapter!

> *Your shoots are an orchard of pomegranates with all choicest fruits, henna with nard, nard and saffron, calamus and cinnamon, with all trees of frankincense, myrrh and aloes, with all choice spices.*

The fruits, spices, oils and incense are recurring images in the Song. We also see them in Exodus, Deuteronomy, Psalms 23, 45, 104, 133, 141; 1 Samuel, 1 and 2 Kings, and Revelation 5, 8 and 18. We also see them in the gospels, connected to the birth, anointing, death, and burial of the Lord Yeshua.

The most foundational references are the holy recipes, which the Lord gave to Moses for the Tabernacle worship.

> *Moreover the Lord spoke to Moses, saying: "Also take for yourself quality spices—five hundred shekels of liquid myrrh, half as much sweet-smelling cinnamon (two hundred and fifty shekels), two hundred and fifty shekels of sweet-smelling cane, five hundred shekels of cassia, according to the shekel of the sanctuary, and a hin of olive oil. And you shall make from these a holy anointing oil* (Ex 30:22-25).

> *And the Lord said to Moses: "Take sweet spices, stacte and onycha and galbanum, and pure frankincense with* these *sweet spices; there shall be equal amounts of each. You shall make of these an incense, a compound according to the art of the perfumer, salted, pure, and holy.* (Ex. 30:34-35).

As I started to research these liquids, perfumes, oils, spices, plants, and the history of their use and manufacture, I realized that this is a very large subject. I saw some disagreements among scholars about which species of plant a certain extract was taken from.

One of the problems is that most of our English translations of the Bible have decided not to translate from the original Hebrew word for the substance; rather, they have chosen the Greek word, found in the Septuagint. The Septuagint was an excellent Greek translation of the Hebrew Old Testament, accomplished by 70 rabbinic scholars, in around 250 B.C. However, in the cases of exact plant species, the word that the rabbis chose in Greek was not always a perfect representation of the Hebrew name of that plant or resin.

In a few cases of finding the ingredients used in the anointing oil and incense recipes, there is some controversy about which plant (or even animal) and processes were used in Israel's ancient Tabernacle. The more I researched, the more I realized that the body of information available on each substance is far beyond the purposes of this book. Here is some basic information about the plants named in the Song, as well as the Tabernacle ingredients, which overlap to some extent.

Anointing Oil: liquid myrrh, cinnamon, cane (calamus), cassia and olive oil

Holy Incense: Sweet spices, stacte (gum resin), onycha, galbanum, and pure frankincense

Myrrh, Henna and Spikenard

We've studied myrrh, henna and spikenard in chapter 3. Myrrh is an aromatic gum resin, which exudes from the inner wood of the balsam tree, grown in India, Arabia, and Ethiopia. Some researchers cite a different species of trees from which the original myrrh was derived, rather than the balsam family.

Spikenard is aromatic oil, extracted from the roots of a perennial herb that grows in the Himalayan mountains of north India.

Henna is a shrub with clusters of aromatic blossoms, fed by an Artesian well in Ein Gedi. From its leaves, red dye is extracted. Its name in Hebrew, *"kopher"* implies covering, or atonement.

Cinnamon: This is the bark of the cinnamon tree (in the laurel family of trees). It is one of the oldest spices in history, and is harvested by stripping the bark and rolling long strips, with layers of bark rolled within. It is ground into powder, and its aroma and sweet-spicy taste is beloved in many recipes.

The stripping of the bark speaks of our need to be stripped of our will and our rights, which is a kind of heart-circumcision. This stripping is necessary for us to "put on Messiah." He will put His righteousness on us as a robe, if we allow Him to strip us of our self-centered ways (see Isa.61:10).

Calamus (Cane): The word "calamus" in Hebrew is *Kaneh*, which means a rod, tube, stalk or reed (Strong's). It is a water plant, growing in marshes. Its fragrance is extracted from the root of this aromatic reed plant.

The Hebrew word *"Kaneh"* means "to purchase." This rare and costly ingredient speaks of the costly price with which Messiah Yeshua purchased us from death. He stood upright, in this bent world, like a measuring rod in muddy waters.[22]

Cassia: This is one of the ingredients in the Holy Anointing Oil. It smells like cinnamon. Like cinnamon, it is also the ground up bark of the cassia shrub. The Hebrew word is *Kiddah*, which means the strips of bark from a tree, which shrivel or roll up after being stripped from the tree. It comes from the primitive root word, *"Kadad,"* which means shriveled, rolled up, or bowed down in deference. This speaks of humility. This fragrance is found in Psalm 45:8, speaking of the scents on the King's garments on His wedding day.

Frankincense: The Hebrew word for this is *"L'vonah,"* which comes from the root word meaning "white." It is named for the milky-white resin that oozes out of the slashed and gashed wood of the shrub, as well as the white appearance of the smoke when this incense is burned. It is a shrub that grows in the deserts of the Middle East.

It was one of the gifts that the Wise Men brought to the child Yeshua, as a symbol of the priestly life He would live. Frankincense was burned on the incense altar in the Tabernacle, and was sprinkled on the showbread. It speaks of prayer and intercession. In Revelation 5:8, we see that the prayers of the saints are being stored in a bowl in heaven as incense.

Saffron is derived from a purple flower from the crocus family. The valuable yellow dye, fragrance and spice are extracted from within the three red stigmas in the center of each flower.[23] It requires 75,000 flowers to make one pound of saffron, and each flower must be picked by hand.

The following three substances are not found in Song of Solomon, but are part of the recipe for the holy incense for the worship in the Temple.

Stachte (Gum resin): *Stachte* is a Greek word. The Hebrew word is *"Nataf,"* which comes from the root word, meaning to drip or form drops. It refers to the liquid portion of the resin which exudes from the Balsam tree, or possibly a different species of tree, after being cut. It is rare and valuable. Some have identified *Nataf* as liquid myrrh.

Onycha: This is the most confusing of all, in terms of possible candidates from nature. *Onycha* is a Greek word which means fingernail or claw. The Hebrew word is *"Shechelet,"* which is extremely difficult to translate, even among the experts in biblical texts. It appears in Strong's concordance as an obscure word, possibly meaning "peeling off by a concussion of sound," as well as a related root word that means the roaring of a lion. This does not help much with finding its identity. There are many candidates for the actual substance, *Shechelet*. Some scholars believe it is the aromatic flap, operculum, or closing membrane of a sea snail or mollusk. This creature is not a "kosher" animal, which makes this theory questionable.

Other scholars and some notable past rabbis have believed that this is a hard and shiny resin or plant distillate; it could include Labdanum (resin from Rose Rock), Styrax Benzoin (distillate from the Styrax species), Bdellium (see Gen. 2:12, Nu. 11:7), or Tragacanth Gum. The extract from these plants can become a hard and shiny substance, and therefore, the Greek word *onycha* was chosen by the translators of the Septuagint. This choice was possibly related to the Onyx stone, which is hard and shiny.

Galbanum: The Hebrew for this substance is *"Chelb'nah,"* which means a fatty, odorous gum. It is identified as a rubbery resin taken from the roots of a flowering plant that thrives in Syria and

Persia. It has been known for its medicinal properties. It is reported to emit an unpleasant, earthy odor when burned, due to its earthiness and greasiness. We might wonder why the Lord chose it for His recipe. Some rabbis have speculated that the Lord deliberately included a disagreeable fragrance, to signify the presence of less worthy, less holy people within the community who should not be ostracized. Or more likely, when this odor is combined with all the other numerous sweet spices, the overall effect is enhanced by galbanum's presence. It was not meant to be burned alone, but as part of the whole mixture, it adds something that the ancient priests understood. In modern times, this gum is used in the perfume industry, and for glue in the jewelry industry.[24]

Sweet Spices: In the incense recipe from Exodus 30:34-38, we also see "sweet spices," and "spices," listed separately from the four key ingredients (stachte, onycha, galbanum and frankincense). We don't know what these spices were. Because of this, the rabbis engaged in numerous discussions and writings about what other spices were used to complete the incense recipe. The respected first century historian, Josephus stated that there were thirteen spices in the holy incense. Some spice candidates proposed by the rabbis were: cassia, cinnamon, costus, myrrh, spikenard and others. For this reason, the exact recipe remains a mystery, perhaps by the Lord's deliberate design.

This gives us a new appreciation for what Moses and the Levites needed to do during their years in the wilderness, and after they entered the Land as well, under Joshua. They had to acquire these rare and expensive oils, spices, aromatic gums, distillates, and powders from merchant caravans from other lands and the Far East. Some of these items came from India, Persia, Arabia or even Ethiopia.

Researching all this made me realize how sacrificial it was to find, purchase and prepare large quantities of these ingredients for the Tabernacle worship system, day and night for 40 years. The Lord was so specific in these recipes, and it made me really think about the reality of the priestly vocation and lifestyle. It took much skill and knowledge to prepare these priestly oils and incense.

Now, we will go back to the heart of the Bride! AMEN.

Chapter 8

NOT FINDING HIM–PART 2 (SOS 5:1-6:3)

5:1 I have come to my garden, my sister, my spouse; I have gathered my myrrh with my spice; I have eaten my honeycomb with my honey; I have drunk my wine with my milk.

Eat, O friends! Drink, yes, drink deeply, O beloved ones!

The Lord desires for you to ask Him to show you your garden, through His eyes. He will show you the plantings, patterns, design and artistry of your life. He will also show you parts of your garden where there are plantings of fear, shame, sin or judgments. The Lord will comment on all the things He loves about the garden of your heart, and He will ask if you would like Him to pull out the dark and chaotic plantings that were not planted by Him. If you agree, He will remove these right away, or in phases, with no condemnation.

The Lord will also begin to pluck painful thorns out of your heart, explaining to you what deep hurts you have received from various things that have come against you, or that are currently wounding you regularly. With your permission, He will pull out the thorns, and will identify them, so that you know what is coming out. This doesn't mean that no one will ever stick a thorn in again – they surely will. But the Lord wants us to come to Him alone, and He will be faithful to pull out those thorns in our heart.

We now see the Lord's response in the first verse of chapter 5. He says, *"Yes, I have come into My garden. I have breathed the sweetness of your myrrh and tasted the bitterness of your suffering; I have tasted the precious* (spice) *and the sweet things* (honey) *in your heart; I have enjoyed the delight of your wine* (the flow of anointing, joy and revelation) *and the nourishment of your milk"* (the substantive and nourishing truths with which our words sustain and refresh others).

Now that the Lord has had His first fruits, His rightful portion, He graciously invites others to share the wealth and treasures of His Bride's fertile and fragrant heart.

He declares, *"There is more than enough to share. Come, my friends, and eat and drink of the wealth and treasures of My beloved's well-watered garden."* There is a feast in our gardens, where others can graze and be revived with our treasures. This is really true: we have treasures that the Lord wants us to give away. They are not just for our benefit, but for others. This is very important to the Lord.

Isaiah spoke out this same invitation, on behalf of the Bridegroom God:

> *"Come, all you who are thirsty, come to the waters; and you who have no money, come, buy and eat! Come, buy wine and milk without money and without cost. Why spend money on what is not bread, and your labor on what does not satisfy? Listen, listen to me, and eat what is good, and you will delight in the richest of fare* (Isa. 55:1-2, NIV).

When we put the Lord first, and give Him our first and best offerings (time, money, love and affection, thoughts and feelings, tears and even our bitter complaints) then He will send us out to minister these transparent treasures to the dry, burned out, hungry, discouraged or empty hearts. Our overcoming grace, even in the bitter trials, will greatly encourage those who are also walking in a bitter season. We comfort them with the comfort with which the Holy Spirit has comforted us (see 2Cor. 1:4-6).

The Clothing and Defilement of Shame

5:2-6 I sleep, but my heart is awake; it is the voice of my beloved! He knocks, saying, "Open for me, my sister, my love, my dove, my perfect one; for my head is covered with dew, My locks with the drops of the night."

I have taken off my robe; how can I put it on again? I have washed my feet; how can I defile them? My beloved put his hand by the latch of the door, and my heart yearned for him. I arose to open for my beloved, and my hands dripped with myrrh, my fingers with liquid myrrh, on the handles of the lock (NKJV).

I opened for my beloved, but my beloved had turned away and was gone. My soul left me when he spoke. I sought him, but I could not find him; I called him, but he gave me no answer (AP).

In this painful third test or challenge, the bride's heart (her spirit) is awake with the awareness of the one she loves. She loves Him deeply, and He is always in her heart. She has proven her love and He has declared her to be flawless and without blemish. The Lord comes unexpectedly to her door in the middle of the night, as one who has been out in the cold, damp night air, alone and needing fellowship with one He trusts and loves. He is looking for companionship, partnership and comfort in His hour of need. This is a side of Him she has not yet encountered, and His vulnerability and neediness catches her off-guard.

In their respective commentaries, both Watchman Nee[25] and Mike Bickle explain that in this visit, the Lord Yeshua is coming to us as "the Man of Gethsemane."[26] This is a picture of One who has been praying alone in the night, and contending for His destiny, and for His inheritance in His bride. He is a Man of Sorrows. He has been to the mountain of myrrh alone, contending for this very hour. He is looking for a companion to keep watch with Him, to share His pain, shame and sorrow. He is about to put on the worst kind of shame and reproach, one that we will never fully experience, but must experience to only a limited degree.

We saw this on the night the Lord was betrayed. He took His disciples with Him, and asked them to keep Him company in prayer, in His lonely vigil in the garden. It was the worst night of His life; His soul was overwhelmed with sorrow and anguish, and His head was wet with the cold night air. His brow broke out with drops of sweat, mingled with His blood, so great were the pressures of this sacrifice.

Yeshua asked them to stay awake and keep watch with Him, as He awaited the greatest trial and suffering of His life. His heart was sorrowful, even unto death. On the worst night of His life, His betrothed let Him down. Three times, He found them sleeping. Then He was taken away, and where He went, they could not follow. Their Beloved was gone!

And so the Beloved comes to Shuli as the Man of Sorrows. He knocks on her door, after she is already asleep in bed. *"I have taken off my robe— must I put it on again? I have washed my feet—must I soil them again?"* Is this statement an excuse not to get up or to delay getting up and going to the door? First, let's look at the natural meaning in the story line, and then let's examine the spiritual meaning and application.

The Natural

In both ancient and modern Israel, your feet get very dirty walking on the floors. They did not have carpets to walk on, and the stone floors would dirty her feet, after getting cleaned for bed. They had no running water inside the house, no showers or faucets. Think about it: It means you would have to go outside to the well and draw water in the cold, in the middle of the night; then you would gather sticks, build a fire and heat the water, bring the hot water to your room and begin to clean your feet again, before you could return to your bed. It was a much larger inconvenience than what we would picture, those of us who might live in heated, carpeted homes, with running hot water, and fuzzy slippers to step into.

157

The bride's heart is awake for Him. At the sound of His voice, she merely hesitates for a moment, to count the cost of getting dressed and getting her feet dirty, before walking outside to open her garden gate to Him. Wouldn't we do the same thing in her position?

The Spiritual

Now let's look at a spiritual interpretation of the Bride's response, when she first hears His knock and His voice.

"I have taken off my robe. How shall I put it on again? I have washed my feet. How shall I dirty them again?"

At the Last Supper, the Lord took off His outer clothing and wrapped Himself in a towel, for His humble act of washing His bride's feet before He suffered (see John 13:3-4).

Peter said, "You shall never wash my feet." But when the Lord told him that He must do this, Peter asked Him to wash all of him. But the Lord answered, *"If you are clean, only your feet need to be washed."* (John 13:8-10). The Lord declared all of His disciples "clean," except for Judas Iscariot. His Bride was clean, her feet were washed, and He had taken off His robe for their sake. He was already uncovering Himself to cleanse His bride.

After the washing, the Lord put His clothing back on. The next morning, after the horrific scourging, the Roman soldiers would remove His clothing, and put on Him a purple, kingly robe of mocking, calling Him, "King of the Jews." (John 19:2-3). After they finished mocking Him, they put His robe back on Him for His torturous walk up the hill to the cross (Matt. 27:31). When they crucified Him, they took off His robe again, a third time, so that they could cast lots for (steal) His clothing.

And so, in this one cataclysmic night into the following morning, the Lord's robe was taken off of Him at least three times. The first time, He put it back on Himself, after finishing His humble act of service. The second time, the cruel soldiers put it back on Him, after they mocked Him. The third time, they stole His robe from Him and crucified Him naked. (There was possibly a fourth removal and putting on, between the first and second time, as it would have also been removed for the scourging).

The Lord was then **covered** in shame and with the sins of the world. The level of defilement which accompanied this third removal of His clothing is unimaginable and unbearable. He who was fully clean was fully defiled. Not only His feet, but all of Him was defiled to the fullest extent that a man could ever be defiled.

Peter had left the Passover purified, having had his feet washed and the Lord declaring him to be fully clean. Soon, he was sleeping during the Lord's worst hour, but his heart was awake, because the Bible says they were sleeping because they were exhausted with sorrow (see Luke 22:45). Then Peter defiled himself three times in his unplanned denials of the Lord. When Peter realized that he had denied the Lord, he was **covered** in shame.

The Shulamite had taken off her robe to go to sleep. Her feet were clean. She loved the Lord, and she was undefiled. Like Peter, she was certain that she would go anywhere and do anything for Him. And although she delayed momentarily, she put on her robe again to go out and open to the Beloved. Her feet had been washed, but for His sake, she got up and dirtied them again. When He was withdrawn from her, like Peter, her soul departed from her (this is the literal meaning of the Hebrew, indicating sorrow to the point of death.) She ran through the streets, getting her feet very dirty, and the cruel Watchmen **took away her covering.** They took her veil, or her robe, or both. They beat her and uncovered her. They left her bruised, possibly bleeding from the Hebrew for "wounded," and **covered** in shame.

Having taken off her robe in cleanness of soul and right-standing with the Lord, she was being asked to put it on again. But this time, putting on this robe would be symbolic of sharing a portion of the Lord's shame, humiliation, and seeming rejection by the Father Himself. This would be her third challenge and her hardest, which parallels our own journey into the pain and shame of dying to self.

1) It is one thing to leave the worldly pleasures and sins behind, and come away to work in the Lord's vineyard, or in whatever field He has chosen for us. In this first level of challenge, we

arise and come away with Him, leaving behind our clothing of defilement from this world's values and stains.

2) It is another thing to come with the Lord into the Mountain View of the events on this earth. To leave behind (take off) our narrow-minded, short-sighted, soulish and human understanding of all events "under the sun." This obedience to come with Him and look from Lebanon is the second challenge. It is a higher level of maturity, and a more trusted stage of partnering with the Lord's plans, desires and purposes for our sojourn on this earth. It is learning to pray from Heaven's perspective, rather from our limited view.

3) But it is fully another matter to put on shame, nakedness, exposure and rejection from the very authorities who appear to be doing the will of God and teaching others the ways of the Lord. If the Lord asks us to put on a robe which will make it seem to others, even to believers, that God Himself is punishing us because we have "evidently" displeased Him, this pill is so bitter, it is almost impossible to say "yes" to. In fact, the Lord's withdrawal of His Presence at this worst of moments will cause us to truly wonder if He Himself is rejecting us, displeased with us, or finding us unacceptable partners. Have we lost His grace? This is real, and every bride must walk through this, in one form or another.

Job's Reproach

Look at Job's suffering and shame, and look at his "comforters." The part of Job's suffering which was even more distressing than the physical pain in his body, was the condemnation of his friends. The following is a brief excerpt from my third book, "The Seduction of Christianity," in the chapter on Suffering.

Job's physical agony is increased by his inability to find the Lord he has loved and served all his life in this terrible trial. His friends have a great deal of insight about God, righteousness, and the justification of suffering. Some of what they say is true, but much of it attempts to find fault with Job, since there is no other logical explanation for this "punishment."

As he continues to answer his friends' theological explanations for punishment and logical accusations, Job is saying,

"You don't understand. If only I could find Him. If only I could schedule a date in court with the great Judge. I know I could plead my case with Him. I know I could show Him the life I've lived. My conscience is clear. This can't be happening to me; this isn't the God I know. This punishment is unjust.

"Couldn't you just stop accusing me, and share my pain? Couldn't you just stand with me in the terrible bewilderment and abandonment I am feeling right now? Do you have to keep telling me this is my fault? Couldn't you pray with me, instead of telling me all the right reasons that this is happening to me, none of which are true?

"I just have to find Him and reason with Him. But that's the problem! **I can't find Him** to talk to Him. He has disappeared, and left me dying in my rotting flesh, with only my three best friends here to tell me what I must have done wrong.

"I am so alone in my suffering, and even God has deserted me. I know I didn't sin, I can prove it. But who will hear my self-defense?"

One of the hardest aspects of Job's third test was that the voice of the accuser came through friends. And one of his friends received his theological wisdom from the visitation of an evil spirit (see Job 4:12-21). He was being used by the enemy, but thought he was "helping" Job see the error of his ways!

Oh, how the Church has fallen from her first love, her first compassion and intercessions. How often the enemy has used Christians to accuse their brothers and sisters, even gloating when those they dislike get sick and die. The greatest woundings often come from the "house of our friends," from the ones who should be comforting us (see Zech. 13:6).

[end excerpt from The Seduction of Christianity].

Job's is one of the most heartbreaking stories of human history, but there is yet One whose suffering is without equal. The Lord Yeshua was punished as a criminal, with even His Father allowing Him to appear rejected, forsaken by God, and rightly executed for His sins. **So His martyrdom was re-interpreted by the highest spiritual authorities, as a righteous execution of a false prophet by God Himself.** When Yeshua hung on the cross, the Father turned

His face away. And the religious leadership concluded that God had smitten Him and afflicted Him, because He was a sinner, a pretender and a blasphemer, claiming to be the Son of the Most High.

> *He was despised and rejected by mankind, a man of suffering, and familiar with pain. Like one from whom people hide their faces he was despised, and we held him in low esteem. Surely he took up our pain and bore our suffering, yet we considered him punished by God, stricken by him, and afflicted.* (Isa. 53:3-4, NIV).

After the resurrection, when Peter is just about to be fully restored to his relationship with the Lord, he is out in the boat, fishing. When John identifies that it is the Lord on the shore, **Peter puts on his outer cloak**, and jumps into the water to reach the Lord as fast as possible. Most people wonder why he **put on** his outer clothing, just to swim to the shore. In the natural, it makes no sense, as normally, we would strip down to jump into the water. In fact, that heavy outer cloak would make it harder and slower to swim to shore.

I believe it was a prophetic picture of Peter's willingness to put on again the robe of the Lord's shame and reproach. He wanted to show that he would pass the second challenge, though he had failed the first.

After the three denials and then the crucifixion of the One he loved, Peter was covered in shame and self-hatred. But when He saw his resurrected Lord serving them breakfast on the beach, he robed himself for that joyful reunion and reinstatement of his precious relationship with His Beloved.

It was in this restorative conversation that the Lord spoke of the taking off and putting on of Peter's clothing, his covering, signifying how he was destined to share in the shame of the cross. For as the bride of the Beloved, Peter would also share in the shame, reproach and suffering of his Lord. Even without the torture, it is humiliating for someone else, especially an enemy, to dress and undress you, and to expose your nakedness.

Very truly I tell you, when you were younger you dressed yourself and went where you wanted; but when you are old you will *stretch out your hands, and **someone else will dress you** and lead you where you do not want to go.* (John 21:18, NIV).

And so, the Shulamite bride was not disobedient, but she protested and delayed, due to her inability to embrace the level of shame and rejection that this new challenge would bring. And then she arises, but He is gone! We will now see that the Lord's withdrawal is not a punishment, but is a planned and deliberate opportunity for her to share in the fellowship of His shame and rejection. She would indeed put on her robe and her veil, and she would dirty her feet. But others would uncover her, and they would consider her smitten by God.

> *You know my reproach, my shame, and my dishonor; my adversaries are all before You. Reproach has broken my heart, and I am full of heaviness; I looked for someone to take pity, but there was none; and for comforters, but I found none. For they persecute the ones **You have struck**, and talk of the grief of those **You have wounded**.* (Ps. 69: 19-20, 26).

The Lovesick Bride

> *My beloved thrust his hand through the latch-opening; my heart began to pound for him. I arose to open for my beloved, and my hands dripped with myrrh, my fingers with flowing myrrh, on the handles of the bolt.*

Something happens when the Lord thrusts His hand into the latch of her door. Something happens in her heart, and it begins to yearn. **Notice that she did not arise until He thrust His hand through the latch opening of the gate.** When He touched the door opening, then her heart yearned for Him. This is a prophetic point about when Love is awakened. The Lord has to touch the door of our heart, before our heart has the capacity to long and yearn for His nearness. And before we will have the strength and resolve to arise and accept the shame and rejection of the Cross.

Prophetic teacher Bobby Conner shared an insight that the Lord had given to him at Shekinah Worship Center in Lancaster, CA, August, 2013.[27] The Lord showed Bobby that when He put His hand on the latch of her door, His own hands were dripping with liquid myrrh (His signature fragrance, from having just come from the Mountain of Myrrh, the hill of contending). So when He withdrew His hand and then departed, the deposit of His liquid myrrh was still on the latch. When she touched the handles of the bolt, **her** fingers dripped with liquid myrrh. She received it from His fingers, and now she was anointed with myrrh, to prepare her for what she was about to suffer. It was then that her heart yearned for Him.

She flung open the gate to find Him, but He had departed. Her heart was unlocked at that moment, because He had touched her with His passion, His sacrifice, His grace to suffer, His commitment to go all the way to the cross. This was typified by the myrrh, the perfume associated with suffering and death.

We cannot say if He departed because she waited too long to answer. Probably, this was not the reason. But if it were me, I would wrestle with my thoughts: *Did I wait too long to answer? Is He displeased with me, because it took me so long to make up my mind? Where did He go, and how long until I can find Him again?*

It is apparent that He did not depart out of any sense of anger or punishing her for not moving quickly enough. One reason why this seems clear is that the next time He speaks, He sings nobler praises than in the first "gladdening the bride" statements (6:4-9).

A second reason why it seems He is not punishing her is that He seems to have come just to anoint her with liquid myrrh. Then He departed so that she could undergo her season of suffering, at the hands of the watchmen. He knew she would need that grace to endure the persecution without bitterness or offense. The watchmen would interpret her inability to find Him as a sign that God has cast her aside because of her sinfulness. Just as Job's friends had concluded.

Sometimes, the Lord seems to "depart," but we haven't necessarily done anything wrong. This could be one of those cases, where He had a particular reason for awakening her heart to love and then vanishing. He awakened love, for it was love's time for the bride to be disturbed, awakened, disrupted and aroused. He initiated this awakening to deposit the grace to suffer, and then departed, to test her heart. Sometimes the Lord withdraws His presence to test our heart, and to see what is inside.

> *However, regarding the ambassadors of the princes of Babylon, whom they sent to him [Hezekiah] to inquire about the wonder that was done in the land,* **God withdrew from him, in order to test him that He might know all that was in his heart.** (2 Chr. 32:31).

Just as Mary of Bethany anointed the Lord Yeshua before He was to suffer, so the Bridegroom anointed the bride, before her time of persecution and suffering would begin.

This was the second time she lost Him. In this second case, it doesn't explain how she found Him again. However, there is a large clue that she will find Him in the place of praise and worship, even while suffering and not sensing His presence (5:10-16). We do not know if this period of not finding Him (in "real time") is days, weeks or months. If it represents our "dark night of the soul," it could last any period of time, even into years for some of us.

What seems to be a short while later, she will tell the Daughters of Jerusalem that she now knows where He is. He has gone to his garden to shepherd his flock among the lilies (6:2). The moment she declares this, the Bridegroom reappears on the scene and pours out His heart to her with the deepest verses of adoration that we have yet heard.

Clearly, by this point, she will have passed her test of suffering, which comes next (5:7-8).

The Persecuted Bride

> *5:7-8 The watchmen who went about the city found me. They struck me, they wounded me; the keepers of the walls took my veil away from me. I charge you, O daughters*

of Jerusalem, if you find my beloved, that you tell him I am lovesick!

So desperate is she to find Him, that she endangers herself, and walks alone in the city streets at night. She no longer cares about her appearance or whether she is clean or dirty. This speaks of the hunger to find the Lord's Presence being so consuming, that we will bypass the natural concerns for comforts, propriety, dignity, even our personal well-being. Once the Lord has awakened Love, normal boundaries become irrelevant.

The "righteous" watchmen of the city find her. They had encountered her during the night once before, when she had also lost her Beloved's presence (3:3). The first time, she had asked them, *"Have you seen the one I love?"* She thought they could help her, but apparently, they either couldn't help her find Him, or they did not wish to search with her.

But now, there she goes again, desperately and recklessly seeking, disturbing the order and the peace of the city streets. This time they thought they needed to teach her a lesson, for her own good. They beat her, wounded her and took away her covering, as the lovesick Bride heedlessly searched for her Beloved. Some translations say that they took away her veil, and others say that they took away her cloak. The Hebrew word is *"radid,"* meaning shawl or veil, something that is spread over. So they wounded her, shamed her and removed her protective covering, that which provided warmth, and a decent covering of face and body. If she was engaged and was wearing the betrothal veil in public, for watchmen to forcibly take it off her implies dishonoring her before her wedding. If they wanted to unlawfully see her beauty, and took away her veil, perhaps they abused her as well.

Wasn't it the job of the "watchmen" to **be the covering** and to keep the safety of the citizens during the night watch? Was she really a threat to the safety of the city? What made them so angry with her? Why did Solomon put this abusive event in the greatest love song ever written? The bride was also abused in her childhood. Why did Solomon put this cruel reality in the Song of all Songs? Is it a normal part of a love story?

The enemy of our souls hates the Bride of Messiah with a perfect hatred. He wants to seduce and deceive us, defile and uncover us, accuse and abuse us, and to rob, harm or kill us, if it would be possible. He will use anyone who permits him, including and especially fellow-believers or spiritual leaders. The wounds we receive in the "house of our friends" are the cruelest wounds of all (see Zech.13:6).

There will always be some guardians of the status quo, who cannot understand our pursuit of the Lord. The lovesick bride is at times an unsatisfied voice within the church community. A holy restlessness consumes these lovesick ones, and they are always pressing for more. They don't fit in.

"There must be more than this," is their heart's desperate cry. They often plead for more bridal purity, humility, repentance and prayer. They take a strong position for Israel and the Jewish people, honoring them through compassionate intercessions. They focus more on the Lord's desires, rather than the programs and praises of men.

The keepers of the walls do not always appreciate the treasure of love that the Lord has put in our hearts. They may be content, secure and even self-righteous. Our excessive passion might make them feel threatened, jealous, or uncomfortable. Or they might find a theological reason to disagree. Those who are self-contained and self-reliant will not be open to our entreaties.

The watchmen beat her and they take away her covering. This means her reputation and protection. In some cases, it would mean that the elders took away her ministry to the younger believers (the Daughters of Jerusalem), who needed to be led into intimacy with the Lord. They leave her exposed and bleeding, with no hiding place for her exposure. There are seasons in our lives when it "seems" that the Lord has stripped us of everything, our ministry, our reputation, even His own presence. We lost friends, although we have not actually wronged them. We are no longer sought after, and people avoid us. Even the Lord seems to have abandoned us. We fear that our broken condition will cause others to think that the Lord has turned His favor away from us. Our lives don't seem to be bringing Him any glory.

But beloved, things are not always as they seem. After the watchmen leave her uncovered and wounded, the Bride doesn't think about this shameful exposure or injustice. She can only think about finding the One she loves.

> *Daughters of Jerusalem, I charge you— if you find my beloved, what will you tell him? Tell him I am faint with love.*

She is so consumed with finding Him, that she even seeks the help and counsel of younger believers, who do not know Him that well. This is how low and humble the lovesick Bride is willing to become, in order to find Him.

There have been points when I've been so low, and in so much pain, that I have asked even little children or backslidden believers to pray for me; I know beyond any doubt that He will hear their prayers, and mine don't seem to be helping at that moment.

After the season of persecution, we will see the bride make a deliberate choice to praise and worship the Lord, despite all that she has been through. And it is precisely this act of worship that brings the awareness of His Presence back to her.

Praise and Worship Bring Him Back

The Daughters wonder what is so incredible about her Beloved, that she would still want Him, when all this sorrow and pain has befallen her, because of her loyalty to Him. They ask her why He is so superior that she would seek Him above all the others.

> *How is your beloved better than others, most beautiful of women? How is your beloved better than others, that you so charge us?* (5:9, NIV).

In reply to their honest question, a torrent of praise and worship flows from the bride, and she sings a new song, unlike any other love song heard in the pages of Scripture. She sings unashamedly of the beauties and qualities of this uniquely excellent Man.

5:10-16 My beloved is radiant and ruddy, outstanding among ten thousand. His head is purest gold; his hair is wavy and black as a raven. His eyes are like doves by the water streams, washed in milk, mounted like jewels. His cheeks are like beds of spice yielding perfume. His lips are like lilies dripping with myrrh. His arms are rods of gold set with topaz. His body is like polished ivory decorated with lapis lazuli. His legs are pillars of marble set on bases of pure gold. His appearance is like Lebanon, choice as its cedars. His mouth is sweetness itself; he is altogether lovely. This is my Beloved, this is my friend, daughters of Jerusalem (NIV).

Each physical attribute speaks of inner qualities that the Lord possesses. His character, wisdom and strength are like the finest gems, the most perfect gold, the most elegant marble, and the sweetest spices of the perfumer. Let's look at these ten attributes that make Him so much more beautiful, kind, holy, powerful and courageous than anyone we could ever hope to meet.

He is dazzling, radiating with light; unique among ten thousand. In John 3:16, the Greek word for "only begotten son" is *monogene*, meaning "one of a kind," or uniquely produced.[28] He is One of a kind, without equal.

That His head is gold speaks of His thought life of integrity, nobility and holiness; His hair represents His Nazirite vow of purity and consecration to God (see Nu.6:2).

His eyes are single-minded doves of devotion for His Father and for the ones He died for. His glance is innocent, humble, tender and transparent. The tenderness and tears in His eyes sparkle like gems.

His cheeks are the tender part of His face and His gentle emotions; cheeks that allowed wicked men to rip out His beard, and to strike them with bruises and wounds. He turned the other cheek, as a sign of meekness under injustice and persecution.

His lips drip with liquid myrrh; His words are sweet, like myrrh. But at times, to eat His Word leaves a bitter feeling inside, like the bitterness of myrrh, due to the painful realities of the prophetic future for the wicked (see Rev.10:9-11). This speaks of the prophetic words that come from His mouth, which we must embrace without offense.

His arms speak of His strength to stretch out His hand of intervention, healing, and protection on behalf of His own people. They also represent His affection to embrace us, and to carry the little lambs in His bosom; His left hand is under my head and His right arm embraces me. Isaiah 53:1 speaks of the "Arm of the Lord" as the revelation of the Father's love. The Father stretched out His Arm, who is His own Son, Yeshua, and His own Arm brought salvation to the world.[29]

His body like ivory set with gems speaks of the perfection, self-control and purity with which He disciplined His bodily conduct during His days on this earth. He lived a perfect life, and overcame all physical temptations and defilements, not as a god, but as man, so that we could know that it is possible to overcome temptation in this life. It is possible to keep our bodies undefiled, and Yeshua has shown us the way. He did it as a man, just like us.

His legs speak of His swift and purposeful striding through each day's assignments that His Father had appointed for Him. His legs walked hundreds of dusty miles to bring healing, help, deliverance, and love to the lost sheep of Israel. His legs brought the Word of the Lord swiftly to all of Israel in only three and a half years. He leaps over mountains to find one lost soul, and will spare no effort to run to His needy ones. It also speaks of His swift return and purposeful reentry into Jerusalem, and into world history as we knew it.

His appearance is as Lebanon; this speaks of His towering virtue, inner strength and majestic character; it is not only about Yeshua's physical appearance, but reflects the superiority of His thoughts, words and deeds. He towers above other men, in His maturity, wisdom and purity. The cedars of Lebanon give us the strong, enduring and fragrant wood, with which Solomon constructed the Temple, and his wedding carriage. Cedar wood does not corrupt or rot, and this speaks of Yeshua's incorruptibility and His enduring fragrance in His Father's house.

In ancient times, people would use cedar oil on clothing to protect it from humidity, insects or bacteria. We also see cedar wood in Leviticus 14 and Numbers 19; it was used in the purification rituals for leprosy and contact with a dead body.[30] So Lebanon speaks of the purification which the Lord offered to those of us who were spiritual lepers and spiritually dead.

His mouth is the instrument of God's Word to convict of sin, to forgive, to heal, to deliver and to perfectly represent and reveal the heart of the Father in a sea of brokenness. His speech is seasoned with heavenly knowledge, wisdom and revelation. He is the kindest Man we have ever known, for His words are full of goodness over our life.

She declares the love and the deep friendship between them, as she completes this song of worship. *This is my Beloved, this is my Friend.*

Just before the bride sang this chorus of His praise, she was asking the Daughters where she could find Him. But now that she has finished her song, the Daughters ask the bride where **they** can find Him. And now, the bride knows where He is, although the only thing that has changed is that she took time to worship Him, even in her state of grieving for His loss.

The very act of testifying of His excellence to those who have not known Him restored the bride's awareness of His Presence. Choosing to worship in a time of seeming abandonment releases the manifestation of His Presence. The awareness of the Lord's Presence was restored to the Bride through the act of deliberately speaking the truth about all we have known Him to be, even if we are not finding Him at this moment.

> *6:1-3 Where has your beloved gone, most beautiful of women? Which way did your beloved turn, that we may look for him with you? My beloved has gone down to his garden, to the beds of spices, to browse in the gardens and to gather lilies. I am my beloved's and my beloved is mine; he browses among the lilies* (NIV).

After embracing the shame and reproach of the cross and enduring persecution, Shuli has come through the trial without bitterness or offense; she has now been restored to her peace and security in His nearness, and her awareness of where to find Him (feeding His flock among the choicest flowers).

We are Waiting, not Forsaken

In this lesson, we saw again that the Lord never really leaves us. The bride passed her test by remembering Him and proclaiming the truth about Him, despite suffering and injustice. Our human nature is to try to control our relationship with the Lord. We want Him to come in a certain way or timing. At times, we might try to manipulate His timing and His seasons in our lives. However, the Lord has ordained all the seasons of our lives: from birth's first breath to our final moments in this broken world – we come to know Him through knowing His seasons. They are perfect, though we will not understand how perfect until we see Him face to face.

There is a season when the Passionate Pursuer, the real and personal God of Heaven, knocks on our door. This is an invitation to encounter; it is like a visit, a tugging on the heart, a new season of springtime in our lives. There follows then a series of astonishing encounters with our very own Beloved, and we feel that the honeymoon will never end. It seems like it will always be this way, and we feel like a most-cherished bride.

But at some point, there inevitably comes a season where it seems impossible to find Him, as if He has turned and gone. And all our cries and searching seem to yield nothing but tears of loneliness and struggle, even a sense of abandonment. But we must know that as surely as the Lord lives, He has not abandoned nor forsaken us. We must stay steady, even if we feel forsaken. We are not forsaken, but we are merely waiting for Him to return in a more manifest form, in His perfect timing. Keep trusting and patiently seeking, for He is worth waiting for. Do not give up or get frustrated, as I have done so often.

There are a number of "markers" in our lives, where we could say, "That was when the Lord knocked on my door." This happens at various points along our journey. He knocks more than once. There are sweet and bitter seasons, and tests that push us to what feels like "the end of ourselves." Later, we will understand why the Lord allowed these terribly hard times of testing, confusion, illness, loss, exhaustion and breakdown.

In my own case, after a long series of crises and complex relational strains, I recently hit a point of ministry crisis, health crisis and emotional breakdown. I had rarely been in this kind of place, where I was ready to quit all of it. I couldn't do it anymore. As always, I cried out to the Lord relentlessly, day and night, in my distress. I remembered His kindness to me in times past, and this has helped me to recover. He has healed me, and I'm back in the army.

Why is this Happening to Us?

It is hard to know the root cause of these mental, physical and spiritual troubles, when you're in the midst of these "beatings and woundings." In this troubled world, there a number of potential causes of our distress, illnesses and mental perplexity. It is wisdom to know which one is at work in our various trials.

- Just natural health breakdowns, both physical and emotional, due to stress, fasting, overwork, relational abuse or sleep deprivation.
- Chastisements from the Lord, in case we have displeased Him in some way. It is wise to check our hearts before Him and repent quickly, if something convicts us. But guilty soul-searching can be destructive if we assume we must have sinned to have caused this problem. Often, the problems are not because we sinned, so we should check our hearts, but not excessively assume guilt that is not ours.
- The enemy attacks God's people. He can attack our health, our finances and family, our minds and emotions. He wants us to blame the Lord for our sorrows, and withdraw from His callings on our lives.
- It can be the Lord's will to allow a season where we come to know a small portion of the shame and reproach of the cross; this can be personal loss, or a stripping of our ministry or reputation. It can include the sudden loss of friends' trust and respect, which we had accumulated over many years of pouring ourselves out for others.

- At times, the enemy will sabotage communication with pastors, ministry partners and friends, creating painful betrayals and misunderstandings, wearing us down to the point of giving up on these relationships.
- When fellow believers gossip or slander us behind our backs, the enemy can use these poisonous words as curses against us. Words are powerful tools, for good or for evil, and in the mouths of believers, our words can do much good or harm. We need to guard our lips far more than we ever realized, as they have far reaching consequences. I have seen the fruit of this, where accusations from believers had their harmful effects on my life. My words have also harmed others.

In my crisis, it was hard to find the Lord's comfort. I felt perplexed, lost, disoriented, and could not figure out what to do in many cases. This is why we must be trained to stay steady and faithful, when things seem to be collapsing around us. The Lord allows and even ordains these hard seasons so that our faith may be proved by the fire. That is why we need wisdom to know if the attack is from the enemy, so that we can resist, rebuke and reject it. But if the Lord has allowed it for our refinement, we need to walk through the test without taking offense. These grievous situations will bring forth the imperishable reward of proven faithfulness.

> *In this you greatly rejoice, though now for a little while, if need be, you have been grieved by various trials, that **the genuineness of your faith,** **being** much more precious than gold that perishes, though it is tested by fire, may be found to praise, honor, and glory at the revelation of Jesus Christ. Beloved, do not think it strange concerning the fiery trial which is to try you, as though some strange thing happened to you; but **rejoice to the extent that you partake of Christ's sufferings,** that when His glory is revealed, you may also be glad with exceeding joy. If you are reproached for the name of Christ, blessed are you, for the Spirit of glory and of God rests upon you* (1 Pet. 1:6-7, 4:12-14).

Meditation

Dear Lord Yeshua, although You have a destiny for me, my agreement is vital and critical. If I do not agree with Your plans, none of this is fatalistic, because You look for my voluntary agreement. You care about my desires, my will, and my free choice. You will not force a particular destiny upon me. I must agree.

I have been scourged, and I know it might yet continue, although I pray it does not. But not my will, but Yours be done in my life. Much has been severely tested, exposed, wounded, and stripped away. Much has been subjected to shame, accusation, misrepresentation, misunderstandings and miscommunication, more than would naturally occur. Then came the betrayals from people I had poured myself out to help, more painful than I could bear. Some of my close friends and colleagues cut me off, or misread my heart completely. I did not defend myself, because You are my defense.

Then, as I lay on my face in sackcloth and ashes, as all hope was lost in the darkest loneliness of an Asian hotel room, Your mercy and kindness arose like the dawn. I saw Your kindness and covering love. I heard the songs of mercy that Your Spirit was singing over my hopelessness; I saw the miracle of new beginnings, and new chances. Impossible mercy. Improbable redemption. That's why I have a Savior! That's what You said to me.

That's who You are, Precious Yeshua, my Shepherd of Mercy. You have dealt kindly with me before, and You will deal kindly with me again and again. Goodness and mercy have followed me, and have redeemed the trail of brokenness I have left behind me. Loving Redemption is who You are and what You do. You are the kindest One

175

*I have ever known, and I am intensely grateful for Your saving grace, Lord Yeshua. **Amen**.*

How long, O Lord? Will You forget me forever? How long will You hide Your face from me? How long shall I take counsel in my soul, having sorrow in my heart daily?

How long will my enemy be exalted over me...But I have trusted in Your mercy; my heart shall rejoice in Your salvation. I will sing to the Lord, because He has dealt bountifully with me (Ps. 13).

Chapter 9

WHO IS THE BRIDE? (SOS 6:4-7:9)

His Bride is a City

6: 4-5a Thou art beautiful, O my love, as Tirzah, comely as Jerusalem, terrible as an army with banners. Turn away thine eyes from me, for they have overcome me (KJV).

At the time Solomon wrote this song, the judgment of civil war had not yet come upon Israel, subsequently dividing Israel into the Northern and Southern Kingdoms. The Lord brought this judgment in 931 BC, after Solomon's death (see 1 Kings 11:9-13). Thus, Tirzah was one of Israel's most beautiful cities, second only to Jerusalem.

In comparing His Bride to the beauty of Jerusalem, the Lord is again revealing that this is not a natural love story; it is the story of a God who chose a people, and took a city to be His own bride. It is a revelation that this song is about the Lord, His covenant people, and His chosen city, Jerusalem. At the end of the book of Revelation, we see the New Jerusalem as His eternal bride.

Jerusalem was where the Lord chose to build the temple. He revealed this to King David during the terrible three days of plague, (see 1 Chr. 21:14-22:1). When David saw that the Lord sent fire from

177

heaven to consume his sacrifice on the threshing floor of Araunah the Jebusite, he knew that this would be the dwelling place of the Lord's house forever.

It became the center of all Israelite worship, and out of the perpetual prayer and worship from this place, David and Solomon's governments and exploits would be successful. It was the place when the Lord's manifest *Sh'chinah* (indwelling presence, which we call "Shekinah glory") would come and dwell permanently. The Lord called Jerusalem the "center of the earth" (see Eze. 5:5, 38:12). The Hebrew word used in Ezekiel 38 for "center" is *"tabur,"* which means "navel." Jerusalem is compared to the place where the umbilical cord from heaven touches the earth.

In the Millennial Kingdom, Jerusalem will be the center of all the worship of the earth (see Isa. 2:1-4; Zech. 14:16-19). It will also be the seat of Yeshua's throne and government. After the Millennium period, the eternal, heavenly Jerusalem is revealed as the bride of the Lamb.

> *Then I, John, saw the holy city, New Jerusalem, coming down out of heaven from God, prepared as a bride adorned for her husband... Then one of the seven angels who had the seven bowls filled with the seven last plagues came to me and talked with me, saying, **"Come, I will show you the bride, the Lamb's wife."** And he carried me away in the Spirit to a great and high mountain, and showed me the great city, the holy Jerusalem, descending out of heaven from God* (Rev. 21:2, 9-10).

Terrible as an army with banners.

In Hebrew, the word for "terrible" is even stronger. It is *"ayumah"* which means, "striking terror or threatening." This is the same Hebrew word which is used in the Hebrew New Testament, when Zechariah (father of John the Baptist) sees the angel Gabriel, as he stands to burn incense. It says, *"Zecharyah saw this and was alarmed, and **terror** fell upon him"* (Luke 1:12, DHE).

The Bridegroom tells His Bride, "You are as terrifying as an army, marching in its divisions (under banners)." This is a picture of the worshiping/warrior Bride in the final battles with evil. She will be a fearful and unified army, marching under all her various regiments (streams) and banners (movements or areas of particular anointings). In ancient empires, victorious armies would display their banners in a military parade, while the defeated armies would be stripped of their banners.

This warrior bride will be as beautiful as Jerusalem, filled with worship, praise and the glory of God. She will terrify satan's troops; she will prevail and overcome, and be found worthy to dwell in the city of God.

His Bride Overwhelms His Heart

Turn your eyes away from me, for they have overcome me.

After comparing His bride to an army, the Lord makes a vulnerable and "weak" statement about His own emotions: that He Himself has been overcome by the love He sees in our eyes. *"Turn your eyes away from Me, for I am overwhelmed with the love I see there – it is more than I can absorb, to see that look in your beautiful, adoring eyes, your dove's eyes of loyal, heartsick love."*

If we knew what we meant to Him, it would change the way we see our own "sorry selves" and our messed up lives. The Lord told Rick Joyner, *"My children are worth more to Me than the stars in the heavens."*[31] The blazing galaxies and heavenly bodies do not move His heart as one adoring gaze from His own beloved ones, His chosen bride, whom the Father chose and gave to His Son as an eternal companion.

We are Yeshua's inheritance. We are the prize that kept Him through the oil press of Gethsemane, as His soul's sorrow burst the capillaries in His forehead. We are the joy that was set before Him through the anguish, the beatings and flaying, the crown of thorns, and the infestation of all humanity's leprous filth upon His soul during the torturous hours on the cross.

179

His Bride moves Him more than the seas, the stars, the mountains. More than the crystal sea, and the myriads of angelic beings adoring Him with symphonic ecstasy. One glance of our eyes moves Him so deeply, He is undone, and asks us to turn away for a moment, so that our Bridegroom can integrate the emotion and our devotion into His heart's reservoir.

He who conquered death and hell is overcome by the love in our eyes. Faithful eyes that remain loyal during the gross darkness that veils us from His Presence, yet we press into this Love. This is a great marvel and treasure that we must never cease to remember, and to meditate on. That weak, sinful, flawed, foolish people like me can move the heart of the Creator of the Universe. Let the songs of this Love never cease, and let the high praises of this LOVER never run dry! We must sing the song of the Bridegroom's love forever and ever, and our love must outshine every star in the heavens. Amen.

His Bride is an Overcomer

During the time that she could not find Him, the bride fell into the hands of cruel men. Her lover had withdrawn from her, even though she arose to open the gate. She could not see Him, find Him, or derive help from Him in her time of suffering.

But when we feel nothing, He feels everything.

She came out of the wilderness of suffering without losing the strength of her love and trust in this Good Shepherd. His heart was overwhelmed with her faithfulness during this dark hour, when His help seemed not to be found. This is infinitely precious to the Lord, and our rewards for this overcoming steadfastness will astonish us on that day.

The painful truth is that many will start the journey of following this Shepherd, but few will finish the race. Many will enlist, but few will follow through with our covenant commitments when the Lord "seems" to let us down, abandon us, or not fulfill our expectations and demands on Him. Many will stumble, be offended and say, "It's not worth it – He let me down once too often."

I have a friend who has just said those words to me and to others. After being a devoted believer for decades, he has thrown it all away (as of this moment, which I pray will be swiftly turned around). He has declared that the Lord did not come through for him, and it has been too many years of broken promises. He is finished, and says he is already in hell, and it can't be any worse than this. This is the painful reality that many will step back, out of our weakness and inability to see the end of the Story.

This is a hard walk, and it will require unusual perseverance and enduring patience. Let us prepare our hearts now, because it will be much harder than we imagine. Get extra oil now for that darkest of dark hours. I am speaking to my own unprepared soul as much as to any precious reader, reading these words.

Yeshua felt abandoned on the cross. He was not truly abandoned by His Father, not in the ultimate sense, but He felt abandoned, as much as any human on earth has ever felt abandoned by God. More, in fact. Because none of us has felt the Father turn His face away from us, due to the cumulative world's sins defiling our souls so completely that He could not even bear to look upon His Son.

The Truth about Polygamy

> *6:8-9 There are sixty queens and eighty concubines, and virgins without number. My dove, my perfect one, is the only one, the only one of her mother, the favorite of the one who bore her. The daughters saw her and called her blessed, the queens and the concubines, and they praised her (NIV).*

Solomon, at the time he wrote this song, already had sixty wives and eighty concubines. He would end up with a great deal more women before the end of his life.

A concubine was very much like a wife, in that she was a permanently committed partner, who was never free to leave or marry another man. The king owned and cared for his concubines financially, and they had a high status as part of his family, though they lived in separate quarters. The queens were legal wives, with higher status than the concubines, although both were legally bound to the king forever. In modern society you could compare a concubine's relationship with the king to "common-law marriage." The couple is essentially married, but without full legal or covenantal status.

Believers are very confused about why the Bible seems to sanction polygamy through the lives of some of the kings of Israel. They wonder why there was a different morality in Bible times. Always remember that although Israel's kings practiced polygamy and Solomon practiced it to the highest level imaginable, **this was not the will of God, nor His original design**.

Just because God blessed a king with many wives, does not mean that He approved of this violation of Genesis 2:23-24. The Lord blesses many believers who are not walking fully in His laws and His ways. Out of His patience and love, He still loves them, uses them, and even grants them many spiritual gifts. **These blessings and gifts are not God's stamp of approval on every aspect of our lifestyle.** He is gracious, but it does not mean He approves of all that we do.

There is one issue that kings from many cultures faced, which "regular" people did not face. Because of this, it is possible that the Lord Himself made allowances for this issue: the issue of needing and having an heir. However, we cannot justify this biblically, and therefore, I still believe it was not the Lord's will. Even though Abraham was promised multitudes of descendants, Sarah was barren. She took matters into her own hands, giving him Hagar, but dear Abraham would have waited forever for the promise of God to be fulfilled. He did not need many wives to get the son God promised him.

Isaac too had a barren wife, but he did not take multiple wives to get the many sons he "needed." He just prayed for Rebecca, and she finally conceived. Jacob would have been happy with Rachel for the rest of his life. We all know how Laban tricked him into marrying Leah, and then Rachel and Leah got into a fertility contest and gave Jacob their maids to impregnate. But this was not Jacob's idea. And so I see that our patriarchs set an example of monogamy, even though they needed an heir more than any man.

In the same way, I don't think the kings of Israel, or the polyg-amous kings of countless cultures, "needed" to take many wives to produce the number of viable sons for them to have a guaranteed heir to the throne. In some cases, this was a king's main obsession, such as Henry VIII of England.

Isaac was righteous and prayed for his wife, and the Lord was gracious. It is so comforting that we have this example of a righteous man who waited for the Lord's healing of his wife's barrenness, rather than manipulating the circumstances.

But it seems that some kings just took dozens of wives and concubines because they were allowed to, so why not? This was not God's original plan, and at least these Israelite kings could have followed the path of their fathers, Abraham, Isaac and Jacob. Nevertheless, we know that God blessed them with great love and favor, and I am in no position to judge them.

My main point was that just because the Lord blessed and loved them does not mean that polygamy was His best and perfect will. It may have been His permissive will, but we know from Genesis that it was not His heart's original intent.

There have been successful ministers, some of whom were very gifted and anointed believers. They have preached to many, and have done healings and miracles. But this will not help them on Judgment Day, if they have not been conformed to the standards and character of Yeshua, and if they have deliberately practiced lawlessness, without repentance. The Lord did not withdraw His blessings from them, but they misunderstood His kindness, and assumed that He approved of their lives (see the chilling warning in Matt. 7:15-23). Blessings are free. Gifts are free. They are not the same as lasting fruit of the Spirit, nor are they a sign that we are "OK" with the Lord. **We need to separate in our minds, the Lord's blessings from His approval.**

This is the same principle that was in operation when God blessed kings who had multiple wives and other partners. He always meant for marriage to be one man and one woman. The Lord allowed much, due to our hardness of heart, including divorce, but it was not His plan. (See Matt. 19:4-9). In fact, Solomon's many wives turned out to be his falling away. They led him into idolatry and he built altars for their demonic gods.

> *For it was so, when Solomon was old, that his wives turned*
> *his heart after other gods; and his heart was not loyal to the*
> *Lord his God, as was the heart of his father David...So the*
> *Lord became angry with Solomon, because his heart had*
> *turned from the Lord God of Israel, who had appeared to*
> *him twice, and had commanded him concerning this thing,*
> *that he should not go after other gods; but he did not keep*
> *what the Lord had commanded* (1 Kings 11:4,9-10).

Because of the Lord's covenant with David, it is clear that the Lord never rejected Solomon utterly, as He rejected Saul. I believe that Solomon came to repentance and was fully restored and saved before his death, due to the promise the Lord gave to David in 2 Samuel 7:12-16. But that does not mean that his lifestyle fully pleased the Lord.

His Nameless Bride Stands Out among the Vast Household

> *There are sixty queens and eighty concubines, and virgins*
> *without number. My dove, my perfect one, is the only one,*
> *the only one of her mother, the favorite of the one who*
> *bore her. The daughters saw her and called her blessed,*
> *the queens and the concubines, and they praised her.*

In addition to Solomon's wives and concubines, there was a large company of young maidens (virgins) who lived and worked among the courts and offices of the palace complex. They were likely girls of special beauty, grace, musical, or artistic skills that had won the approval of the king's staff. Or possibly, the king owed their parents a favor, and allowed their daughters to have access to the king at this level. These girls may have had various jobs in the royal administration, or they attended banquets and helped to entertain heads of state who visited Jerusalem.

These hundreds or thousands of girls may have been "in line," or contending for a future status as a queen or concubine, in case

Solomon would notice them and choose to make them more than a courtier. They may have had a status comparable to the thousands of virgins that were brought to the king's complex in the days of Esther. Which one might catch his eye? What was he looking for, that would make one girl stand out in the crowd?

Despite the vast company of women who were in Solomon's royal harem and courtiers, there is one mysterious girl, **who is never named**, but is only referred to one time in the entire Song, as "the Shulamite." Solomon never calls her that, but the Daughters of Jerusalem call her by that title once (6:13). The King calls her "his dove, his perfect one, his love," and we see that she holds a place in his heart, unequalled by any other relationship. By the way, the Hebrew word that is translated "my **darling**," or "my **love**," is the same word that is found in Leviticus 19:18, "You shall love your **neighbor** as yourself." It comes from the root word for "shepherd," and means a close friend, associate, intimate companion, as the closeness of a shepherd with his sheep. For male believers, this will help you to know that the Lord is not calling you "Darling," but is calling you a bosom friend, the closest of companions.

And so, the maiden does not even have a name, although she is the center of it all. This speaks of the nameless bridal company, whose hearts embody the rare attributes that are compelling enough to get the Lord's attention in a sea of people claiming to be part of His greater household. Have you ever read another love story where the Lover has a name, but the beloved girl remains hidden and nameless?

There are millions of professing Christians on the earth today. Many call themselves by that name, meaning that theoretically, they have received the Lord Jesus as their Lord and Savior. However, there is a huge spectrum of heart commitments among this vast body of "Christianity." Within this population, there are multitudes of denominations, sects, and movements.

Only the Lord has the wisdom to sort out every motive of every heart on the earth who uses the title, "Christian," or all the other names we give ourselves. And there are levels of sincerity, commitment, transparency, and righteousness.

No human can judge another heart, but the Lord, who sees every heart, sees the brides, the warriors, the harlots, the hypocrites, and the innocent children. The Lord loves every single person who He made and designed to be in relationship with Him. It's not a matter of love. The Lord loves even those who hate Him. He would have died for any one person on earth, whether lover or hater. In fact, He did.

But there are certain hearts that catch His eye and capture His emotions. They move His heart and cause Him to be drawn toward these particular hearts. There's something about single-mindedness. There's something about passionate commitment and about reliable, trustworthy, faithful, loyal love.

There's something about those who behave and think just as excellently when they are alone in their room, when no one is watching, and the integrity that is contained in that testimony. There's something about transparency, humility, vulnerability, and a torn and lowly heart. Despite our weakness, sinfulness and brokenness, there is a sincerity that the Lord can feel, and it feels very different from all other religious activity. Do you want to be one that catches His eye?

The Original and Eternal Plan of God

The original and eternal plan of God was an intimate relationship with His people. He arranged a marriage for His son Adam, as a picture of His own marriage to His future bridal company. His plan was that an *ezer* (helper) bride would be taken out of Adam's side, and she would be "suitable" for him. In Hebrew, the word for suitable is *"k'negdo,"* which means "like him, comparable to him, after his kind." When Adam saw his wife, he was joyful to see that she was compatible with him, "bone of his bones and flesh of his flesh." So much like him in every way.

Paul understood that the relationship between the Lord Yeshua and His *ezer* bride is a great mystery, which corresponds to Adam's relationship with his bride. Paul wanted to convey to the church that the Bridegroom-Bride relationship between the Lord and His people was God's original plan. Thus, he deliberately compared the Lord's relationship with us to Adam's relationship with Eve. **He quoted**

186

Genesis when explaining the "great mystery" of the bridal paradigm, just to make sure we didn't miss the point.

*For no one ever hated his own flesh, but nourishes and cherishes it, just as the Lord does the church. For **we are members of His body, of His flesh and of His bones**. "For this reason a man shall leave his father and mother and be joined to his wife, and the two shall become one flesh." This is a great mystery, but **I speak concerning Christ and the church**.* (Eph. 5:29-32).

And again, Paul reminds the Corinthians about the bridal relationship, and that the goal of all things is the Wedding of the Lamb to His people.

> *For I am jealous for you with godly jealousy. For **I have betrothed you to one husband**, that I may present you as a chaste virgin to Christ.* (2 Cor. 11:2).

Our salvation is our most valuable treasure, but it is not the ultimate goal of our life. It is the beginning of beginnings. No relationship with the Lord could ever be possible, apart from our Savior purchasing us with His blood. But the Lord Himself is our true treasure. Our salvation is the first step in restoring us back to God's eternal purpose: To find a worthy Bride for His Son, with whom He will enjoy intimate love and governmental partnership, now and in the ages to come.

Sometimes believers feel satisfied just to know they are saved – they see no need to press on further. But is there more than this "common" Christianity? Is there such a thing as "uncommon devotion?" **This uncommon devotion should be normal Christianity**, for this is the Lord's passionate and urgent desire.

The invitation is to each individual believer, as this is about our private relationship with the Lord. We will stand before the Judgment Seat of Messiah alone. This is the judgment (evaluation) for believers, not the judgment (condemnation) for unbelievers. This judgment is where the Lord tests the quality of our love and our lives. No other opinions will help or hurt us on that day. His righteous eyes will see who we are, and He will evaluate our lives with perfect truth and righteousness.

*We shall all stand before the judgment seat of Christ...
Then each of us shall give account of himself to God.*
(Rom. 14:10-12)

*The Lord...will both bring to light the hidden things of
darkness and reveal the counsels of the hearts. Then each
one's praise will come from God.* (1 Cor. 4:5)

*For we must all appear before the judgment seat of
Christ, that each one may receive the things done in the
body, according to what he has done, whether good or
bad.* (2 Cor. 5:10)

Just as the Lord took a bride for Adam out of his own body,
in the same way, He will take a bride for His Son Yeshua, out of
His Body. The Body is the larger redeemed household of faith; the
bride will be taken out from among the Body of Messiah. The Lord
will take a corporate bride comprised of individual brides, who have
made their hearts wholly devoted to Yeshua and His heart's desires.
Their hearts are fully in love, thus fulfilling the First Commandment
(see Deut. 6:4).

This is not about an elite company. The invitation is to all. He
stands at the door of His own church and knocks. Whosoever will,
may come. It is an equal opportunity beauty contest. No one will be
refused. All it takes is a heart that is fully in love.

And remember Esther, and the two banquets. In the first banquet,
she and the King refreshed and renewed their love for each other. In
the second banquet, Esther ruled and reigned over her enemies, in the
midst of the King's table. Remember the reality of your Bridegroom
and the Wedding feast. Prepare yourselves for this moment. It is
more real than anything we have yet known on this earth.

The Privilege of Esther

Even the hosts of heaven in all their beauty do not move the King's heart as one of His redeemed on the earth. He left Heaven's glory to become one of us, and to take on all the frailties of human flesh. He empathizes with our frame and our weakness. He has felt and walked in all the temptations and trials that assail us. There is nothing we have ever suffered that He did not taste. His heart is moved by human beings more than all the others in His vast household.

The mystery of the Lord's love for His people is a marvel, even to the angels. They see the way we redeemed ones overwhelm the Lord's heart, with one glance of our eye. We have great favor and influence with our Bridegroom King. Our prayers and songs cause Him to intervene in the affairs on the earth. We have an audience with the King. This is the privilege of prayer, which we have never appreciated fully. At least I haven't.

Who will be the rare and precious Esther company, whose character and beauty found favor with the King, and delivered millions of innocent lives from death, due to the favor that she found? This, beloved bride of Yeshua, is our inheritance. To move the King's heart through the favor that we have found, and to rescue millions from death by the authority of the golden scepter of mercy that He extends to us.

We are Esther, the unknown orphan who rose to royalty. The Bride of Yeshua has great influence in the courts of heaven. We are being prepared for the day when we will be trusted with more power and authority than we can now imagine. We have an audience with the King. Our favor and influence with the King will spread salvation and restoration among our nations, as we move His heart with our love, prayers, songs and tears.

The Rising Warrior Bride

> *6:10 Who is she that appears like the dawn, beautiful as the moon and clear as the sun, terrible and fearsome as an army?* (AP).

The voice of the Bridegroom continues His praise for His bride. She appears like the dawn in the dark night sky. Is this not how Rebecca's bridal caravan appeared to Isaac, as he rose up from praying in the field, and lifted up his eyes into the darkening night sky? *"Who is this, coming from the wilderness, appearing as the dawn, fair as the moon and clear as the sun? Could this be my bride?"*

Her light is rising, her hope is rising, and her visibility in the darkness is arising like the brightening dawn. She is on the horizon as a champion, waiting to run her course in this final hour. **Esther's obscurity has been unveiled, her opportunity has arisen, and her authority to expose the darkness has reached its maturity.**

> *Arise, shine, for your light has come, and the glory of the Lord rises upon you. See, darkness covers the earth and thick darkness is over the peoples, but **the Lord rises upon you** and his glory appears over you. **Nations will come to your light, and kings to the brightness of your dawn.*** (Isa. 60:1-3, NIV).

She is as fair as the moon. The moon is the brightest light in the night sky. The Lord God made the moon to govern the night, as He made the sun to govern the day. The light of the white moon is but the reflection of the greater light, the Sun of Righteousness. She has no true beauty or light of her own, for without the sun, she would be a dull and pockmarked body in space. But with the light of the Lord bathing her in His shared glory, the strength of her light dispels the darkness. The moon must turn her face to the sun, or she will not have His light. Her reflection of Yeshua's light captures the second heavens, and the darkness flees before her.

She is clear as the sun. She is accessible, transparent, vulnerable and pure. Her light is pure, and without spot or blemish. She has been cleansed of her bent motives and uncircumcised heart. The bride of Yeshua is now a body of light and truth that cannot be hidden. The lost and hopeless world will be drawn to her light.

You are the light of the world. A city set on a hill cannot be hidden. Nor do people light a lamp and put it under a basket, but on a stand, and it gives light to all in the house. In the same way, let your light shine before others, so that they may see your good works and give glory to your Father who is in heaven (Matt. 5:14, ESV).

She is as terrible and fearsome as an army with banners. This is the same phrase which He spoke over her in 6:4. She is the worshiping warrior bride, like Joshua and the Levites. The singers and musicians went ahead of the army, and the high praises of God brought down the sword of the Lord upon their enemies. This last days' worshiping warrior bridal army is perfectly portrayed in Psalm 149.

Praise the Lord. **Sing to the Lord a new song,** *His praise in the assembly of his faithful people...For the Lord takes delight in His people;* **He crowns the humble with victory...May the praise of God be in their mouths and a double-edged sword in their hands, to inflict vengeance on the nations and punishment on the peoples, to bind their kings with fetters, their nobles with shackles of iron, to carry out the sentence written against them —** *this is the glory of all His faithful people.* (Ps.149, NIV).

The Bride Contends for the Harvest
We now see the bride in her role as both gardener and warrior.

6:11-13 I went down to the garden of nuts to see the verdure of the valley, to see whether the vine had budded and the pomegranates had bloomed (NKJV). *I did not know it, but my soul set me among the chariots of the noble volunteers of my people. Return, return, O Shulamite; return, return, and we will gaze at you. Why do you need to gaze at the Shulamite? For this is the dance of Mahanaim* (AP).

191

Verses 6:12 and 13 have been difficult for both translators and interpreters. It is hard to know with certainty who is speaking in this conversation, and what important points are being conveyed. This is the only place in the Song where the bride is called "the Shulamite," and she has no other name in the rest of the Song.

I believe it is the bride speaking in verses 11 and 12. She is busy with the ripeness of the harvest. She is taking responsibility to watch over the budding of the nut trees, the grape vines and pomegranates. This will culminate in the end of the summer harvest. No one told her to go into the groves and vineyards – she is a willing volunteer.

Notice the contrast between this scene and the opening scene from her childhood. Her mother's sons were angry and made her labor in their vineyards, causing her to lose her beauty. Now, as a mature bride, she willingly works in the orchards, inspecting for the readiness of the fruit. This speaks of the bridal responsibility for the harvest of souls. The Lord's bride shares His concern for the integrity of the harvest, and she willingly takes part.

The bride now says, "My King's people are my people. My Beloved's vines are my vines. We are partnering to bring in the full harvest, and I am in full agreement with caring for His fields. We are raising children together."

During Israel's long years in Egypt, they were forced to labor in Pharaoh's fields, but when they came into their own Land, they gladly labored on their own properties.

The Bride Arises as a Military Commander

6:13 I did not know it, but my soul set me among the chariots of the noble volunteers of my people (AP).

You can find a number of translations of this verse, but most do not make sense, because it is so difficult to translate and interpret. I went back to the original Hebrew, and prayed for the Lord to help me understand what is happening here. (I am not claiming to have the authoritative meaning of this passage, but only that I tried to make sense of it.) That is why I have used my own personal translation of the Hebrew here, because it sheds more light on the meaning. In the previous verse, the bride is a willing volunteer in the harvest, searching for the ripeness of the fruit.

In this verse, now she is saying that without realizing it, her soul has thrust her into a leadership role in an army (chariots), where all the soldiers are voluntary fighters from among her people, Israel. When I read the Hebrew phrase, "the chariots of *'ami-nadiv,'*" I worked on some possibilities. I chose the words "noble volunteers of my people" to translate this phrase. *Ami* means "my people," and *nadiv* is from the same root as *"mitnadev,"* meaning, to volunteer. It is often used for soldiers who fought voluntarily, and also for those who are generous and noble. As a noun, *nadiv* means noble or ruler, and implying generosity, such as a good leader would show toward his people.

As I read this, I remembered a similar phrase found in the book of Judges, referring to Deborah's military leadership over the volunteer soldiers of Israel. It struck me that Solomon was comparing the bride to soldierly Deborah.

When the princes in Israel take the lead, when the people willingly offer themselves— praise the Lord! My heart is with Israel's princes, with the willing volunteers among the people (Judges 5:2, 9, NIV).

Deborah is saying that when the noble leaders set an example of voluntary sacrifice to enter a battle, the people will also rise up and volunteer to fight. This brings praise to the Lord. Isn't that what the Lord Yeshua did? He was the royal Prince of Heaven, and He volunteered to enter the worst of earthly and cosmic battles. As a result of His voluntary sacrifice, a multitude of willing volunteers have now followed this great One into the battle fields. This brings praise to His Father, who is in heaven.

Before Deborah was thrust into the battle in the north, she was holding court as Israel's judge (ruler) in the area near Bethel. She was teaching the Israelites the ways of the Lord, and maturing them. This would be like the bride, first tending the vineyards and flocks of Israel. Then the Lord urged her into a military role. Deborah says, "I arose, a **mother** in Israel," (Ju. 5:7). Do you see how she moves into a parental role, raising up the Lord's children as an army?

The Shulamite says that although her mind did not know what was happening, she was somehow placed within a volunteer army of Israel's royal chariots. She is thrust into the midst of a battle for her people Israel's princely destiny.

About 800 years after Deborah arose for her people, Esther was also placed in a noble position of leadership. Without knowing it, she was thrust into a deadly war game, where Israel's survival was at stake. It was her intercessory warfare that caused the Jews to be given the right to bear arms and defend themselves in the coming battle for their survival. Mordechai became a prince overnight. The Jews in the Persian Empire became a princely people as a result of that victory. It says that "many become Jews in the Persian Empire, for the fear of the Jews had gripped them."

The Shulamite is also taking responsibility and contending for Israel's destiny, through finding favor with the king. This speaks of the bride of Yeshua arising into exactly this position in these last days. The Lord will give us courage, strength, and a responsibility to care for the welfare of Israel, as well as for the whole One New Man flock of the redeemed from the nations.

The Bride's Weapons are Spiritual Weapons

The name *"Israel"* means "struggles with God," but it also has another meaning: "Prince of God," or "rules with God." Israel was meant to be a prince among nations and under the reign of Solomon, Israel came closest to walking in that princely role. However, it will not be until the end of this age that Israel will rise up into her greater prince-nation status, when Jerusalem becomes the capital of the earth, under the government of Messiah Yeshua, the Son of David.

The bride finds her soul in a battle to save her princely nation. Shuli, like Deborah, finds herself contending in the spirit for what will become of Israel in the present or future. She represents the last days' warrior bride, moving in prophetic intercession in the realm of the Spirit. This will affect the outcome of spiritual and physical battles on the earth, as well as governmental powers. She has stood on the mountains and looked with the Lord from Lebanon. She has taken leadership, training and equipping the last days' Daughters of Jerusalem. She is taking the lead in an army of volunteers, who desperately need leadership by example. This is the role the Lord will give to His last days' bride.

The One New Man Bride

Joel speaks of a future restoration of Israel's relationship with the Lord, and her prophetic destiny. The Lord compares Israel's destiny with the blossoming of the fig tree (Hos. 9:10, Matt. 24:32-33). He likens the Body of Messiah to branches of the Vine, who is the Lord (John 15:1-2). Both believing Israel and the Bride from the nations will come into their fullness (full numbers and full maturity in Yeshua) at this time. The Jewish Bride and the Bride from the nations (*"goyim"* in Hebrew, also translated gentiles) will finally become One Bride in Messiah. This will fulfill Paul's statement that we are "One New Man" in Messiah (see Eph. 2:15b). This is already a present reality, but not yet in its full expression. Paul's word will be fulfilled at the greatest measure when all Israel is saved and joined to all those who have been grafted into her own original olive tree (see Rom. 11:25-26).

Do not be afraid, you wild animals, for the pastures in the wilderness are becoming green.

The trees are bearing their fruit; ***the fig tree and the vine yield their riches. Be glad, people of Zion, rejoice in the Lord your God, for he has given you the autumn rains*** *because he is faithful. He sends you abundant showers, both autumn and spring rains, as before. The threshing floors will be filled with grain;* ***the vats will overflow with new wine and oil*** (Joel 2:22-24, NIV).

The Bride's Elevation to Royalty

> *7:1 Return, return, O Shulamite; return, return, and we will gaze at you. Why do you need to gaze at the Shulamite? For this is the dance of Mahanaim* (AP).

This is one of the most difficult and confusing passages in the Song to interpret. I thought very hard about this passage before writing this section, because it raises some questions.

The first question is: Who is saying, "Return, O Shulamite?"

The second question is: Who is saying, "Why do you want to gaze at the Shulamite?"

The third question is: What are they talking about?

Let me attempt to answer these three questions with my "thesis" of what this passage is about. Below is my exact/literal translation of the Hebrew text, which is a little different from the regular Bible translations. I believe the first sentence is spoken by the Daughters of Jerusalem and the second sentence is spoken by the Bridegroom in response.

Daughters: *Return, return, O Shulamite; return, return, and we will gaze at you.*
Bridegroom: *Why do you need to gaze at the Shulamite? For this is the dance of Mahanaim.*

To understand this dialogue, we need to study the word *Mahanaim*. Literally, *Mahanaim* means "two camps" in Hebrew. However, what is more important is to understand how an Israelite in Solomon's day would understand the word *"Mahanaim."* They might simply think it means, "Two camps," or "two opinions," or "two groups of people."

But I suspect that an ancient Israelite would think immediately about what their father Jacob meant when he said, *"Mahanaim."* Jacob had spent 20 years of hard labor under his devious father-in-law, Laban. He finally fled from Laban with all his flocks, herds, daughters, servants and little ones, and escaped to the mountains of Gilead, a fertile area east of the Jordan River, southeast of the Sea of Galilee and north of the Jabbok River. Laban tracked them down. After some tough negotiations, they made peace; Laban went back to Syria and Jacob's family continued southward, to prepare for the dreaded confrontation with his potentially vengeful brother, Esau (see Gen. 31:22-32:2).

As Jacob's family and flocks approach the campsite near the Jabbok River, they are astonished to see that a group of angels has already set up camp there, and have been waiting for Jacob's family to arrive! Jacob is overjoyed that the Lord has provided a heavenly "boost" to support him through the coming trip to meet Esau. In his joy, he exclaims, "This is the camp of God!" How would you like to camp out in God's own campground? Sounds like Tabernacles to me!

And it says he named that place, *"Mahanaim,"* meaning two camps. Two groups were camping at the river that night: One from heaven and one from earth. Jacob's family and a group of angels. In the cool night air, they all sang and danced around the campfire. Heaven and earth had a camp meeting! It was the dance of *Mahanaim*. This time of worship, with a supernatural component, encouraged Jacob, so that he would not lose heart at the thought of meeting Esau.

But a day or two later, Jacob was so afraid of Esau's approaching "army" of 400 men, that he separated his own household into "two camps." He felt that by dividing them, at least one half would escape from possible attack. But when he named the campground *"Mahanaim,"* he had not yet divided his household. They were still one group.

It is likely that Jacob thought of the strategy of dividing his family into "two camps" because of the angelic visitation, and the naming of the campground, *"Mahanaim."* He prayed and told the Lord, "You promised that You would protect me on this journey, and now I have become 'two camps.'"

So, what does the Bridegroom mean when He says, *"Why do you need to gaze at the Shulamite? For this is the dance of Mahanaim."*

Well, the Daughters of Jerusalem know that the Bride has gone away on a special assignment, whether in the physical or spiritual realm is not clear. But she is somewhere else, contending for Israel's destiny, among the royal chariots of the willing troops of her people Israel.

And the Daughters miss her counsel, her companionship, her wise instruction, her beauty and kindness. They look up to her and feel like things are not the same without her wisdom and passion for the Bridegroom. So they urge her: "Return, return, O Shulamite, so that we can enjoy and admire you. Come back to the pleasant routines of life in the palace, and the comforts of the courts. We want to discuss with you all that you have experienced in your times with the King. We want to emulate your beauty and wisdom, and to absorb what you will teach us. Come back!"

I'm sure that in the days of Deborah, Israel also felt somewhat lost when their spiritual mother, ruler and judge, was off in a dangerous battle in the north country. What would they do without her wise and just counsel? What if she was killed in battle?

But the Bridegroom would answer them:

> *"No, why do you need to gaze at her, as if she is your focus? It is not about gazing at her. She has been entrusted with a holy assignment in the camp of God, because My bride has matured and overcome persecution and scorn for My sake. She is standing in the place of warfare and intercession, even in the courts of heaven, and she is pleading the cause of her people. She is engaged with angels, who are encamped round about her, and they are preparing her for her confrontation with the spirit of Esau (compromise with the pleasures and mixture of this world).*

> *"Trust Me, it is for your good, O Daughters of Jerusalem, that she is fighting for you at this time. All of Israel will be glad and rejoice later, when they realize the critical battles she is fighting on your behalf. This is more important than your enjoying her wisdom and counsel at this time. Pray for your leaders.*

> *"Esau is jealous of what My Bride has inherited, and she will need courage to stand in the blessings of God.* **She has now been elevated to royalty, and she is in the place where heaven and earth meet. She is partnering with heaven. It is the dance of Mahanaim that Jacob, our father, experienced, and this joining of Heaven and earth is the inheritance of all My bride."**

The angel of the Lord encamps all around those who fear Him, and delivers them (Ps. 34:7).

Three Banquets of Wine, Three Praises of the Royal Bride (SOS 7:1-8)

This passage (SOS 7:1-8) is the third chorus, where the Bridegroom sings of the beauty of the bride. For the third time, He sings of her virtues and all her desirability. Like Esther, the bride is lovely of form and beautiful to behold. The King desires her beauty. The three passages in the Song where He praises the bride's beauty can be likened to three particular banquets found in the book of Esther.

In the first banquet, Esther is chosen as queen (Est. 2:18). This first banquet was initiated by the King, and it was a feast to which all were invited. The purpose was to "gladden the bride," that is, to display Esther's favor and beauty with the King. It was called "the Feast of Esther."

Spiritually, this shows that the Lord loved and chose us first, and because of His kindness, we can return His love and love others as well. The Lord's love song (feast) first announces His love for us, and then we respond.

Likewise in the Song, the first chorus of praising the Bride is sung immediately after the bridal wedding carriage arrives in Jerusalem (SOS 4:1-5). All the Daughters of Jerusalem were invited to come and see the King on His wedding day, and so it is like the feast that the King gave for Esther.

The Second Banquet

In the second banquet, Esther delights the King (and Haman) without revealing the desperate intercessions of her heart (Est. 5:4-6). The King had not called Esther for many days and thus, she was insecure about where she stood with the king (Est.4:11b). Esther risked her life to initiate this second banquet. During this banquet, Esther secured and renewed the favor that she had previously enjoyed, after a long time of separation. This step was necessary, before she could reveal the deeper intercessions of her heart. She needed to make sure that she had the King's favor, before asking him the life-and-death question. Remember the biblical examples, when a prophetic intercessor is about to petition the Lord for a critical issue. He begins his plea with the phrase, "If I have found favor in Your eyes, O God..."

Likewise, in the Song, the second chorus of praising the bride takes place just after the Bridegroom has left her alone, and she has gone through a painful period of separation, persecution and not knowing where to find Him (SOS 6:4-7). As with Esther, as soon as the bride has passed her test of courage, the King praises her and reminds her that His favor is securely upon her.

The Third Banquet

In the third banquet, the Lord had gone ahead of her, knowing she would be entering real warfare. Esther had entered into spiritual warfare with fasting and intercession. Without knowing how this happened, she was thrust into a life and death battle, figuratively among the chariots of her people, Israel. She was now in a position to move strategically in the war zone. Esther raised one warrior finger, and pointed at Haman. She exposed the enemy, dooming his murderous scheme against the Jews, and sentencing him to execution (Est. 7:3-6). It was Esther who initiated this third banquet, after securing the favor of the king. His wrath was released after she exposed Haman as a wicked enemy of herself and her people. New and righteous laws were written, and positions of power were overturned on earth, because Esther touched heaven.

In the same manner, in the Song, we see this third chorus of bridal praise taking place after she has become "terrible as an army," and has found her soul among the war chariots of her people, Israel (SOS 7:1-8). The bride has now been elevated to royalty, and with military honors. Thus, the Bridegroom lavishes the third and highest exclamations of her perfect beauty in His eyes. He is praising the victorious, overcoming, warrior Bride. **She is like Esther, perfect in inner beauty, for her love was stronger than death and her intercessions more unyielding than the grave.**

Likewise, the King permitted Mordechai to write a new decree. This was the Word and authority of the Lord, authorizing His bride to be prepared and armed against the enemies of God's people. The Bridegroom and His bride partnered together to overturn the schemes of destruction.

The Feast of Purim celebrates the victory and deliverance of Israel's people, through the warfare, fasting and intercessions of His bride. The result is a time of feasting, to remember and celebrate our victory over the Lord's enemies.

Solomon's Descriptions of the Human Body

It was Esther's physical beauty that won the King's heart, and thus, her elevation to royalty. However, it was her faith in the Lord, courage, intercession and willingness to be a martyr that saved her people. In the same way, Solomon highlights the physical features of the bride that attract him. However, it is her noble character, willingness to suffer, and warrior-like courage that have placed her in the position of contending for Israel's destiny.

Solomon's expressions of his bride's beauty tell us much about the Lord's view of beauty, and His creative work in designing the human body for beauty, strength, worship, functionality and for love. The Lord would not have included this book in the Bible if it were not pleasing in His eyes. He rejoices in the beautiful work of His creation, and the magnificence of the human face and form. **He created them in His image and His likeness; male and female He created them. And He saw that it was very good.**

Therefore, He put it in Solomon's heart to express this magnificence in this biblical love song, in a way that no other biblical book expresses.

Solomon was a poet, philosopher and a wisdom teacher. He was also a diplomat and a king. He pioneered new territory in art, music, architecture, and biblical literature. He was a man of diverse talents and was extravagant in all he built, wrote and accomplished. What he did, he did it all the way. He has shared with us the Lord's heart for His perfect dove. As the rabbis wrote: "All the writings are holy, but Song of Songs is the Holy of Holies."

The Lord has made it clear that He loves this Song. He will sing it over you and me one day very soon. He is a Bridegroom in love, and we too, have ravished His heart. Amen.

Chapter 10

THE SHARED INHERITANCE (SOS 7:8-8:14)

7:8b-9a Oh may your breasts be like clusters of the vine, and the scent of your breath like apples, and your mouth like the best wine.

9b-10 It goes down smoothly for my beloved, causing the lips of sleepers to speak. I am my beloved's, and his desire is for me (ESV).[32]

In verses 8b-9a, the Bridegroom is still speaking, as part of His praise for the beauty of His bride. But halfway through verse 9, even halfway through a sentence, the speaker changes to the bride, as we observe the Hebrew gender changes. This confuses translators, as we would not have expected the speaker to change halfway through a verse. There are two possible explanations:

The original Hebrew Bible does not have our chapter and verse divisions. Therefore, one easy explanation is that whoever inserted the verses in this Song, centuries after it was written, made a mistake in 7:9, and broke it up in the wrong place, thus changing speakers in the middle of a verse.

The other explanation is funny, and might end up being true. We could conclude this: The bride is literally finishing His sentence! Wives do that to their husbands all the time – he starts a thought, and she interrupts and finishes his sentence. Of course, in real life, the husband gets quite irritated when his wife finishes his sentences. At least my husband does. (I hope you're laughing at this point.) I don't think that the King got irritated with His bride finishing this beautiful sentence, about her wine going down smoothly into His heart, soothing him with her devotion.

On a spiritual level, it could actually mean that at times, the Lord will speak part of a sentence and pause – He is waiting for the bride to finish His sentence, so their hearts and thoughts can flow as One. This is entirely possible, as to why Solomon switched speakers, midway through a sentence.

In fact, there was a sentence that the Lord once spoke to Rick Joyner in "The Final Quest," where the Lord stopped midway through the sentence and paused. Rick knew that the Lord expected him to finish the thought. Rick thought for a while, and then realized that the second half of the sentence was, "...if I put my confidence in You." And he was correct.[33] The wine of his full confidence in the Lord, and not in himself, went down smoothly into his Beloved's heart. So I guess that proves the point that at times, the bride can finish her Bridegroom's thought, if she is aligned with His heart.

Then the next phrase, 9b-10, spoken by the bride, would read: *"It goes smoothly to my Beloved, and causes the lips of sleepers to speak. I am my Beloved's and His desire is for me"* (AP). Let's return to study the first part of this passage.

Nurturing Love

Oh may your breasts be like clusters of the vine

Breasts are a picture of nurturing love. One of the names of God in Scripture is *"El Shaddai."* In Hebrew, *"Shaddaim"* are breasts. Therefore this title of God describes His motherly, nurturing, gentle and loving nature. It gives us a sense that we are like little babes, earnestly drinking His Word and His ways, as nourishment for our spirits. The Lord often compares Himself to a mother in the Scriptures.

*Can a woman forget her **nursing child**, and not have compassion on the son of her womb? Surely they may forget, yet I will not forget you* (Isa. 49:15).

*But we were gentle among you, just as a **nursing mother** cherishes her own children* (1 Thess. 2:7).

*...As newborn **babes, desire the pure milk** of the word, that you may grow thereby...* (1 Pet. 2:2).

*O Jerusalem, Jerusalem, the one who kills the prophets and stones those who are sent to her! How often I wanted to **gather your children together, as a hen gathers her chicks** under her wings, but you were not willing!* (Matt. 23:37).

The Treasures of our Mouth

...the scent of your breath like apples, and your mouth like the best wine.

The breath of the bride is compared to the sweetness of apples, and her mouth to wine. Our mouth reveals what lies in our heart.

A good man out of the good treasure of his heart brings forth good things, and an evil man out of the evil treasure brings forth evil things. (Matt. 12:35, NIV).

We have seen that the apple tree was compared to the Lord's place of rest, shade, and sweet fruit. Here, the Bridegroom compares the words that come from His bride's mouth to apples and to wine, flowing out from the treasury of her heart. Her love satisfies His heart more than the finest wine. May we fulfill this high standard of the Lord – that the words of our mouth and the overflow of our hearts would be fully pleasing to Him. This is a hard level to attain, purity of motives and speech. It will not come automatically.

205

How beautiful is your love, my sister, my bride! **How much better is your love than wine, and the fragrance of your oils than any spice!** (SOS 4:10).

9b-10 It [the wine]goes smoothly to my Beloved, and causes the lips of sleepers to speak. I am my Beloved's and His desire is for me.

This means that our thoughts, emotions and words are compatible with the Lord. He can receive them with ease, without His holy heart being jarred or grieved by any incompatible thoughts of our heart. Thus, we are found to be a "suitable partner" to Him. As we pour out worship, prayer and love songs to the Lord, sleepers begin to awake. Dreams and visions stir them in the night, and their lips move in prayer and revelation. This has happened to me a number of times, where I can feel that my lips are murmuring things to the Lord in my sleep. I'm sleeping, but my heart is awake, and I am praying and receiving from Him in my sleep.

When the priestly bride ministers to the Lord, the sleeping (immature or lukewarm) bride awakens, and becomes aware of her priestly responsibilities. The bride begins to pray out of intimacy, rather than mere duty.

As Yeshua is magnified by our love, others begin to wake up and recognize His beauty and His jealous love. We saw that the Daughters of Jerusalem were awakened to love by seeing the passion of the Bride. We come out of spiritual slumber and awaken to the purposes for which the Lord placed us on the earth, for such a time as this.

Mike Bickle also offers this thought: "The proof that the Spirit has awakened the sleepers is that their speech comes under His leadership. He will move the sleepers so that they speak in purity and righteousness. The Spirit gently woos us to speak on His behalf with subtle impressions. He calls us to voluntary love; therefore, He will gently move us without violating our free will."[34]

Awake, you who sleep, arise from the dead, and Christ will give you light (Eph. 5:14).

Partnership Requires Consecration

> *7:11-12 Come, my beloved, let us go out into the fields and lodge in the villages; let us go out early to the vineyards and see whether the vines have budded, whether the grape blossoms have opened and the pomegranates are in bloom. There I will give you my affections*[35] *(ESV).*

This speaks of a season when the Bridegroom and His bride spend time together in refreshing their relationship, consecration and intimacy. Then in the early morning, signifying the beginning of the harvest time, they go out to seek for the signs of the blossoms on the vines and fruit trees. When the flowers bud, the fruit cannot be far behind. They go to check for fruitfulness together, because the bride is a partner and helper to the Bridegroom in all things.

Let's review the history of Shuli's maturing process, to get the bigger picture. The Lord has been calling us into partnership from the beginning, both in human history, and in our personal journeys. In her earliest stage of knowing the Lord (salvation), the bride said, "Draw me after You, and we will run." However, in 2:10-14, the Lord tried to draw her away. He invited her to come into the harvest fields, but she wasn't ready at that time.

In 4:8, He urged, "Come **with Me**, from Lebanon **with me**, from the mountain tops…" Here, she was ready to partner with Him, and see things from the Mountain View (heaven's perspective).

In 5:6-7, she suffered persecution, seemingly without Him. He had withdrawn, or so it seemed. She shared a portion of His shame and reproach at the hands of spiritual leaders, who should have known better. But after the test and trial had passed, she realized that He had never left her; He was with her all the time, but her awareness of His presence needed to be restored.

In 6:11, Shuli went down to the garden, taking responsibility to supervise the growth. At that time, the Lord promoted her to a military partner, and she fought for her nation's destiny, like Deborah, like Esther, and like the last days' overcoming Bride of Yeshua.

Now, in 7:11, she is inviting the Lord of the Harvest, beckoning Him to intimately partner with her, so that together, they can nurture, equip and gather the end time harvest of souls, both Israel and the nations. It is not presumption that the bride invites the Lord to join her. The Lord loves our pursuit of Him, and our invitations to seasons of intimacy and partnership. That is like saying to Him, "I can't do any of this without You, Lord." A mature Bride has freedom to initiate partnership with the Lord, because she shares His heart's desires.

Running in the Pure Streams of God

This passage is also about consecration. It speaks of our need to be separated from the mixture found in some segments of professing Christianity. There is a cry in the bride's heart to come away from all the many systems that are not the pure streams of God. There are many diverse ministry works that we can be involved in, but not all are the pure streams of God.[36]

Sometimes, at a moment we might not be expecting it, the Lord will sovereignly lift us up, out, and away from a ministry, a church or network of churches, into which we have poured years of intense labor. It feels frightening and lonely when the Lord abruptly pulls us out, but in some cases, He is doing this as a deliberate act of separation.

It is not always that He is separating us **from** something, although that might be the case, depending on where we are laboring, struggling, or stagnating. But His heart is more to separate us **to Someone**: to Himself, as an act of setting us apart **unto** the Bridegroom King, our jealous God. To be holy, to be set apart, is not just **from bad things**, but rather, we are set apart **to the One who desires us to be His alone**. He might separate us from a "good thing," which is not best for our growth, nor for the destiny He has planned for us. Most readers can identify with this work of separation.

In some cases, friends, leaders or ministry partners might become exclusive, controlling, or unbalanced. They might begin to embrace mistaken doctrines and teachings, based on wrong research or false revelation. In these cases, if we are close to these ones and wanting to please them, they can draw us into mixture, or unbalanced focus. Sometimes, you can be caught up in several streams at the same time, and they are all pulling you in different directions. Sometimes we are asked to choose between one prophetic stream and another, which both have strong and compelling leaders. Or people will want to use us to lend our gifts and talents to their goals, but not allow us freedom to be who He made us to be. All that I have just described have been serious and troubling issues to me, a number of times in my journey.

If the Lord sees that we are becoming fragmented, confused, used or spiritually abused, He will take steps, which we might have never asked for. He is a good and caring Father, and if He does this, it is for our good, and for our future with Him. Yes, the Lord Himself will carry us away into a time or space of separation. It will feel lonely and scary, to be taken out of the familiar faces and places, where we are so accustomed to ministering, being fed, or just fellowshipping. But when He separates us, it is for our good, and we should not let our emotions rob us of this new season's purposes. Remember in 3:1-3, the bride searches in all the familiar places and among the familiar faces of watchmen, hoping to reconnect to the Lord. But it is not through these familiar places or faces that she finds Him.

Maintaining Intimacy while Serving

The bride has now come to a new level of maturity. In previous phases, she was able to enter into times of intimacy with the Shepherd-King, while at places of rest and comfort. One restful place was at the King's table, dining on the meat of His Word.

Another place was under the shade of His apple tree, representing resting in the finished work of the cross. There we learned that we are secure under His shade (His commitment). There, we began to taste more than mere salvation, but we also saw His kindness to help us in our tiniest problems.

Another place of security was within the wall of our own garden. The Lord watched her from behind the wall, and gazed at her through the window. He surprised her with an invitation to come away into ministry, which she was not ready to accept. She stayed in her comfort zone, and asked Him to run on the mountains till the night was over. **And so, at times our security is a hindrance to obedience.**

Another invitation to encounter came was while she was sleeping. But when He knocked this time, it was in the hour of the Lord's sorrow, loneliness, and anguish of heart. This invitation was to share the Lord's suffering and shame. He anointed her with myrrh, to give His bride the overcomer's grace to endure, and through the hard trial, she passed her test without bitterness.

The bride has now come to a point where she is going out into the Lord's harvest, while still maintaining their shared times of intimacy and friendship. It includes rising up from the privacy of their shared love, and beginning to do the work of the harvest, including hardship, rejection, and at times, even persecution.

This maturity means that we don't have to choose between resting in the secure place and serving His children in the hard place of ministry. We are learning to serve, without sacrificing the needful times of rest in the Lord's Presence.

*7:13 The mandrakes send out their fragrance, and at our door is every delicacy, both **new and old**, that I have stored up for you, my beloved* (NIV).

What is the bride saying? The Lord and His bride have spent precious time together, renewing their covenantal commitments. The Lord, of course, does not need to "recommit" to us. He pledged Himself at the final Passover, and gave it all for His bride. He signed the marriage covenant in His own blood, so He needs no reminders for His sake.

But for our benefit, the Lord enjoys our times of re-consecration, going down "memory lane," and rehearsing our journey together. We remember His kindness, deliverance, help in desperate moments, and funny little things that we laughed about at the time. And remembering tears, disappointments, emotional storms, tests of our faith, nights of sorrow and suffering, times of supernatural rescue – these are very dear to the Lord's heart. **It makes Him feel valued, as we intentionally remember Him by rehearsing our**

history. These are precious, private treasures from the deep well of our history with Him. The Lord wants us to take time to open our "journals of journey," and let Him know that we have not forgotten all that has transpired. Isn't the Bible a book of remembrances of what the Lord has done for His people, so that we never forget how good He is?

Treasures from the Bride's Hope Chest

Because of the urgent pace of life, and the chores consuming us, days turn into weeks and months, in the blink of an eye. How often I forget something that the Lord told me or did for me. Even something major that happened a week or two ago, feels like months ago to me, due to the amount of consuming activities that have occurred since that recent memory. These remembrances of the Lord's faithfulness are like old treasures from the Bride's hope chest, and we bring them with us to our Wedding Day.

The Lord measures wealth by the depth of our heart and the strength of our love. He will deck Himself in these "old treasures," like putting on the finest antique jewelry and embroidered robes from an elegant period of royal history (see Isa. 61:10). The Lord is waiting and hoping to receive these unique and valuable adornments that each of us alone can bring to Him. No one else on this earth has the unique wedding trousseau ("hope chest") that we have. Each one has a deep well and a testimony, along with pearls (acts) of love, which were our responses to His love.

And so the bride tells the King: "As we go into the harvest fields, we will see, smell and taste the fruit of our labors, and the rewards of Your suffering. We are on the threshold of Your inheritance, the nations of the earth, and Your own portion, Israel."

> *Indeed He says, "It is too small a thing that You should be My Servant to raise up the tribes of Jacob, and to restore the preserved ones of Israel; I will also give You as a light to the Gentiles, that You should be My salvation to the ends of the earth"* (Isa. 49:5-6).

The Bride continues, "At the very gates (threshold) of our house (the Kingdom household of the faithful from all nations), we are reaping pleasing and satisfying fruits. These are the reaping of many souls in the harvest field of the earth. As I have brought to You my **old treasures** from the race we have run together, now we are bringing in the **new treasures** (harvest), and seeing mighty acts of salvation and deliverance such as have not yet been seen. Before our eyes, Bridegroom King, we are now **reaping** the new harvest, faster than we can sow the seeds. The plowman is overtaking the reaper! Behold, they have reached our very gates."

Behold, the days are coming," says the Lord, "when the plowman shall overtake the reaper, and the treader of grapes him who sows seed; the mountains shall drip with sweet wine, and all the hills shall flow with it (Amos 9:13).

The Kingdom of God's New and Old Treasures
This statement about the old and new treasures is so similar to a parable that the Lord shared.

*Then He said to them, "Therefore every scribe instructed concerning the kingdom of heaven is like a householder who brings out of his treasure things **new and old"** (Matt. 13:52).*

This parable was the eighth one, after the Lord had delivered a series of seven parables about the Kingdom of God. All eight parables are found in Matthew 13.

The Lord speaks of the scribes of Israel – those who faithfully copied the Torah, the prophets and writings, by flickering candlelight, with laborious and meticulous attention to detail. Even the smallest stroke of each letter of the Hebrew alphabet was given much care, so as not to alter the text in any way from the manuscript from which they copied. With such value and holiness did the scribes copy the scrolls handed down.

Do you ever think about how we got these accurate, printed Bibles, telling stories that are thousands of years old, with pinpoint accuracy? These Bibles contain both the **Old and New Testaments**. I picture these learned Hebrew sages, trained from early childhood in every tiny nuance of the written Word of God, producing one copy at a time, over a period of months or years. This precious scroll, when completed and checked many times for errors, would be placed in the possession of the rabbi of their town. And it was guarded and handed down for thousands of years. Archeologists are often uncovering older fragments of scrolls, revealing again and again, the accuracy of the Hebrew scribes in capturing the eternal histories of God and His people. *"In the beginning, God..."* From eternity past to eternity future, so wide is the sweep of the written Word of God.

And so, the Lord is saying that the scribes of Israel were guardians of **old treasures**, as the Lord had given a wealth of revelation to Israel, before the Son of Man came to the earth. Then the Lord tells us that those scribes who carry these **old treasures** in their hearts, but who now have also been instructed in the Kingdom of God, through His own parables (**new treasures**) – these are carrying the fullness of God's redemptive purposes for the earth. To have hope in our hearts, we need to know where all this is going, and why we are on this earth at this time. We need the full revelation of God, both old and new.

Finding a Bride at the Well

The mention of mandrakes reminds us of the story of Jacob and Rachel. We remember from the story of Jacob's long period of service in Laban's household that he ended up with essentially two wives, two concubines, twelve sons and one daughter by Leah. But Rachel was his perfect dove – the one who caught his eye from that first moment at the well. Like the Shulamite maiden, Rachel was also a shepherdess (see Gen. 29:9). It was in the watering of the sheep at the well that Jacob found her, wept, embraced and kissed her at their first joyful meeting. Jacob's father Isaac (through Eliezer's mediation) also met his mother Rebecca at the well. Later,

Jacob's descendent Moses would also marry a shepherdess, whom he also met at the well, as she was tending her father's flocks.

The Lord Yeshua shared the gospel for the first and only recorded time with a Samaritan woman, whom He met at **Jacob's well** (see John 4:5-6). The Lord stated on other occasions that He was sent only to the lost sheep of the house of Israel, and He commanded the disciples not to enter the towns of the Samaritans when He sent them out. And yet here He was, early in His ministry, taking more time and conversation with this Samaritan woman at the well than any other personal encounter we read in the gospels.

It is significant that this unusual, early outreach to non-Jews takes place at Jacob's well, where the Samaritans became the early first fruits of salvation to the gentiles. They were not excluded from the harvest. In fact, the Lord uses the whole village in Samaria as a picture of the plentiful white harvest fields for whom He came, and told His disciples that they would reap what others had labored for. This is the early "new treasures" of the harvest that we have been sharing.

The King of Israel foreshadowed the inclusion of the gentile bride, for whom He poured out living waters into her entire village, springing from their encounter at the well. The Lord has painted this awesome prophetic picture. He will meet both His Jewish Bride and His Gentile Bride at the well of His living waters, and it is here, at the well, where we pledge our betrothal to Him, the Jewish Bridegroom of the Ages. We are already One New Man, but the Jewish/Israeli Bride has not come forth yet, except in a remnant. Then, the two will become ONE BRIDE.

The Bride Promises Children to her Bridegroom

Rachel was distraught over her infertility, and in ancient times, it was believed that mandrakes improved one's fertility. She asks Leah for some of her son's mandrakes, hoping for the blessing of children. Rachel did conceive and give birth to Joseph shortly after that incident, but the Bible makes it clear that God had compassion on Rachel and opened her womb; it was not about the mandrakes. When Jacob's family fled from Laban, Rachel stole her father's household idols. I realized that she had a superstitious belief about the power of the mandrakes, and I connected it to why she would have stolen these idols. She must have believed that they would help her conceive a second child. She named her first son "Joseph," because she said, "May the Lord add to me another child." In Hebrew, Joseph means, "He will add."

Perhaps Solomon was thinking of Rachel when he penned these words in the mouth of his shepherdess-bride. Along with mentioning the vines and the pomegranates, she speaks of the ripeness of the mandrakes, and then she promises her Beloved pleasant fruits, both new and old, that she has laid up for Him. **There are only two places in the Bible where mandrakes are mentioned: Genesis 30, in Rachel's fertility battle, and here in Song of Solomon 7:13.**

It is possible that the bride mentions mandrakes as a sign that she will be fruitful and will bear Him many children. As a bride to the Lord, we are expected to be fruitful and multiply, and to have dominion over the earth. Our spiritual children will fill the earth, and our Bridegroom will rise up and call us blessed, this bride who has brought Him comfort and the children which His Father promised Him.

Isaiah speaks of the Lord Yeshua being cut off from this life, without having descendants, but he also prophesies of Yeshua having a spiritual "seed" or descendancy, despite not having physical children.

> *By oppression and judgment He was taken away, and* **who can speak of His descendants? For He was cut off from the land of the living;** *for the transgressions of My people He was stricken...***He will see His offspring, and prolong His days,** *and the will of the Lord will prosper in His hand. After the suffering of His soul, He will see the light of life and be satisfied* (Isa. 53 8,10b-11a, NIV).

The Lord Yeshua will have offspring, and His days will be from everlasting to everlasting. His Bride will be fruitful and multiply, and the Lord will have His children around His table, like fruitful olive shoots.

And again, Isaiah declares:

Here am I and the children whom the Lord has given me! *We are for signs and wonders in Israel from the Lord of hosts, who dwells in Mount Zion (Isa. 8:18).*

Chapter 11

SET ME AS A SEAL (SOS 8:1-10)

He is Not Ashamed to Call us Brothers

SOS 8:1-2 If only you were to me like a brother, who was nursed at my mother's breasts! Then, if I found you outside, I would kiss you, and no one would despise me. I would lead you and bring you to my mother's house— she who has taught me. I would give you spiced wine to drink, the nectar of my pomegranates (NIV).

F irst, let's look at this statement from the natural understanding of the story, and then we'll look at the significance for the bride of the Lord.

At the beginning of the Song, we looked at Shuli's "mother and brother issues." Those who made her labor in the fields were not called her brothers, but were called "my mother's sons." This implies that they were the product of the same father, but a different wife, and that she uses the term "mother" to refer to a step-mother. It was acceptable in those days for a man to have more than one wife. At times, the father would expect the children to call the other wife "their mother," out of affectionate respect, even though she was not their mother, nor could she love them like a mother.

Thus, among the children of this one father and several wives, there could be rivalries, rebellion, or abuse. The Bible is such an honest book that it does not hide these problems, nor does it sugar-coat the lives of the men and women we read about. We are allowed to behold the weaknesses and sins of those we respect, in the pages of the Bible, so that we will not lose heart, when we behold our own weaknesses and faults. I love that the Scriptures do not idealize these heroes and heroines of the faith. James says that Elijah was a man "with a nature just like us."

We've already seen the damages done to both David and Solomon, due to David having multiple wives, resulting in many half-brother and half-sister relationships. One of Solomon's half-brothers, Amnon, raped his half-sister, Tamar. Then another of Solomon's half-brothers (Absalom, who also tried to usurp David's throne) murdered Amnon in revenge for his full-blooded sister's disgrace.

And so, Shuli laments that if only her beloved were like a true physical brother, one who had nursed at her own mother's breasts, she would be allowed to show him love, without appearing to break the protocol of unmarried female behavior. In the same vein, a man in our society would not be allowed to show much physical warmth and affection for another man, because of the fear and shame that people might misinterpret this affection as something else. But if he were our biological brother, we could hold hands, run through the fields, hug, jump up on his back, play in the ocean's waves to our heart's content, and no one would judge us or despise us.

She never knew the affection of a full, biological brother. This is the significance of her longing for one who nursed at the same breasts. Just as all of us have a built-in need for a father's and a mother's love, I am convinced that we have a deeply rooted need for a **true brother**, one with whom we share a bond that only a brother and sister can share, or only a brother and brother can share.

Our earthly parents, no matter how good they might be, cannot fill our deepest need for a perfect parent. In the same way, our need for a true and perfectly loving brother cannot be fulfilled by our earthly siblings, even if we are blessed to have a close family. I was the older of two children in our family. I had one little brother, very close to my age, and we fought all our lives. We were always competing for everything; he was rough with me physically, and I got him in trouble by always telling our mom what bad things he had done.

After I got saved, I began to long for a true brother, with whom I could entrust my soul, and show real affection, in a safe atmosphere. (Just in case you are wondering, I did share about the Lord with my brother right after my salvation. It was an encounter which the Holy Spirit initiated, and He told me the exact moment to go into his room, in the midst of a horrific family battle. My brother received the Lord at that time, and hung on for a short time, but then when I went back to college, and wasn't at home to disciple him, he changed his mind, to my great sorrow.)

Much later in my spiritual journey, I began to encounter the Lord as my big brother. I saw an affectionate and playful side of Him that was astonishing, and yet freeing and "fun" to be with. On the spiritual level, among the many roles and titles which our Lord Yeshua rightly holds, the one that is the most humble and endearing is that He desires to be "our brother."

> Both the one who makes people holy and those who are made holy **are of the same family. So Jesus is not ashamed to call them brothers and sisters.** He says, "I will declare your name to my brothers and sisters; in the assembly I will sing your praises."
>
> And again, "I will put my trust in him." And again he says, **"Here am I, and the children God has given me"** (Heb. 2:11-13, NIV).

Lord, I always wished I had a brother like You. You are like the best big brother to me, and I wish I could show and tell the world how much I love You, without being despised.

He Became as One of Us

As we look through spiritual and prophetic eyes at this statement (*If only you were to me like a brother*), there is a remarkable insight about what Solomon was telling us here. The Song was written before the Lord entered human history as a baby, born of a woman. Solomon knew that he was a fulfillment of the promises that God gave to his father, David, about a son who would reign after him. But Solomon was aware that portions of the prophecy that David received spoke of a greater Son of David, who was not Solomon himself. There was a promise of an eternal throne and an eternal Kingdom, and of One whose reign would endure eternally.

Solomon, like all those in Israel who were godly and knew the Scriptures, was longing for this One to be born, to become like one of us, and to save us. Even Job, a very ancient non-Israelite, was longing for this One who would stand upon the earth – his Redeemer! This One would inherit the throne of His father, David, and would establish the Kingdom of God on the earth.

Let's look at this phrase now through prophetic eyes:

> *If only you were to me like a brother, who was nursed at my mother's breasts! Then, if I **found you outside,** I would kiss you, and no one would despise me. I would lead you and bring you to my mother's house— she who has taught me.*

This speaks of the Israelite's desire for the Incarnation, beating in the heart of every godly Jew! We were longing for a **real brother,** who would be like us, and who would sympathize with our weaknesses and temptations. This would bring the Lover of our Soul, who had always been distant and invisible, known in the Spirit realm only – now He would become flesh.

We would **find Him outside** (Yeshua was born "outside the inn," and He died "outside the camp,") and we could embrace Him, kiss Him, and bring Him into our mother's house. On the first level, our mother's house – she who has taught us, is Israel. For both Jews and Christians, we learned the truth from the covenants, patriarchs and Scriptures entrusted to Israel – she is the one who taught us about the one true God (see Rom. 9:4-5).

We could gather Him into the household of Israel (our mother's house) and claim Him as our own Jewish Messiah. He became one of us. He would feel the pains and sorrows of this broken world, and would be compassionate towards our struggles. We would have a true and real brother, when this One would come. And we could kiss Him and touch Him, without being despised and rejected.[37]

Please Do Not Pass Me By!

I would lead you and bring you to my mother's house —
she who has taught me. I would give you spiced wine to
drink, the nectar of my pomegranates.

When we find the Lord, so real, vulnerable, and deserving, we desire to give Him our best offerings. If He came to our house, we would bring out for Him the finest foods, the choicest refreshments that our culture would consider the most elegant treats that a weary traveler could enjoy.

Do you remember when Abraham was sitting at the entrance of his tent in the heat of the day, and he lifted up his eyes and saw the three Visitors approaching, he ran to meet them and bowed low. He immediately implored them, "If I have found favor in Your eyes, please do not pass me by. Please rest and be refreshed, and let me take care of you. Honor my home, and stay awhile." And he and Sarah rushed to prepare the finest meal that they had to offer. He recognized that the Lord had come in bodily form to visit him, along with two mighty angels, who later destroyed Sodom. And Abraham kept them with him and offered them refreshing physical sustenance. This is exactly what the bride is expressing about finding the Lord "outside," and bringing Him into her home and refreshing Him with the finest things.

We saw the bride express this same desire in 3:4, and the theme is the same: Welcoming Him without shame, knowing that He belongs with us (ownership,) sealing Him unto ourselves, closure from past broken relationships, the intimacy of a true brother, freedom to spend time with Him and express the full passion of our heart without being shamed, hated or ridiculed. (*"I held him and would not let him go till I had brought him to my mother's house, to the room of the one who conceived me."*)

She clung desperately to him, holding on for dear life. She desired to make sure she would never lose him again, and tried to keep Him all for herself. This signified two things, in the earthly story line: It represented her desire to secure his permanence, or even a formal engagement. It was also an official statement of a binding commitment, to bring the betrothed into the mother's inner room, as a kind of **setting Him as a seal upon her heart**.

The Bride: Broken to Herself, Enduring to the End

8:5a Who is this coming up from the wilderness, leaning on her beloved?

Here we find the third time in the Song, where someone asks: **"Who is This?"** The first was Solomon's carriage coming up from the desert, like a troop of priests, worshipers and warriors, carrying the golden Ark of the Covenant on their shoulders.

The second **"Who is This"** was the picture of the bride like a city set on a hill (Jerusalem). It was the arising warrior bride, as an army with banners, striking terror and dismay in all the enemies of the King and in those who hate His bride. She is rising like the dawn, humble as the moon and clear and dazzling as the sun.

Now we come to the third **"Who is This."** How amazing that Solomon returns a third time to this theme. Two-hundred years later, Isaiah would write these same words. He would ask, *"Who is this, coming up from Edom, with the Day of Vengeance in His heart?"* It is the Bridegroom, coming to judge and make war, for the year of His redeemed has come and the day of vengeance is in His heart.

Solomon ends this Song with the Bride's most vulnerable, dependent, broken and tender moment. Like John the Beloved at the final Passover, she is leaning on the breast of her true brother and best friend. The night of his Beloved's martyrdom, John was the only bride leaning on His heart.

This is the last days' Bride, broken to herself. She is utterly dependent on the Lord, leaning on Him for all her needs. She is relying on Him, fully trusting in Him, and leaning against His breast, as He is her only hope. He is her only provision and source. She can no longer buy or sell, and the beastly world system has vomited her out of its mouth, like the sea-beast vomited Jonah out of its belly. The bride will have fled to the wilderness.

The Daughters of Jerusalem have seen the transformation of the Bride. She is shining and confident like the sun, yet humble and luminous as the moon in the night sky. She has become bold and unafraid, diligent and vigilant, like an army. They had seen her abused and rejected by the watchmen, but now the Daughters barely recognize her. They had seen her set among the chariots of the willing volunteers of her people, Israel: awesome, fearsome as an army, marching under its banners and divisions like the last days' army of the Lord. But now, she is vulnerable and tender, weak and dependent, just like a loving Bride, leaning only on the strength of the One she loves.

This is a picture of the returning Bridegroom, coming back to the war-torn earth, as His enemies have taken many of His people captive into remote prison camps in other places. Many others have fled into the wilderness refuges, hiding from the soldiers; only the supernatural provision of the Lord has kept them from starvation. Food was multiplied; angelic messengers brought bread, meat and water, as families bowed their heads at empty tables, and simply asked and trusted for supernatural provision.

The Lord is bringing her back from the wilderness, into the fullness of her inheritance. She has been broken but not destroyed. Crushed, but not hopeless. Like a tree, blown over by a hurricane, yet still rooted in the ground, and not snapped off, such is the overcoming Bride in her final ascent from the wilderness of the tribulation. The Bridegroom-King-Judge-Warrior has come to rescue her, finally and eternally, from the cruelties of sinful man. The world was not worthy of her, but she gave it all. No one will ever abuse us again. No one will ever separate us again. The accuser of the Bride and her Beloved is finally silenced and sentenced. Oh, Halleluiah, for the One we've waited for has come to us!

New Life is Born under the Apple Tree

Under the apple tree I roused you; there your mother conceived you, there she who was in labor gave you birth.

We saw in SOS 2:2-3 that the apple tree is a picture of rest, shade, covering, security and sweet fruit. It is a picture of the cross, which provides shade and rest from our striving to make ourselves clean and pure.

"Your mother brought You forth" can refer to Israel, who brought forth and birthed the Messiah into this world, through the Hebrew genealogy which the Father chose (see Rom. 9:4-5, Rev. 12:5)

Another possible meaning of "Your mother" is the company of the faithful and obedient disciples throughout the ages.

He replied to him, "Who is my mother, and who are my brothers?" Pointing to his disciples, he said, "Here are my mother and my brothers. For whoever does the will of my Father in heaven is my brother and sister and mother" (Matt. 12:48-50, NIV).

It was the faithful bride, who would do His will to the end, whom the Lord set before His eyes as He hung on the cross. So it could be said, figuratively, that the obedient bridal company was His mother, who **brought Him forth through the travail** of that agony. Dying on the cross was a type of the Lord being born into the fuller purposes of God, for which He was sent to the earth. **His travail, death and resurrected life brought new birth, new life and ultimately, a new creation, for the whole earth and its inhabitants.**

For the joy that was set before Him, He endured it all. We who were set before His eyes (the bride of the ages,) awakened or aroused His zeal and strength to go all the way, through the humiliation, scourging, stripping, crucifixion, and the filth of all the sins of the world, which caused His Father to look away in rejection. He kept our face before Him during the travail, and He set our hearts as His great prize.

Remember also that as the Lord hung on the cross, **only a few faithful ones, including His earthly mother, stood at the foot of the cross.** They stood under the shadow of the cross, and would not leave until He had accomplished the birthing of the new order of creation. His death would give way to the new humanity who would be attired in His righteousness, who would be fruitful and multiply His spiritual DNA into the earth's harvest fields. It was these ones, "His mother, His brothers and His sisters," whose love and faithfulness helped Him not to give up, but to overcome, until:
IT IS FINISHED.

A Seal of Ownership

> *8:6-7 Set me as a seal upon your heart, as a seal upon your arm; for love is as strong as death, jealousy as unyielding as the grave. Its coals are coals of fire, the very flame of YAH[38] (AP). Many waters cannot quench love, nor can the floods drown it. If a man would give for love all the wealth of his house, it would be utterly despised (NKJV).*

In the Hebrew text, from the gender, it is the bride who is speaking to the Bridegroom in this passage. She is imploring the Lord to seal her in permanent remembrance, upon His heart and His arm. She is also asking Him to mark her with His mark of ownership. The heart is the seat of His emotions, and the arm of the Lord signifies His actions, deeds of help and deliverance. It is a plea for remembrance, permanence, and for help in the day of trouble. It is a desire that the Lord's jealous love will stir Him to fight for us, and to keep us from falling in that day.

In the ancient world, kings put a seal of wax on important documents. The scroll was closed with wax, and then it was stamped with the king's signet ring. The royal seal spoke of the king's exclusive ownership and protection.

Jealous Love

Love is as strong as death, jealousy as unyielding as the grave.

The Lord is a Jealous God, and He wants to consume our heart. The enemy is trying to pull us down into a pit of defiling thoughts, discouragement, pride, independence, or other ways to separate us from our Beloved. The Lord God is also drawing us and separating us to Himself. With fervent desire He draws us. There is a pull, a tugging on the heart, a force which draws us, which proceeds from His very heart. It is like a tug of war for the souls of men.

The Lord desires for us to spend eternity close to His Person, as close as we desire. It is not He who determines how close we will be to His Person. Believe it or not, we determine that, based on the choices we make now. **However much we want Him now, is how much we can have Him then.** The Lord's desire is a consuming fire. He wants to possess you more than the devil wants to steal your eternal soul. As with a tug of war, the stronger party wins. God's love wins!

> *I am he that liveth, and was dead; and, behold, I am alive for evermore, Amen; and have the keys of hell and of death* (Rev. 1:18, KJV).

Nothing in the natural realm escapes the power of death. Its grasp is comprehensive. Even more so, God's jealous love will not allow the grave to have the last word. The Lord holds the keys of death and hell. His love is stronger than the power of sin and death, and His keys open the grave. The Savior came into the world to rescue millions from the pull of sin, death and hell.

Floods of Tribulation

Many waters cannot quench love, nor can the floods drown it.

The floods of the enemy will rush in, to swallow up and sweep away the bride.

> *The serpent poured water like a river out of his mouth after the woman, **to sweep her away with a flood.** But*

the earth came to the help of the woman, and the earth opened its mouth and swallowed the river that the dragon had poured from his mouth. (Rev.12:15-16, ESV).

*When the **enemy comes in like a flood**, the Spirit of the Lord will lift up a standard against him* (Isa. 59:19b).

The kinds of floods that the enemy will send are onslaughts of sexual defilement and temptation; discouragement, despair and suicidal impulses; thoughts of infidelity within marriage; covetousness; blasphemous thoughts that would not normally be in our minds; coldness of heart; disease and pain; lawlessness and crime abounding, which will cause fear and paralysis in the bride.

These and other onslaughts will continue to increase against the bride, like a flood, so that we struggle to keep believing that His love is stronger. We will need to stand firm in the knowledge that the Lord is fighting for us. We must resist these torrents of trouble and temptation that will assail the Lord's chosen ones, with more strength than ever before. This is not the time to be "too tired to fight." We have no choice, beloved. We must fight the good fight. He will raise up a standard and swallow up the floods, as we pray and prophesy.

Because of His faithfulness, we know that the floods of tribulation cannot overcome the flames of love which burn in our Bridegroom. The floods will come, and we must be prepared. But this promise that "many waters cannot quench this love," is going to be the song of our soul in the day of trouble.

The bride, in her brokenness and dependency, makes this appeal to the Bridegroom: "Remember me in the day of trouble. Remember my love, though it is poor and small. Do not forsake me in my darkest hour. On that day, do not turn Your face from me, on the day when my pain is more than I can bear. If I am sealed in Your heart, then I know Your jealous love will hold onto me, fight for me, and nothing will be allowed to pluck me out of Your hand."

We should also pray this prayer in the reverse direction: "Lord, I choose to set You as a seal in my heart. Come and take Your place, rooted and grounded in my heart, so that I will never deny You.

Make your Name burn in my heart like a jealous flame, so that Your love will be stronger in me than the fear of death and persecution."

Meditation

Lord, we will come through the wilderness of the tribulation victorious. We will face death every day, as sheep to the slaughter. The devil is not only trying to kill us, but he is trying to lure us out of our faith in God. Even in our last moments, he wants to shatter our faith. He is whispering lies in our ear – we who are the suffering for Your sake.

Satan says, "God isn't concerned about you. He used you like a slave, and now He's abandoned you to this hell. Deny Him, and I'll take care of you."

He says, "You served Him in vain. There is no resurrection. It's a nice myth for stupid people. This is all there is, this rotting stench of pain and death. There is no Jesus, because no one good would ever let you suffer like this, without lifting a finger to help you, without one word of comfort. **You served Him for nothing!**"

In that day, we will be fighting for our belief in a GOOD GOD, in One who loves us and will gather us into His arms, in the blink of an eye. We will be reeling from the enemy's taunts, trying to wear us down, in our weakened condition.

We will cry out to God, "Remember me in Your faithfulness! Do not turn Your face away from me, in the day I cry to You. Remember me in this place, right here, right now. Your love is stronger than death itself."

*"Lord Yeshua, set me like a seal on Your hand, like a mark of ownership on Your heart. You are not distant, but You are near, and I am written on Your heart. The enemy wants to wear down my soul. He is taunting my faith, trying to drag me down to hell. He is scorning me into the grave. But Your love is stronger than death, Your jealousy stronger than the grave. **You want me more than satan wants me!** Remember me, for my soul is overwhelmed."*

Does the Lord Really Feel this way about Us?

Take a moment and think about the depths of emotions and passion that the Bridegroom has expressed, all through the Song. Add to these the statements of the Lord Jesus Himself. Before you read these Divine declarations of love, ask yourself a question:

Can I really believe that the King of Heaven, seated at the right hand of the Most High, the real, historic, Jewish Man who was born to die for the sins of the whole world – **do I believe that He truly feels these emotions of desire for me?** How could He love me like this? I don't feel worthy or loveable – why would someone like Him want someone like me? Is **this love** too good to be true? Or is it true anyway?

How much would we give to have someone love us like this, unconditionally and with great longing to spend time with us? Is there any amount of money that could purchase this love? Are these more than words in an ancient book, and are these accurate representations of the Lord's heart for me and for you? Let the Word speak for itself.

- How delightful is your love, My bride, how much better is your love to Me than wine and your fragrance than any spice.
- Father, I desire for those you have given Me to be with Me where I am and to see My glory.
- You are altogether lovely, and I find no flaw in you.
- I have loved you with eternal love; with gracious kindness I have drawn you to Myself.
- Set Me as a seal upon your heart, and as a seal upon your arm.
- The Father Himself loves you, because you have loved Me and have believed that I came from God.
- How beautiful you are to Me, My friend, and how delightful is the joy of being with you.
- You are a fountain of gardens, a well of living waters, streaming down from Lebanon.
- I have inscribed your name on the palms of My hands; I will never forget you.
- Turn your eyes away from Me; they overwhelm Me.

- Having loved My own who were in the world, I have now shown you the full extent of My love.
- You have overwhelmed My heart, My sister, My bride; you have captured My heart with one glance of your eyes.
- You are beautiful, My beloved! Your eyes are like doves, loyal and single-minded.
- In the same way that the Father loves Me, so I also love you.
- Like a lily among thorns is My beloved among the all the other hearts in this world.
- Many waters cannot quench this love, nor can many floods overwhelm it.
- As I have loved you, so you must love one another.
- Oh My bride, you are as beautiful as Jerusalem, fearsome as an army with banners.
- He who loves Me will be loved by My Father, and I too will love him and show Myself to him.
- Open to me, My sister, My dearest, My dove, My flawless one.
- For the Wedding of the Lamb has come, and My bride has made herself ready.

The deepest need in all people is the need to be loved, accepted, wanted, and enjoyed by someone worthy of our respect, love and admiration. From birth to the end of life, we need unconditional love. Most of us never find it. There is only One in the universe who is capable of giving us the love that we were designed to need, to crave, to search for all the days of our lives. Not just *giving* us the love – actually, He Himself IS this love that we crave.

One of the aspects of the brokenness of fallen mankind is that when we begin to recognize this part of our nature – this need for love – we sexualize this need for love. This often happens in adolescence, or just prior. I have interviewed people who have lived with various forms of sexual addiction all of their lives, even as believers. And one of the testimonies I have heard is that when they were in their teens, they sexualized their need for love, and found what seemed like a solution in sexual behavior. They couldn't distinguish between love and sexual behavior. It is very important that parents teach their pre-teens that there is a difference between real, permanent and God-given covenantal love and sexual behavior. This is a huge key in their ability to navigate the challenges of adolescence: both the physical changes in their bodies and chemistry, and the changes in their emotional search for "the love of their life."

Why do we all need this love so desperately? We were made in the image of God, male and female He created us. We are emotional because the Lord is emotional. We need love because He is a lover, who designed us NOT to be fulfilled or satisfied, apart from the love that only He could give us.

He gives this Love freely, pouring it out upon an ungrateful world, most of which does not even recognize His love when they receive it. He gave us the covenant of marriage to help us get a picture of His relationship with His people. Love, loyalty, trust, friendship, shared authority, shared inheritance. This is who He is in the Song of Songs. It helps us see Him as a Bridegroom King, Shepherd, and passionate Lover of our souls.

I must admit, it has been a long struggle for me to believe and receive that the Lord truly feels this way about me – that all these love declarations are really His emotions towards me. It took me a long time to begin to trust in His love to this extent. I'm getting there, which is possibly why He asked me to write this book for your benefit.

He wants to make sure that no one would waste their life as I did, not having a clue of how this Yeshua loves so intimately and intensely, even jealous for each one who is reading this book. This truth is especially comforting to those whose heart is leaning towards His heart and pressing in towards Him, even if in small measure.

One of the strongest themes in the Song is the intensity of love with which the Shepherd-King loves His bride. He is a Man of affection, joy, adoration, and appreciation; His heart is ravished by our love. The Lord feels tenderness, generosity, jealousy, desire, possessiveness, longing and yearning for our companionship. Though we are dark of heart, He finds us desirable, lovely and lovable.

What is the Value of This Love?

If a man would give for love all the wealth of his house, it would be utterly despised

Some people who are important and wealthy in this world think that "money talks." They believe that the power and influence of their wealth can literally buy people, buy popularity, buy votes. It is true that in this corrupted and broken world, the power of money is huge. You can buy a lot of power and influence with money. Some even believe you can "buy love."

I once had a friend whose husband died when she was middle-aged. She is a very attractive woman, and after many years of widowhood, she began to consider dating again. One of the men who began to court her was very wealthy. He often mentioned to her the kind of life she would have if she were married to him. He described many benefits, comforts, memberships, and the level of income she would enjoy if she would agree to become his wife.

She spoke with me one day and said that she couldn't picture herself happy with him. She wasn't in love with him, and she sensed that he did not truly love her, as he imagined that he did. He loved her beauty, and loved the thought of having her as a wife, by his side in church and in all his social situations. But she began to sense that married life with him would not be the life that her deepest soul was crying out for. She declined his proposal eventually. This man thought that his significant wealth could purchase her love. Who wouldn't marry for this kind of lifestyle? My friend wouldn't. Much later, she met a humble man, and they fell deeply in love and were married.

The Lord's love cannot be purchased with money, gifts or even sacrifice. Nor can He be mocked, manipulated, bribed or black-mailed. People are foolish who think that they can fool God, when it comes to their motives. This love that He came to earth to reveal is given freely. This love that He desires, deserves and requires must be freely given back to Him, out of our sincere and voluntary heart.

This means that there is no currency in this world that is valuable enough to "buy" or earn His love. If love can be bought, it was never really love, because real Love is freely given, out of the overflow of One whose heart is Love. What price could you pay for real love? What could you offer? It would be despised by Heaven, as if you could buy the free gift of God, the Love that is worth more than all the riches in the world. *"If a man would give the wealth of his house"* – **if someone would offer all they own to buy a love like this, the offer would be dismissed, disdained and despised.**

For Solomon to write this word of Wisdom at the end of the Song is awesome, because at that time, he was possibly the wealthiest man in the world. He could buy anything in the world that he wanted, as many as he wanted. He could "acquire" as many women as he desired, but Love could not be purchased. **The perfect dove, the one his heart yearned for had to love him for himself alone.** She could have no ulterior motive, such as position, houses, lands, ease of lifestyle, wealth or admiration of others. She could not pretend to love him for his benefits package. Many women in the King's courts would do exactly that, so great was their ambition. They knew how to make him *feel* loved, but they did not love him for himself alone, but rather, what he could do to enhance their lives.

In fact, isn't this exactly what the enemy accused Job of, before the throne of God? Didn't he say, "Of course Job loves You, God. You give him money and houses, wealth, health, prestige and influence. Anyone would *seem* to love You when Your benefits package is so generous."

And the Lord God allowed satan to strip away the benefits package in its entirety. Job's wealth, possessions, and all his children were destroyed, robbed and lost. Then his very health was ravaged with a particularly painful disease, which would normally have led to a slow and agonizing death. And satan would taunt God and say, "Now let's see how much he loves You, God!"

But Job did not relent in his integrity, and though he reached the bottom of himself, and sank into despair, he did not waver in his love and loyalty to His Beloved. He said, *"I know that my Redeemer lives, and my eyes shall see Him stand upon the earth."* That is a picture of one with Dove's Eyes: loyalty and Kingdom-minded vision, even in the depths of agony and anguish of soul and body.

The Lord proved to satan that Job did not merely *seem* to love Him for His wealth. Job's love was freely given and voluntary, and was not contingent on the benefits of His "husband," the Lord God.

Guarding the Young Harvest

We have a little sister, and her breasts are not yet grown. What shall we do for our sister on the day she is spoken for? If she is a wall, we will build towers of silver on her. If she is a door, we will enclose her with panels of cedar. (SOS 8:8-9, AP).

This is an incredibly powerful statement about our responsibility to guard and protect the young and immature believers from those who would seek to defile them before they are mature enough to walk in bridal love. Obviously, the fact that their breasts have not yet developed is a picture of innocent childhood, as opposed to one who is ready to be a betrothed bride.

These younger ones are primarily little children, teens and youth, who are increasingly being targeted by the enemy and wicked men whose hearts are yielded to the enemy. But they also include those who are not physically young, but are new in their relationship with the Lord, and have not learned how to walk in bridal love – as a chaste virgin before their Betrothed (see 2 Cor. 11:2-3).

Some years ago, I had a dream which made these verses come alive to me. This was the dream: I was with a large group of friends and others, and we had travelled quite a distance to reach a kind of retreat or vacation spot. We were all spending a few months, like a summer together in a large house, on what seemed to be a rural and secluded piece of land.

Somehow, I knew that I would only be with them for a short time, and then I would depart for a different direction, while they would continue on together to somewhere else. I think this part represented my soon-coming move to another country, where I was called by the Lord.

234

Some of the families there were close friends of mine, but there were others there that I didn't know at all. One of the families was one close to me in real life. They had three young children, two of which were daughters, and all their children were being raised in a very loving, yet strict and holy environment. They were not allowed to watch what other kids watched, or to play the same games as their friends. Their parents were zealous for their devotion to the Lord at a young age. They were protective of the children's radical discipleship at an age where most parents would think, "Oh, let the kids have fun, and we'll train them in the Lord later." At the time of this dream, these girls were about six and eight years old, but unusually mature for their age.

I began to notice a man who was there, seemingly as part of our group. I didn't recognize him, and for some reason, I felt wary about him. He seemed to be a Christian, but I didn't trust him. Then I noticed he was watching me, and paying too much attention to where I was and what I was doing at a given moment. I felt he had prying eyes, and he made me uncomfortable.

At one point in this lengthy dream, I was in my private bedroom, getting ready for bed. I was getting in my pajamas, and for some reason, there was no door on my room, although it was in a secluded part of the house. The man showed up at that moment and stood in the doorway, just staring at me. I turned my back to him, in an attempt to hide my body from his sight.

Then my friend's two little daughters came to my room, and they sensed I needed protection from him. I was so relieved when they came. I think the man left when they came, as he wasn't there for this next scene. They knew I needed something to block the doorway. They ran off and found a panel of wood, with which to block the entrance of my room, so no prying eyes could see me. But the board they set up was far too low – it only reached about three feet above the floor. I was so touched by their love, but I knew this board wouldn't keep the man from seeing me. I asked them to go get a higher board to block the door with, one that would give me privacy. These little darlings ran off to find me a taller piece of wood.

I awoke from the dream, and I felt the Lord speaking to me, from this verse in Song of Solomon.

235

If she is a wall, we will build towers of silver on her. If she is a door, we will enclose her with panels of cedar.

It was like I suddenly saw the little children, and their innocence, and how desperately it needs to be guarded and protected. I thought about all the forms of assault, defilement, predators, and the unclean internet environments that promote filthy and violent sexual acts against youths and even young children.

I was not only thinking about physical and sexual abuse, although this is a huge issue in our broken and sexualized culture. But I thought about influences that would defile their eyes and minds at a young age. I saw images or words or "stories" that would lodge in their mind forever, and poison their view of love, marriage, sexuality and their identities as the holy people of the Lord.

This happened to me as a Jewish pre-teen, who was not raised with any spiritual training (apart from Hebrew school), due to the "enlightened" secular attitudes of my parents. At a critical stage in my mental, emotional and sexual development, though quite young, I was taken to see movies, and given articles and books (there were no personal computers in those days) which formed images in my mind that were impossible to remove. They affected my emotional development, and the subsequent decades of my life, more than I can describe, nor would I wish to describe this defilement. But how I desperately wish that I had never read those words, seen those movies, or heard those "stories" from friends who also knew nothing of the Lord or of His ways. Yes, the Lord has healed and cleansed my mind, but most of my young adulthood was poisoned with fear, shame and defilement, and it affected my most precious relationships.

I'm not blaming anyone for my own damage, but this culture is much worse than when I grew up. Someone we don't even know can send a message to our cell phone that contains a filthy or obscene picture. Before we even figure out what it is, our eyes have been defiled, and the image has been captured in the "hard drive" of our brain. Unwanted images suddenly pop up on our computers, defiling our families. **Things our eyes were never designed to see**. How can we guard our "little sisters and brothers" from defilement? God help us, and save this generation. Set apart a generation of young people for Your holy army, dear Lord. Guard them and guard their innocence, and raise up a Nazirite company in the field of thistles and thorns. Amen.

Hide Them from Prying Eyes

As I thought of these girls and their generation, I considered prying eyes, even well-meaning people, who would be curious about their walk, intimacy and development in the Lord. And yet their very curiosity would harm the privacy and sanctity of the children's maturing process. Some relatives, adults or friends of the family, who are not walking in radical purity, might make comments that would damage the children's thought processes. This is why Solomon wrote, *"Do not disturb or arouse love until it so desires."* Until the Lord comes to marry these precious ones, how can we keep them for their wedding day, as a pure and spotless virgin? (2 Cor. 11:2)

It gripped me, as to how much their walk with the Lord needed to be protected, almost enclosed behind panels of cedar (incorruptible wood from Lebanon) or secure in a tower of silver (which speaks of redemption and purity). In my dream, the little girls were protecting me. But I realized that it was about the parents, grandparents and caregivers building walls of innocence around them, and building towers of truth and holiness upon them, and millions just like them.

When the Lord found Israel in the desert, He described her as a newborn, with uncut umbilical cord and kicking in her own blood. Then He cleaned her and gave her protection while she grew up. When He saw that she had matured, and was ready for a bridal relationship with Him, **He covered her** (see Eze. 16:1-14). Isn't it interesting that as a Husband with a new bride, the Lord **covers her** when He sees that she is ready for love? The Lord says, *"I spread My wing over you and covered your nakedness."*

The Bride Takes her Stand

> *8:10 I am a wall, and my breasts like towers; then I became in his eyes as one who found peace.*

If the little ones are a wall, then the mature bride will build battlements of silver upon her, redemptive safe places, from where they can defend and counter- attack. The wall is a defense to a city, but it requires soldiers stationed on the walls, to be alert for danger, and to shoot through the battlements on the top of the wall.

If the little ones are a door, the mature bride will build panels of incorruptible cedar on her, that the thief may not break into her mind, heart or body. The bride will help them remain undefiled, childlike lovers of Yeshua.

Here, the bride speaks of herself as a wall. Her breasts represent her nurturing strength and spiritual food to the immature. We saw this nurturing, jealous and fierce protection of the Lord's children rise up in Moses, Deborah, Elijah, Esther, John the Immerser, and the apostle Paul, who was jealous for the church's purity. The Lord will stand alongside His bride to protect them, and to quickly raise them to maturity.

The Bridegroom's eyes see in His bride one who has found peace. She is a soldier, and she is an army, willing to give her life for His Kingdom purposes. But in all this, she has found the peace that only the Holy Spirit can give, in the midst of the battle. In the Song, the King's name is Peace (*Sh'lomo*) and the bride's name is Peace (*Sh'lomit*, or *Shulamit*). She has found rest in the heat of the noonday sun, and she knows where He rests His flock. Our Good Shepherd gives us His peace. Praise the glory of His kindness. Amen.

Chapter 12

UNREQUITED LOVE (SOS 8:11-14)

8:11-12 Solomon had a vineyard at Baal Hamon; he leased the vineyard to keepers; everyone was to bring for its fruit a thousand silver coins. My own vineyard is before me.

You, O Solomon, may have a thousand, and those who tend its fruit two hundred.

This passage is speaking of stewardship and accountability. King Solomon is a type of King Yeshua in the Song, and he has always been considered a "messianic" forerunner, in terms of his wisdom, authority, Davidic sonship, and "millennial" government, as we have studied in previous chapters.

The Lord has repeatedly compared Himself to the owner of a vineyard, who leases out the vineyard to tenants. He expects to receive the fruit of His labors, His investment, and His sacrifice. There are fearful consequences to those who will not give the King His fruit in its season. This statement of Solomon's is so reminiscent of Isaiah 5:1b-4 and SOS 2:15.

The vineyard of King Yeshua could be compared to one of three possibilities:

1) To Israel and the Jewish people, the original vineyard of the Lord

2) To the entire population of the earth, which the bride is responsible to tend

3) To the entire company of the covenant people of God throughout all generations. This would include all faithful and upright people from the beginning who were pre-Israelites (like Enoch, Noah or Job), godly and believing Israelites (like Joshua, King David, Esther, Daniel), God-fearing gentiles (like Ruth or Cornelius) and the entire New Covenant company of believers from all the nations.

There are specific ways that each of these interpretations will be fulfilled, but this is a larger topic than we can study in this book. Let us simply say that they were spoken specifically about Israel, and Israel's spiritual leaders, but will also have application to the larger body of believers from all the nations. Essentially, what was true for Israel will be true for the church.

> *My Beloved has a vineyard on a very fruitful hill. He dug it up and cleared out its stones, and planted it with the choicest vine. He built a tower in its midst, and also made a winepress in it; so He expected it to bring forth good grapes, but it brought forth wild grapes.*
>
> *And now, O inhabitants of Jerusalem and men of Judah, judge, please, between Me and My vineyard. What more could have been done to My vineyard that I have not done in it? Why then, when I expected it to bring forth good grapes, did it bring forth wild grapes?* (Isa. 5:1-4).
>
> *Catch for us the foxes, the little foxes that ruin the vineyards, our vineyards that are in bloom* (SOS 2:15, NIV).

Israel is an Example to the Church

It is interesting that the Bible commentaries cannot find any location called "Baal Hamon." While it might have been a real region in ancient times, it is just as likely that the name itself has meaning. In Hebrew, *"Baal Hamon"* literally means, "Lord of a multitude," or "Lord of an abundance."

The passage in Isaiah 5 is a difficult warning, originally given to Israel, the beloved vineyard of the Lord. However, it also has a parallel application for the New Covenant people of God. All of the Lord's dealings with Israel are vital and relevant messages to the church, for understanding His standards, His heart and His expectations for all those who are called by His Name. In fact, there are several passages in the New Covenant that reveal that **the New Covenant church is actually more accountable than Israel**, and that she will face higher standards and a potentially more difficult judgment, depending on her response to the Lord's pleadings and warnings.

> *See to it that you do not refuse Him who speaks. If they did not escape when they refused Him who warned them on earth, how much less will we, if we turn away from Him who warns us from heaven?* (Heb. 12:25, NIV).

Paul tells us that everything that happened to Israel, both the good and the bad, was written down as an example for the believing church, so that we might not fall into the same punishments as befell Israel.

> *For I do not want you to be ignorant of the fact, brothers and sisters, that our ancestors were all under the cloud and that they all passed through the sea. They were all baptized into Moses in the cloud and in the sea. They all ate the same spiritual food and drank the same spiritual drink; for **they drank from the spiritual rock that accompanied them, and that rock was Christ.** Nevertheless, God was not pleased with most of them; their bodies were scattered in the wilderness.*
>
> ***Now these things occurred as examples to keep us from setting our hearts on evil things as they did.** Do not be idolaters, as some of them were; as it is written: "The*

people sat down to eat and drink and got up to indulge in revelry." We should not commit sexual immorality, as some of them did—and in one day twenty-three thousand of them died. We should not test Christ, as some of them did—and were killed by snakes. And do not grumble, as some of them did—and were killed by the destroying angel.

These things happened to them as examples and were written down as warnings for us, on whom the culmination of the ages has come. So, if you think you are standing firm, be careful that you don't fall! (1 Cor. 10:1-12, NIV).

In the same manner, all believers have come under the cloud of God's glory, through coming under the glorious atoning work of the cross, having the Living Word tabernacle among us, and receiving the Holy Spirit into our innermost being. We have all passed through the waters of baptism. We have all eaten the spiritual food of His body and have drunk the spiritual drink of His blood, the spiritual provision for partaking in His substitutionary death and resurrection. We all drink of the living waters that pour out from the Rock, who is Messiah Himself.

And yet, will most of us cross over into the Land of Promise or enter His rest? Paul warns us that we too will fall in the desert of unfulfilled destinies, and the wilderness of missed opportunities, if we do not walk in the Fear of the Lord, holiness and purity of speech and heart before Him.

And so, Isaiah's warning about the vineyard of His Beloved is very much for us, and not only for Israel. The New Covenant believers are co-heirs with Messiah, and we know that the "wild branches" have been grafted into the "natural olive tree" of Romans 11, and thus, are co-heirs with Israel as well.[39] But just as we are fellow-partakers with Israel of her blessings, so also we are under a higher accountability than Israel, due to the greater glory of the New Covenant (see Rom. 11:17-21, Eph. 3:6, Heb. 12:25, Heb. 4:2, 2 Cor. 3:9-10).

242

A Transfer of Authority

Let us look at the vineyard parable which the Lord spoke. The wording is so similar to Song of Songs 8:11, as well as to Isaiah 5, it seems certain that the Lord was building on these two foundational vineyard parables, and taking it to the next level.

Listen to another parable: There was a landowner who planted a vineyard. He put a wall around it, dug a wine-press in it and built a watchtower. Then he rented the vineyard to some farmers and moved to another place. When the harvest time approached, he sent his servants to the tenants to collect his fruit.

The tenants seized his servants; they beat one, killed another, and stoned a third. Then he sent other servants to them, more than the first time, and the tenants treated them the same way. Last of all, he sent his son to them. "They will respect my son," he said. But when the tenants saw the son, they said to each other, "This is the heir. Come, let's kill him and take his inheritance." So they took him and threw him out of the vineyard and killed him.

Therefore, when the owner of the vineyard comes, what will he do to those tenants? He will bring those wretches to a wretched end, and he will rent the vineyard to other tenants, who will give him his share of the crop at harvest time."

When the chief priests and the Pharisees heard Jesus' parables, **they knew he was talking about them.** (Matt. 21:33-41,45, NIV).

Some teachers have interpreted this parable to mean that the Lord will take away the stewardship of the Kingdom of God from Israel (the Jewish people,) and will give it to the Gentiles. I have heard this before, as it is a common interpretation, based on this sentence: *He will bring those wretches to a wretched end, and* **he**

will rent the vineyard to other tenants, *who will give him his share of the crop at harvest time.*

However, if we read this carefully, we will see that this is not what the Lord is saying. What is the vineyard? Who is He taking it away from, and who is He giving it to?

Firstly, the chief priests and the Pharisees rightly understood that this parable was directed against them, the spiritual leadership of Israel, and not against the whole nation of Israel. **Israel was the vineyard**, but the stewards or tenants of the vineyard were being replaced. We read in the gospels that many thousands of Israelis, and in Acts, tens of thousands of Israelis (those "zealous for the Law of Moses") followed Yeshua and the witness of His apostles after His resurrection.

From the accounts, scholars estimate that the number of Israelites (whether living in the Land or dispersed) who received the Lord Yeshua during the first couple generations after His death and resurrection could have reached one million. Many of them were scattered at the time of the destruction of the Temple and took the gospel to many lands. In any case, it was a very significant number. This was still a minority of the nation, and yet there was a foundational company of Israelis who were impacted by the Lord in His generation. The Word says that He had compassion for the sheep of Israel, because they were harassed and helpless, like sheep without a shepherd. It was the shepherds who were the problem.

Secondly, the Lord made it clear to His own Jewish disciples that He was conferring a kingdom on them and giving **to them** eternal spiritual authority in the Kingdom of God, and over the nation and people of Israel, in particular. Consider these promises to them.

> *Peter answered Him, "We have left everything to follow You! What then will there be for us?" Jesus said to them, "Truly I tell you, at the renewal of all things, when the Son of Man sits on His glorious throne,* ***you who have followed Me will also sit on twelve thrones, judging the twelve tribes of Israel*** *(Matt. 19:27-28, NIV).*

> *And **I confer on you a kingdom**, just as My Father conferred one on Me, so that you may eat and drink at My table in my kingdom and **sit on thrones, judging the twelve tribes of Israel*** (Luke 22:29-30, NIV).

This means there will still be an Israel, with the twelve tribes identified and distinct.

> *And he ... showed me the Holy City, Jerusalem, coming down out of heaven from God... It had a great, high wall with twelve gates, and with twelve angels at the gates. **On the gates were written the names of the twelve tribes of Israel...The wall of the city had twelve foundations, and on them were the names of the twelve apostles of the Lamb*** (Rev. 21:10-14, NIV).

The names of the twelve tribes and the names of the Lamb's apostles are twenty-four Jewish men. **And so, even in the heavenly Jerusalem, the spiritual authority has not been removed from Israel.**

Therefore, the parable meant this: The Lord would remove from the chief priests and Pharisees of His generation, the spiritual authority over the people of Israel. Israel is the vineyard here, and the chief priests and Pharisees are the tenants of the vineyard. They did not produce fruit worthy of the owner of the vineyard. Therefore, the Lord takes the vineyard of Israel away from their leadership. Instead, He confers the spiritual leadership of the vineyard (Israel) to His own Jewish apostles, who had followed Him and laid down their lives for Him. Essentially, we see a transfer of authority from one population of Jewish leaders to a different company of Jewish leaders.

Who is the Faithful Steward of My House?

But as with the other two vineyard parables, this one will also be fulfilled at a higher level – one that goes beyond the spiritual leadership of Israel alone. Ultimately, the vineyard becomes the global company of the redeemed, and the Lord will appoint a vast company of overcomers from all nations (His bride) to rule over His (international) household. Thus, He will give to His bride authority over portions of His vineyard, and they will be made rulers over cities, regions and even nations, according to the rewards which the Lord appoints to each one.

In the Millennium, the vineyard is actually the entire earth, as the resurrected overcomers co-rule with Messiah over all the earth. While the majority of earth's population will be saved at this point, even the "as yet" unsaved survivors on the renewed millennial earth will be under their spiritual authority, both before and after they are saved.

As those trusted with spiritual authority, we need to honestly look at what kind of fruit we are producing. Are we producing humility and purity in those under us? Are we drawing the people into radical discipleship and closer to the Lord's heart, or are we calling attention to ourselves and our own ministries? Are we producing a harvest of humble, transparent, bold and prophetic worshipers, who walk in purity in their private lives, as well as in public? Are we exercising control over those under us, or are we humble and teachable servants to all?

It won't matter how large our ministry is, if the people under us are not growing in holiness, intimacy with the Lord, and meekness of heart. Who is raising up the mature bride, and who is going on with business as usual?

If the Lord finds us to be worthy shepherds that produce fruit for the Master, we will be given even more authority. If we fail to give the owner (the Lord) the fruit He requires, He will remove us from our place of authority and will give it to a more worthy company of leaders, from all ethnic backgrounds. Overcomers will not be given their rewards based on whether they are Jewish or gentile, or any ethnic background. The rewards will be based on their hearts' responses to what the Lord entrusted to them, during their days on this earth. He is looking for fruit, and is no respecter of persons or of ethnic background. Nevertheless, the Scriptures teach us that Israel will always be a nation before Him (see Jer. 31:35-37, 33:23-26).

The Lord has "gone on a long journey" and will be returning soon to collect His harvest, His fruit, His wages, as it were. Will the Son of Man find faith on the earth?

The quality of our life and fruit will be judged at that time. Sometimes we spend years and much effort building something, establishing something, leading something; our motives are good, and the work is seemingly "good." The problem is that if it is not the vineyard that the Lord gave you to tend, it might not stand the fire of testing on that day.

Sometimes we do things He never assigned for us, but we didn't know it! This is a surprise we do NOT want to hear when we stand before the Throne. We would rather Him correct us now if we are running in the wrong field, or climbing the wrong ladder, which is leaning against the wrong building.

What matters is that we are faithful workers in whatever vineyard He has put us in, from the lowliest to the most public – that doesn't matter. All that matters is that we bear good fruit in the vineyard where He has placed us. Now is the time to make sure our work will stand the fire which tests the quality of our work. Don't wait till "that day" to find out if your work is what He has chosen for you. The Lord will gladly show you, if you seek His face now, so there will be no regrets later.

> *For no one can lay any foundation other than the one already laid, which is Jesus Christ. If anyone builds on this foundation using gold, silver, costly stones, wood, hay or straw, their work will be shown for what it is, because the Day will bring it to light. **It will be revealed with fire, and the fire will test the quality of each person's work.** If what has been built survives, the builder will receive a reward. If it is burned up, the builder will suffer loss but yet will be saved—even though only as one escaping through the flames (1 Cor. 3:11-15, NIV).*

Let us live every single day on this earth in preparation for the Judgment Seat of Messiah. Nothing else will matter, except His evaluation of our entire life. Run the race with endurance, so that we will be able to stand before Him without shame and regret.

> *For we must all appear before the judgment seat of Christ, so that each of us may receive what is due us for the things done while in the body, whether good or bad* (2 Cor. 5:10, NIV).

One Thousand Shekels of Silver

> *Everyone was to bring for its fruit a thousand silver coins. My own vineyard is before me.*
>
> *You, O Solomon, may have a thousand, and those who tend its fruit two hundred.*

The mature bride realizes that the Lord expects much return on His investment. The number "one thousand silver coins" seems to mean a very high return on His vineyard. It reminds us of the parable of the talents (see Matt. 25:14-30). There, the master left a trust of money to His various servants, and He expected a large yield on what He left them to deposit or invest.

The servant who merely gave Him back His original amount was cast out into outer darkness, and the little he had was taken away from him. From this we know that the Lord expects us to be fruitful and multiply. This does not necessarily mean that we must multiply the number of people we influence or draw to "our ministry." In fact, it rarely means this.

It will look like a multiplication of inward transformation in the souls for whom the Lord has given us varying degrees of responsibility. We might be caring for them, teaching, counseling, or helping in a practical way, from time to time. When we help these ones to draw closer to the Lord, purify their lives, or to lead others to deeper commitment, it will be counted to our account as multiplied good fruit. It might be a very tiny circle which is the vineyard the Lord has given us, even our own children that we are raising. It's not about the size or the numbers.

One time the Lord told me, *"I measure success one heart at a time."* This was so awesome for me to hear, since I was not selling many books, for sure! He doesn't look at success the way the world does. One changed heart means more to Him than a thousand shining stars in the heavens. What an intimate Maker we serve!

What the Lord looks for is our response to what He gave us. Did we "make much" of the little He gave us? If He gave us much, then more will be expected of us. That's kind of scary, but it's just the way it is in Heaven's protocol.

Some have been given so little, but they make so much of it, that their reward will shock them. Another person might look more successful, but their reward will be less, because they did not multiply and make much of the large amount they were given. This can apply to gifts, anointings, finances, even how much love we were given to give out to others.

The Lord judges our fruit justly, so we only have to compare ourselves to what He invested in us, not to anyone else we see around us. Isn't that freeing to know? That He will only compare our results to the amount He invested in us? I think it is good news, although still a very high accountability. It is still a fearful reality, to be honest.

Blessings on the Willing Volunteers

And for those who tend its fruit, two hundred.

In this passage, the bride offers the King the required thousand shekels for the fruit He left in their care. But she goes further. She also offers an extra 20% (two-hundred shekels) for the laborers who helped her tend the vineyard. This shows that she is generous to her fellow workers, and not merely giving the Lord His due. She shares extra from what she gained from the fruit. Without our fellow laborers we could not accomplish what we do. They might be intercessors, administrative assistants, translators, those who help us clean and cook, or those who help us with the children, so we can attend a meeting which is important to the Lord's work. It could be those who help us with our ministry, our business, our personal needs if we are sick or injured, or those who will pray over the phone for us when we are in despair.

The bride is giving over and above the required amount, for the sake of the laborers. They may seem lowly and unimportant to others, but the mature bride deeply loves and appreciates every single one who, according to their own motivations and giftings, voluntarily helps tend the vineyard.

I don't have a staff for my ministry, but I have several extremely dear friends who help me with this ministry, in the perfect roles that the Lord has called them to. I could not do this without them, and they are so worthy of their "hire," which is actually volunteer service. "May the Lord bless the willing volunteers," as Deborah declared.

We Only Have One Heart to Give

My own vineyard is before me.

The bride once again considers her own vineyard and its condition. This is the garden of her heart, and its fragrance will prove more important than all the other work she did in the harvest fields.

In the beginning of Shuli's spiritual journey, she was coming out of family hardship and abuse and into a new relationship with the Lord. She lamented that she had neglected her own vineyard (her heart's condition), due to working for her step-brothers. She had poured out her strength for others, but the garden of her own heart, she had not tended.

My mother's sons were angry with me; they made me the keeper of the vineyards, but my own vineyard I have not kept.

But now, after much growth, testing, blessing and seeking, she has attained the intimacy of a mature bride. But we are never so "mature" that we do not need to carefully take stock of our own heart. She is aware of the great accountability for what depth of love He will find in her heart. No one else can answer for our own hearts: it's just the Lord and us on that day.

We now come to the end of the Song; to the end of the matter.

My own vineyard is before me, my Bridegroom-King.

A Bride for the Son of Man

When the Bridegroom comes for His bride, what is He seeking? What will He find? What qualities will distinguish the worthy bride from all the others from the vast company of the redeemed? Some will protest against this very question. They might say, "All of the redeemed are the bride; why do you insist that there are different categories, among the redeemed?"

In chapter 9, we looked at how the Lord took out a bride for Adam from out of his body. She was taken out from Adam's opened side. In the same way, the entire company of the redeemed comprises the Body of the Messiah. He is the Head, and all the truly saved are His body (see Eph. 1:22). Paul calls Adam "the first Adam," and he calls Yeshua "the last Adam" (see 1 Cor. 15:45-47).

And so from among the body of Messiah, the Lord will take out a Bride for the last Adam, who is the Son of Man. Figuratively, the Lord takes the bride out of Yeshua's wounded side, as He did with Adam. This was the seventh wound in the Lord's body, which the soldiers thrust into Him; blood and water poured out of His opened side.

In chapter 1, we saw that positionally, all who receive the Lord unto salvation are "betrothed" to Him; salvation is the first step in a long journey towards the wedding day. However, during a long engagement period, there are many days, months and years to conduct ourselves. Some conduct themselves as one getting ready for the Wedding. Others just take this great salvation, and then use their lives as they wish. They do not behave as an engaged person, waiting for that day with intense devotion and purity. Therefore, the Lord will not marry one who has not conducted themselves as befitting an engaged person, one who is keeping themselves pure and chaste, and one who has no other lovers besides Him, until that day.

All from among the saved are invited and welcomed to be the bride. It is a choice. But it is not automatic, upon receiving the salvation of the Lord's work on the cross. This is because at the moment of our salvation, we do not automatically become a suitable marriage partner, equally-yoked to the likeness and character of our Lord.

Eve was created a perfect bride. But since the fall, the bride of Yeshua must make herself ready, by her own choices and behavior. The Lord Yeshua can only marry a bride who is "according to His kind," those who have been transformed and conformed to His image. The Lord will not arbitrarily shut anyone out of the marriage of the Lamb. But those who have neglected to make themselves ready cannot enter, based on their own choices prior to the wedding.

The Holy Spirit will run to help anyone who desires to be clothed in bridal garments. If we ask, He will make sure we are clothed beautifully for the Bridegroom's coming. Never think that you have to accomplish this transformation in your own strength. None of us can do that. But we have to yield our hearts and lifestyles to the Spirit of God, so that He can cleanse and purify us for the Wedding.

Our proper dress as Yeshua's intimate bride is the holy clothing we receive from Him. These spiritual garments are betrothal adornments, which we receive through our intimate and transparent relationship with Him. Clothing is mentioned because our cloak of shame and filth must be replaced with His bridal garments (see Isa. 61:3).

He has sent forth His Seven Spirits into the earth to adorn the bride with Wisdom, Understanding, Counsel and Mighty Power, the Spirit of the Lord, Knowledge and the Fear of the Lord (see Isa. 11:1-3, Rev. 5:6). These seven burning torches of God's mighty, seven-fold anointing will equip the bride, and help us to prepare for the hardest season ahead. The Lord Yeshua is the Good Shepherd, and He gives the best to His sheep.

He shall feed his flock like a shepherd: he shall gather the lambs with his arm, and carry them in his bosom, and shall gently lead those that are with young (Isa. 40:11, KJV).

But even as the Bridegroom has provided the clothing and adornments, it is our responsibility to receive them and wear them faithfully until that day. The Lord requires us to be equipped, properly dressed and adorned for that day. In fact, He gives a harsh warning for those who enter the banqueting hall without the wedding clothing He had provided for them (see Matt. 22:11-14).

We need much grace and help from the Holy Spirit to have our hearts transformed into the character of the fullness of the stature of Christ (see Eph. 4:12-13). The Lord desires this for us more than we do, but still, it is our choice to become a bride, worthy of this Man. It involves dying daily to self, laying down our will and our rights, and other types of yielding. It is our choice, but He will help us and give us grace to win the prize. Whosoever will may come.

> *For the wedding of the Lamb has come, and **His bride has made herself ready.** Fine linen, bright and clean, was given her to wear* (Rev. 19:7b-8, NIV).

Our Response to Him — The Key

The Lord is a real Person. He has personality, feelings, thoughts, and desires. He walked this earth as real man, and He will always be a human being. Yes, He is glorified and lives in His glorious resurrected body, the first fruits from the dead. But despite all the unimaginable glory of His Person and position in Heaven, He is still a real Man.

This is part of the mystery of the incarnation; He did not merely put on human flesh for a brief moment, and then become a Spirit-being after His death. No, the Father raised up His body from the grave, and His physical, resurrected body ascended through the skies and the clouds, in the presence of hundreds of witnesses. And His perfected body ascended upwards, and entered the heavens as a glorified Man.

The Lord has no desire to marry a robot who is programmed to be perfect. What pleasure would that bring Him? How could that be real love? Our free will is infinitely precious to the Lord. He respects our free will so much that in some cases, He will not intervene, even when He knows our choices will bring us pain and sorrow later.

We were made in the image and likeness of God, destined to rule and reign with Yeshua, **equally yoked in love, bridal love.** But if love isn't voluntary, it isn't real love. Doesn't the Lord deserve a bride who loves Him with the same passion and intensity with which He loves us?

This is why I have continually emphasized that He has intense yearnings and passion for us, deeper than we can grasp or imagine. If we knew, if we got just a glimpse of the emotions of His heart, it would change everything. That is why the Father placed the Song of Songs in the Bible, even though He knew that some would put it on the shelf as some kind of romantic poetry, and certainly not relevant to our Christian lives.

In fact, it is the most relevant of all, as our heart's response to His love will be the measuring rod before His throne. Did we believe in His love, trust in His love, and respond equally to This Love? That is the question. It affects all of our words, choices, behaviors and motives. Our response to His love is underneath every motive in our heart, and He will lay it all bare on that day. Now is the time to adjust our hearts and align our emotions to match His. It will be too late on that day, or on the day He suddenly demands an accounting of our soul, on a day we do not expect it. We do not know how many days we have on this earth – let us not presume on many years ahead to make things right.

Would an earthly bridegroom marry a woman who did not love him as much as he loved her? Doesn't Yeshua deserve a bride who loves Him as much as He loves her? It's really almost common sense. *For I have betrothed you to one husband, that I may present you as a chaste virgin to Christ.* (2 Cor. 11:2)

Because the time has come to awaken love, we will now see this covenantal, loyal love rise up in the heart of the lovesick bride, before the return of the Lord. He will have a mature Bride who will stand in covenant, with priestly purity, unity, deep humility and loyalty that has rarely been seen on the earth. This bride will terrify satan's kingdom, because nothing, not even death can quench this love. He will have a people who will love Him with all our heart, soul and strength. This is the first and greatest commandment in the whole Bible, and this is confirmed by the Lord Yeshua Himself (see Matt. 22:37-38).

You shall love the Lord your God with all your heart, with all your soul, and with all your strength. (Deut. 6:5).

A Bride of His own Kind

Eliezer was a "friend of the Bridegroom." His assignment was to search for a bride worthy of his master's son, Isaac. Isaac is a type of the Lamb of God, because his father Abraham was willing to sacrifice his beloved son, to obey the Lord. He was not permitted to find a bride from among those who were not "Isaac's own kind." Even if the bride was not willing to come back with Eliezer, he was under oath not to take Isaac out of Israel, even to marry.

In the same way, the Holy Spirit must find a bride for the Bridegroom, the Son of the Father. The Spirit is a friend of the Bridegroom, and He cannot choose a bride from among those who are not "*k'negdo*, according to His kind." This means that the bride must be pure and holy, and must love the Lord with all our heart, soul and strength.

There are many people who call themselves born-again Christians, but they practice spiritual mixture in their lives. They mix God's truth with the world's falsehood. They mix true worship with "strange fire."[40] They mix prayer with occult practices, such as horoscopes, lucky charms, masonic societies, and divination. They read books and watch movies and TV shows that glorify witchcraft and wizardry, even vampirism, and think that this is harmless entertainment. They also entertain themselves with violent, blasphemous and sexually immoral entertainment, movies and video games, taking all this filth into the gates of their spirits. This is like being a spiritual Canaanite, who practices detestable forms of worship and sacrifice.

There is a fine line between being culturally relevant to win the lost, and compromising the standards of the Lord. I do not have the right to judge any church or individual, but I am presenting here

255

some observations, and sharing my biblical convictions. Take this point to the Lord, and do whatever He shows you. Regarding "alternative Halloween services" at churches, I fully support programs that are godly, without the evil elements of Halloween, and where they present in some way, the true gospel of the Kingdom to the youth that attend. It could be a drama, a message, or music. As long as the theme is the Lord's atonement and salvation, we have freedom to be creative.

However, some churches hold "Halloween outreach services," but the church kids dress up as witches and vampires, or in sexualized costumes, and no true worship music is heard in this "outreach." Is this not the blind leading the blind? Even if someone would get "saved" at such a meeting, what picture of the Messiah and His holiness are they getting? How can they know the cost of following Him, to make an informed decision for Jesus? In the Lord's eyes, these practices are idolatry, and He will surely not marry this mixture. He must marry a bride who is bone of His bones and flesh of His flesh – His perfect counterpart. Just like Him.

> *For we are members of His body; we are **bone of His bones and flesh of His flesh**. For this reason a man shall leave his father and mother and be joined to his wife, and the two shall become one flesh. This is a great mystery, but **I speak concerning Messiah and His bride*** (Eph. 5:29-32, AP).

The Lord is looking for His image when He gazes at us.

> *But we all, with unveiled face, beholding as in a mirror the glory of the Lord, are being transformed into the same image from glory to glory, just as by the Spirit of the Lord* (2 Cor. 3:18).

That is why Eliezer had to find a bride from Isaac's own kind. It will be the same with our Bridegroom, Yeshua. He cannot be mocked or fooled, so remove anything from your life or library which contradicts the holy Word of God. The Lord Yeshua has high standards for zeal and purity for His Name, and for the worship of His Father.

Friends of the Bridegroom

John the Immerser (the "Baptist") called himself a "friend of the Bridegroom."

> *He who has the bride is the bridegroom; but* **the friend of the bridegroom,** *who stands and hears him, rejoices greatly because of the bridegroom's voice. Therefore this joy of mine is fulfilled.* (John 3:29).

John was filled with burning zeal for the people of Israel to turn from their sin and hypocrisy, and to purify their hearts and lives for the Lord. He was a zealous friend of the Bridegroom. He lived to prepare a bride, worthy of his Lord, who was coming soon.

In Hebrew, "jealous" and "zealous" are the same word. Elijah also was very zealous for the Lord, and poured out his strength to bring Israel to repentance. He knew their tendency to idolatry and unfaithfulness. He went ahead of the people, in jealous love, to prepare the Lord's way, as did John, hundreds of years later.

The apostle Paul was a friend of the Bridegroom, as was James, the Lord's brother. Paul burned with jealousy that the bride would keep herself pure and undefiled. He knew that they would stand before the Lord, and Paul couldn't bear to see their shame and bitter remorse, if they were found to be immoral, idolatrous, running after other lovers. He promised the Lord that they would remain pure for their wedding day!

> *For I am jealous for you with godly jealousy. For* **I have betrothed you to one husband,** *that I may present you as a chaste virgin to Christ.* (2 Cor. 11:2).

James was fierce and uncompromising with the New Covenant believers – he was angry at compromise, and the fear of the Lord gripped him. He knew that the Lord's standards were much higher than the believers realized, and that they would be wailing in bitter shame and mourning, if they did not quickly align themselves with this holy God that they claim to serve. Think about James' words below, and ask yourself how you would feel if a modern pastor spoke to the church in this tone, and with these choices of words. Most of us would be offended. But isn't it better to be insulted now than rejected by the Bridegroom later, when it is too late to change the way you lived?

> *Adulterers and adulteresses! Do you not know that friendship with the world is enmity with God? Whoever therefore wants to be a friend of the world makes himself an enemy of God. Or do you think that the Scripture says in vain, **"The Spirit who dwells in us yearns jealously"**?*
>
> *Draw near to God and He will draw near to you. Cleanse your hands, you sinners; and purify your hearts, you double-minded. Lament and mourn and weep! Let your laughter be turned to mourning and your joy to gloom. Humble yourselves in the sight of the Lord, and He will lift you up* (James 4:4-5, 8-10).

Let Me Hear Your Voice

> *8:13 You who dwell in the gardens, there are friends listening to your voice—Let Me hear it!* (AP).

This is the final word that the Bridegroom speaks to the bride in the Song. The Lord is speaking this to His last days' bride, with an urgency that we must apprehend. He acknowledges that she is now mature and well-situated in the various gardens of the Lord's plantings. The bride is now caring for them, as she rose up and began to do in 6:11 and in 7:11-13. She is continuing to assume responsibility for tending and guarding the Lord's harvest.

Part of her work is to teach and lead the Daughters of Jerusalem in the ways of intimacy, righteousness and holiness; this group could also be called "friends." In this verse, the Hebrew clearly says that "friends" are listening to your voice, O bride of the Lord. They have been listening intently to all she has taught them and shared with them during her worst moments. She has been transparent with them all through the Song, and has even sought their prayers and support in her weakness. But primarily, the bride is their "big sister," or "big brother," showing them the way through this difficult journey of faith and love.

And so the Bridegroom would say, *"I see that there are friends grazing in your garden; they are also learning to labor in My harvest fields with you. They are harkening to your voice, My bride. They have gleaned much from you, and they are closer to Me, due to your testimony, even in your weakest times..."*

But He does not stop there. He hesitates a moment, and then in a pleading voice, with an urgency and desperation that surprises her, He cries out, *"Let Me hear it! Let Me hear your voice – I am listening more intently than the friends that surround you. I must hear your voice, for your voice is sweet and your face is lovely."*

Unconditional Love

The Lord Jesus is a Man of deep yearnings and inward suffering, due to His desire to fellowship intimately with His people. We cannot know or feel the pain His heart feels, due to His people's lack of affection, desire, passion, commitment, or intimate longing to be with Him, **with Him, with Him**.

Can you think of anyone more deserving of unreserved, unashamed, abandoned love than this Yeshua? Is there anyone who loves like He loves? Is there anyone who cares for the welfare of our souls like He cares? Have you ever met a kinder, more selfless person?

The truth is that it is easy to "use" the Lord Jesus for what we need from Him. We're not trying to use Him, and we really do love Him, but we fall into a need-based love at times. Many people's love is rooted in our neediness (including mine); only the Lord is powerful and capable enough to fix our messes, and only He can heal us or provide for us. He is so powerful, that underneath our love is often our need for what only He can do to help us.

259

Once the Lord gave me a vision. I saw hundreds of people, all over the world. They were kneeling at His feet, and each one was crying out, "Help me, Jesus." "Heal me, Jesus." "Save my family, Jesus." "Provide for what we need, Jesus." And it just went on and on, in rapid fire requests. Everyone was clinging to His legs or grabbing the edge of His robe, and begging for His help.

I saw the Lord's attitude – He was kind, gentle and patient. He didn't mind hearing every cry and answering them, to help, heal and answer all these prayers. Then He spoke to me, saying, *"My children use Me. I love serving them, and I am happy to answer their requests, but there are few who ever ask Me what I desire."* I sensed that the Lord felt used, and did not feel loved just for who He is, nor for just the pleasure of the relationship itself, apart from what we need from Him. Does this make sense?

Thus, it is not in itself wrong that we need the Lord so desperately. In fact, it is right to need Him, and foolish not to. He loves to serve us and help us. He has a servant's heart, and the Lord is glad to answer thousands of prayers, cries and requests every day or every hour. So please don't misunderstand what I'm saying. I need Him more than anyone, and this is not wrong.

But the point that the Lord wants me to make here is this: Who loves Him just for who He is, rather than what He can do for our lives? Do we love Him unconditionally, just for who He is, no matter what is wrong in our lives? If He never gave us one more thing, would He still be the One we cling to? Hard question, right?

Yesterday, I was waiting on the Lord before writing this last chapter. I was thinking very hard about how and why I love Him. I was searching my heart and motives as deeply as I could. I was also searching His heart at the same time, wondering what He wanted me to share with the reader in this painful final chapter of our love story. I knew the title of the chapter had to be called, "Unrequited Love." Just the title alone is so very painful to contemplate, let alone to feel the pain in His heart.

I wrote this in my journal:

"When You love Your bride, and she doesn't love You back with the same intensity, it is hurtful to Your heart."

Then I began to think about my blessings and provisions that I live with daily: my home, my family, my ministry, my bank account, my friends, my health, my safety, my car – it went on, as I am greatly blessed by the Lord. Of course, I instantly thought of Job. My thoughts often turn to Job, and what he went through. I realize that we might find ourselves in a situation where it will be hard to love and trust the Lord. I often wonder how I would do under such a trial as Job's, and I cringe in fear and shame, realizing I would not do well at all, apart from a massive infusion of grace, faith and courage.

I continued writing in my journal: "If everything were taken away, house, money, health, family, loved ones – would I still love You with the same intensity? I want to be found faithful. 'Lovesick' hurts You more than it hurts us."

Then the Lord reviewed the past 14 years of my life, and showed me the flow and development of my maturity through this period. He again showed me how my life has paralleled the spiritual journey of Shuli the Shulamite, who is all of us.

Then He spoke to my heart: *"This last chapter is very important to Me. Do not hold back – this is your last chance to impart **urgency** to My Bride. Warn her, love her, shake her. Make it real. I yearn for My children to grow up and become My bride. I desire relationship that goes beyond, goes deeper than they can yet imagine. Tell her how I feel. Tell her how she will feel if she has not loved Me equally, when we meet. Her regret, sadness and remorse will be impossible to bear, though I will cover her in My grace, mercy and love.*

*She will never be condemned, but the pain in her heart for not requiting My love, not being equally-yoked in fierce and jealous, possessive, even **demanding** love, will be a terrible pain I do not wish for her to endure. Her pain will be My pain on that day.*

Tell them how I feel, and hold not back."

A Visitation

I'd like to share a dream that my dear friend, David Michael received, in which the Lord came and expressed His feelings about this painful subject.

My Dream, in which The Lord Jesus Appeared to Us, January 1997

Adoni-Yeshua gently and powerfully came to me in a dream in early January 1997. I was standing with my oldest son and some other people, all of them godly people, but I don't know them by name. We were outside a huge arena/conference center auditorium, which was as large as a small stadium.

There was an older gentleman, unknown to me by name, who appeared to be in his late 60's at least, and had walked with God for years, and was very meek. His persona was rather like a curator or librarian – and he announced to the several of us standing there on the pavement, "The Lord Jesus is going to come here today, and He wants to speak to you personally; He has a very important announcement to make, and it is very serious."

We were astonished and excited at the amazing news that the Lord would come personally to meet with us. After a short while of waiting, He suddenly appeared, and my heart was in my throat – I could barely believe it was happening. But He looked very sober, almost sad – and one could tell that the matter He came to discuss was weighing heavily on His heart. He wanted to go inside the arena/auditorium, and speak to us there.

The next thing I knew, we were inside the auditorium, which was filling up with tens of thousands of the Lord's most devoted people, all of them filled with the Spirit, all of them following after Him. These were not miserably defeated saints, struggling to cope and to survive each day – they were awesome believers. And I thought, "These people are definitely the cream of the crop! They are the healthiest, finest group of saints I've ever seen."

The ones who were summoned to stand around the Lord, and hear Him disclose the burden of His heart, appeared to be eight in number. It was seven men, of whom I was one, and there was one woman in that group. It appeared that these eight were very much like a "cabinet" of a head of state, or a security team that surrounds a president. I, of course, was astonished, in that I didn't know how it had even become possible that I could be included in such a group. And I felt more chagrined, in that I didn't recognize even one of these people by name. I felt that I should know who they were – they were so important to the Lord's purpose, that it seemed oddly out of place that I couldn't name them. They were not any of the well-known ministries I could have mentioned at the time, but they were like royalty in the eternal evaluation.

We found ourselves gathered around the Lord, standing down towards the front, in perhaps the second or third row from the very front of the auditorium. The seats were the type that folds straight up when no one is sitting on them; they were padded, and one could simply fold them down in order to be seated. Thus, we were kind of squeezed in, and clustered around Him as He spoke in the quietest, gentlest voice, that only the eight of us gathered around Him could hear.

The Lord looked very concerned and somewhat heavy-hearted, almost disappointed, really – and began to speak to us. He said:

> *"I am here because it has become necessary to let My Bride know that I don't feel that she loves Me the way I love her. My people all say they love Me – and I am sure they do. They really do mean well. But they don't have the intense devotion, the zeal, the passion, the faithfulness and intensity that I do when I think of them. I yearn for my people, but My yearning for them is not matched by their desire for Me."*

The Lord looked sad. It was almost an embarrassed look, like in modesty, He didn't want to have to point this out. We felt pangs of remorse and sadness for Him as He said this, and as He continued.

> *"My people are not even as eager to hear Me talk to them, or as desirous to have Me come and visit them, as a human fiancée is, when she sits hour after hour by the phone, waiting breathlessly for her love to call. At this point, I*

would be happy if My people could be even as eager for My call as this young woman is for her fiancé to call her. If they could match even that level of ANTICIPATION, I would consider it an improvement. It needs to be much more than that, but if they could be brought even to that level, it would be progress."

We were heart-broken. I looked at the Lord's face, and He was so perfect, so beautiful, so approachable, so vulnerable it seemed – in that He opened up His heart on such sensitive personal issues. His very skin was of a glory that was like perfection: like gold; like light; like something I can't describe, because there are no words in any language to explain how magnetic, attractive, divine, and drawing one into Himself it was. I can picture it still, but it's really frustrating to be unable to verbally describe what it is, because I don't know the words for it. But a person could fall into looking at Him forever and never be tempted to turn their eyes away. I was standing less than two feet away from Him (we were all gathered closely about Him, but I and two others seemed to be standing as closely as we could, and each of the others who stood closely around Him were no more than four feet away from Him. We were truly collected or huddling or gathered as closely around Him as we could, while He spoke of His serious concerns.

At this moment, I could not help but look closely at each of the other "ambassadors," or "diplomats," or princes, or representatives (which is probably the best word to describe this cabinet of officers, or this team of people). As I was noticing them carefully, I was astonished at their physical perfection, their beauty, their wisdom, their dignity, their princeliness, their sterling character – and their height! They seemed to be about 6 feet 4 inches tall, which struck me as taller than average. And they were unblemished, noble and stately, as you might picture King Solomon, or possibly Michael or Gabriel or some glorious being. But they were very undeniably HUMANS, and it perplexed me even more, realizing that I was supposed to know who they are, but didn't recognize them as anyone I knew.

And true to form, when someone is having such an encounter and has so little awareness of his own being or self, I did not know if I was also tall and perfect like these majestic officers. I wondered, "Am I also this tall, like the rest of them? And if so, when did I grow to such height?" (I am normally just six feet tall).

Not only did I not have any awareness of my own physique, but I wasn't even aware that the Lord had selected me to be the spokesman (or 'recording officer' perhaps is a way to put it) or leading officer of the group. I only found that out by what the others were saying to me, and what the rest of the encounter revealed, concerning the assignment that the Lord had given me to do. Truly it was as much an absence of self-awareness as one could hope to have. And it was effortless! All we could do is to focus our full attention on His heart's needs. And thus the Lord continued to speak:

> *"I didn't WANT to come down here and say this. I didn't want to HAVE to say it. I was hoping My people would just sense the urgency of the matter. They are just sup-posed to KNOW....."*

We felt even more grieved, truly sorry for Him. Grieved for His sake.

> And then He said, *"I didn't want it to come to this, but the time has gotten so LATE that it really can't be put off any longer. I had to let My Bride know how I am feeling."*

At this point, I was made aware that all of us, this multitude of people gathered in the auditorium, were going to need to come forward to the front, to come and declare our response and our acceptance of His beckoning; that we would RESPOND to His invitation/message/summons/appeal/heart's petition.

The thousands of people I could see filling the stadium seats, many just now coming into the building to take their seats, were eagerly craning their necks and looking with intent eyes to see and to hear what would soon be announced. They hadn't heard what we heard the Lord say, and strangely enough, they hadn't seen Him, because of the way we were gathered around Him. It looked like a gathering of people, just standing there talking.

By this point, I was so overwhelmed with the desire to repent, the urge to go running to the front, the determination to respond to this Appeal, this Invitation, that I thought I was nearly dying. The stress of wanting to RUN to get to the front before the opportunity closed, was such that I was in a great strait between two points. I felt nearly physically sick.

But the immediate problem was that I could not squeeze back out of those tight seats to get out of that row, without turning my back on the Lord, who was standing not 24 inches away from me. And I instinctively knew that somehow, I MUST NOT and could not, and should not do that! But the conviction of His message was so intense I thought I would die if I didn't do something to respond in the way He was asking all His Bride to do! So I felt very much torn apart inside.

Several others of these "ambassadors" sensed the conflict that I was feeling, and the woman spoke assuringly to me as follows: "No, David, you are not supposed to leave. You need not leave, because the Lord called you HERE to attend to this matter, and you are standing in the task He appointed for you. He knows you want with all your heart to respond, and to gather at the front with every one of these people who are pledging themselves to Him. He knows that, and it is all right that you stay here. You wouldn't want to move away from Him. There will be time enough for you to go with everyone, so just stay here for now. That's what He would want." And as soon as she said that, my heart settled, and I knew that it was true, that it was wisdom, and that it was necessary. So I was much relieved, and stayed close, to hear the rest of what He would say.

> And the Lord said, *"Well, that is what I came down here to speak today. That is the main thing on My heart. There will be more, but this is enough to start things in the right direction for today."*

And as He said that, He brightened a little bit. He seemed much relieved, mainly to have unburdened His heart, AND to see that we so intensely received and took His words to heart ourselves.

He knew His desires had been understood, and His message had been received.

Now here was the most amazing thing of all: in each of the statements that the Lord made, my assignment was to simply repeat what He said. He spoke a sentence, and it was in a very quiet voice; then I spoke the sentence after Him, repeating the message, also in a very quiet voice. But it was as if there were a hidden microphone in my clothes, so that once I spoke it, it was "radioed" to the platform, where there was a huge, wooden brown box that was like a speaker box.

And next to that box was a modest looking man, a technician, almost an anonymous, obscure person, because the people didn't notice him either. But he took what was transmitted as I spoke what the Lord had just said, and he broadcast it to the ENTIRE auditorium, and it went over the loudspeakers. And the people, row by row by row, were pierced by the same poignant conviction that we had felt, and they began streaming to the front by the thousands.

I looked up into the highest balcony, and you could actually see the exact moment that the MESSAGE reached them! They wept, or their bodies shook, or they got a fierce look of determination on their faces, or they began to make their way to the front. As soon as the word reached the upper rows, the people began to come forward.

So here is how it was:

Jesus said, *"My people don't yearn for me the way I do for them."*

I said, "He is saying that His people don't yearn for Him the way He does for them".

The man by the speaker equipment repeated my sentence, and everyone could hear it. The congregation hadn't heard the Lord speak, nor could they hear me speak, but everyone could hear the general announcement as it was broadcast.

Jesus said, *"At this point, I would be happy if My people could eagerly wait for My visit as much as a young lady does that of her fiancé."*

Again, I repeated His words, and the man on the platform announced my words to the audience.

> Jesus said: *"I didn't really want to have to come down here and say this. My people are just supposed to KNOW how I feel. But it has gotten so late, that I must say it Myself now."*

Again, I spoke and then the technician broadcast to everyone present.

Now this whole process remains very mysterious to me. Jesus spoke it, and only the eight of us heard it. Then I repeated His words so that the others standing around me could confirm and ascertain that I had exactly spoken the sentences that Adoni Yeshua had declared. Yet other than those of us standing there, no one else heard me except this nameless man up by the speaker box. What a mystery! There was a "process of transmission" of the message, so no person's name was on it, and no one was conscious of anything other than that the Lord had come to address His people (MEEKLY) through these nameless, nearly invisible spokesmen. And yet the integrity of the words that the Lord spoke was provably guaranteed and maintained! And in the end, EVERY person heard the Heart Message from the Heavenly Bridegroom.

The Lord Jesus, relieved and satisfied, smiled, and having said that this is what He had come to deliver, turned and went to walk away, and was gone before we could say how. He just somehow walked away and seemed to disappear. At that point, I turned and hastened to the front to make right, along with the thousands of others. And in that very moment, I woke up.

For weeks I couldn't even attempt to tell this in a comprehensible manner, as all I could do was to break down and cry. Still after these years it continues to move me to the depths of my being.

Sincerely, David J. Michael, Hemet, California, USA

Unrequited Love

We may think that we are lovesick for the Bridegroom. But the truth is that He is more lovesick than we are. His pain is greater than ours, yet we do not know it. Have you ever seen a movie or read a book, where the theme was "unrequited love?" This is where one person is deeply in love with the other, but the other one does not return their feelings. They just don't feel that way. It is one of the saddest themes you could ever read about or watch in a drama.

This is reality, and it is sadder than fiction, because it is about the One who loved most, loved first and loved best. Yeshua loved us at our worst. He gave His all, His blood, His tears, His life to secure our love. He didn't even stop giving after the cross. He poured out His Spirit to comfort and counsel us while the Bridegroom was away.

And the Lord is still giving Himself away, day after day, night after night. He is still investing in our lives, our destinies, even investing in the earth that we have so corrupted. The Lord pours forth love, healings, guidance, provision, deliverance, help, miracles, whispers of love – relentlessly He gives Himself away. He is the gift that keeps on giving.

He waits for a response from the ones He came for, lived for, died for. Our bridal love was the joy set before Him as He hung on the cross. The Lord Yeshua waits patiently for a response that will match the intensity and passion of His heart towards us. But the response does not come to Him, because His people are caught up with themselves and their own affairs. When will He have a bride who will love Him just for who He is, with an intensity of love and desire that matches His? It is time. The Lord has waited for a long time, O bride of Yeshua. It is time that we love Him as He loves us, and as His Father loves Him.

*And I have declared to them Your name, and will declare it, that **the love with which You loved Me may be in them**, and I in them* (John 17:26).

269

Enlarge My Heart to Love You

On our own efforts, I am convinced we are not capable of loving the Lord in the measure that He loves us. And yet He desires and requires this, so what can we do? We must ask the Lord to enlarge our hearts' capacity to love Him more. He can instill and install this love in our hearts. The Lord prayed that the love with which the Father loves the Son **will be in us.** This is a prayer He delights to answer: Father, put Your love for Your Son Yeshua in my heart, so that I can love Him as He deserves and desires. Enlarge my capacity to love Him fully and freely, apart from the benefits of His kindness. Take this heart of stone and give me a heart of tender flesh, one that is capable of giving back the love that Your Son so freely gave. I desire to love Him more, Father. I desire to love Him better, love Him deeper, and to love Him more consistently, with a love which will not be dependent on my circumstances or my needs.

The Lord will answer this prayer, if we begin to pray it sincerely. We cannot do this on our own, and it requires His grace and help for us to love with this heavenly love. Amen.

All He Ever Wanted was an Open Heart

And so, the Bridegroom's last request of the bride is this cry:

> *"Your friends in the garden are listening to your voice.* ***Let Me hear it!*** *Let **Me** hear your voice – I am listening more intently than the friends that surround you. I long to hear your voice, your prayers, your songs, your tears, your worship, your laughter, your affection. I long for conversation, pouring from our open hearts, one to another. Give Me your time. Your voice is sweet and your face is lovely to Me."*

The bride hears the Bridegroom's last declaration of commitment. Suddenly, a torrent of memories floods the bride's mind and senses. She hears their history, their journey, which is theirs and theirs alone.

She sees how far she has come, without realizing how she sprang up so tall. The bride sees so many snapshots of the Bridegroom's longing and affection flashing before her eyes. How many ways He came, He saved, He intervened with His kindnesses. Scenes play out before her mind: laughter, struggles, repentance, long walks in the wind and tears, desperation, cups of coffee, journal entries, unanswered questions, new songs, raised hands, private jokes, vows, whispers in the long nights.

Then the bride hears His desperate cries again, ringing in her remembrance, but she hears them in a new way, with a new passion. She hears His voice, singing over her of His hunger and thirst to hear from her, to meet with her, to speak with her face to face, to draw her away into the secret place. She remembers how many ways He is saying the same urgent request:

> *Arise, My love, come away, for the time of singing has come.*
> *Your eyes behind your veil are doves.*
> *Let Me see your face, let Me hear your voice.*
> *Come with Me from Lebanon, with Me, My bride.*
> *I am gazing at you through your window.*
> *You have ravished My heart with one glance of your eyes.*
> *How much better is your love than wine.*
> *Honey and milk are under your tongue.*
> *My bride is a locked garden.*
> *My bride is a blocked spring, a sealed fountain.*
> *Open for Me, My perfect one, open to Me!*
> *My Beloved thrust His hand through the opening.*
> *His fingers dripped with liquid myrrh, and I touched the lock.*
> *My heart began to yearn for Him.*
> *There are friends, who are listening to your voice – let Me hear it!*

The Spirit and the Bride cry "Come!"

> *Come quickly, Beloved. Be like a swift and graceful young stag, and come for us quickly, leaping upon the mountains of incense* (AP).

The bride responds to the Bridegroom's urgent request to hear our voice: We begin to call for Him to come to us, and to come for us. We had a foretaste of His ability to cross impossible distances in the blink of an eye (2:8-9).

He will come, bounding over the stars to be with us again. The bride remembers His sudden appearance, when He came to us, leaping over the mountains of separation, doubts, and obstacles to our intimacy. Running like a swift gazelle or a young stag. But first, we heard the voice of our Beloved from afar.

So it will be for us: first we will hear the sound of the shofar, and the voice of the Bridegroom thundering through the universe, erasing distance and time. He will come swiftly to us, bounding across galaxies to gather His bride, His darling, bone of His bones and flesh of His flesh.

The Bridegroom is waiting to hear the unified, desperate cry of His bride from all the nations. He must hear our voice, calling Him to come back to us, come back to this broken world and reclaim what is rightfully His. The nations are Yeshua's inheritance and the ends of the earth are His possession (see Ps. 2:8).

When we desire Him to return to the same degree that He longs to return, heaven can retain Him no longer! He will come and marry His pure and spotless, equally-yoked bride.

The Lord will drink the cup anew in the Kingdom of His Father, with His bride. His fragrance will fill the mountain of spices, and our love will spread across the wedding garden.

A river will flow from His throne, rippling crystal water through our garden. We will be married under the banner of Love, the *chuppah* prepared for this very hour. His banner over us is love.

He has prepared a table before us, in the presence of our enemies. We are seated with princes at the places He chose for us before the foundations of the world.

The fragrance of our love will fill the skies. Our alabaster jars of perfume will be poured upon Yeshua's head, running down His beard, and spilling down to the corners of His robes. And we will rule and reign with our Beloved forever and ever. No one will ever separate us again. He will be our God and we will be His people. Glory to the Righteous One! Amen.

The Spirit and the bride say, "Come!" And let the one who hears say, "Come!" Let the one who is thirsty come (Rev. 22:17a, NIV).

Even so, come quickly Lord Yeshua. (Rev. 22:20). AMEN.

ENDNOTES

Chapter 1

[1] http://www.myjewishlearning.com/texts/Bible/Writings/Song_of_Songs.shtml?p=2

Chapter 2

[2] Rick Joyner. The Final Quest, p.117. Whitaker House, 1996.

Chapter 3

[3] NIV Study Bible footnotes, p. 1022. HOLY BIBLE, NEW INTERNATIONAL VERSION® Copyright © 1973, 1978, 1984 by International Bible Society. Used by permission of Zondervan. All rights reserved.

[4] Helene Rudolph. "Bridal Preparation Series: Fragrance. Tal Zion Biblical Oils. www.tal-zion.org

[5] The Hebrew word "ezer" means "helper." In Gen. 2:18, the Lord used this term to describe the woman He would create for the man. She would be "a helper comparable to him." In modern Hebrew, the military uses the term "ezer" to refer to an adjutant or high level assisting officer to the commanding officer. Likewise, the Lord considers His bridal company to be suitable military partners who will assist him in judgment, execution and governmental authority.

[6] NIV Study Bible footnotes, p. 1022. HOLY BIBLE, NEW INTERNATIONAL VERSION® Copyright © 1973, 1978, 1984 by International Bible Society. Used by permission of Zondervan. All rights reserved.

[7] Pastor and director of IHOPKC Mike Bickle has commented on the biblical appearances of myrrh, in his teaching series on the Song of Songs. www.ihopkc.org

[8] This process was described in a teaching by Pastor Steven Brooks at the Open Heavens Conference, Jerusalem, 2010. www.stevenbrooks.org

[9] Helene Rudolph. "Bridal Preparation Series: Fragrance. Tal Zion Biblical Oils. www.tal-zion.org

[10] Wade E. Taylor. "The Eye of a Dove." A portion of this article was used here. www.openheaven.com Also see www.wadetaylor.org for more awesome teachings.

Chapter 4

[11] Leeland: "Sounds of Melodies." Marc Byrd, Steve Hindalong, Leeland Mooring

Chapter 5

[12] Many of my struggles and experiences with finding intimacy in the Lord's Presence are shared in depth in my first book, "Coffee Talks With Messiah," Gazelle Press, 2007. www.coffeetalkswithmessiah.com

[13] "Closer Still" is the title of the magnificent painting, which artist Nancy DeWind painted, as a glorious offering to the Lord, for the purpose of gracing the cover of this book and of the new worship CD, "Song of the Beloved," which is the worship music to accompany the teachings in this book. www.coffeetalkswithmessiah.com

Chapter 6

[14] This full journey into intimacy is shared in my first book, "Coffee Talks with Messiah: Where Intimacy Meets Revelation." Gazelle Press, 2007. Available at www.coffee-talkswithmessiah.com

[15] For a detailed teaching on the return of the Lord and the route that the Lord and His armies will take, before entering Jerusalem, read "Israel's Prophetic Destiny," by Jill Shannon. www.coffeetalkswithmessiah.com

Chapter 7

[16] http://people.ucalgary.ca/~elsegal/Shokel/940217_Glad_Bride.html

[17] http://www.worldweddingtraditions.com/ethnic_wedding_traditions/jewish_traditions.html

[18] Rabbi Dan Juster is the founder of Tikkun Ministries. To read his awesome books and for other Messianic resources, go to: http://www.tikkunministries.org/

[19] http://www.morfix.co.il/

[20] This awesome prophetic insight was shared by prophetic intercessor Robert Misst at a bridal conference at Eagle Rock, MO, during Feast of Trumpets, 2013.

[21] For Neville's awesome teachings and revelations, go to www.lwf.org.au

[22] Helene Rudolph. "Bridal Preparation Series: Fragrance." Tal Zion Biblical Oils. www.tal-zion.org

[23] Ibid.

[24] Ibid.

Chapter 8

[25] Watchman Nee. "Song of Songs." Translated by Elizabeth K. Mei and Daniel Smith. Christian Literature Crusade. Fort Washington, PA 19034. In his teaching on this passage, Brother Nee believes that the bride made delaying excuses as to why she could not put on the deeper level of the shame and

reproach of the cross. This aligns with what the Lord showed me as well.

[26] For Mike Bickle's awesome teachings on Song of Solomon, go to www.ihopkc.org In his teaching on this passage, Mike believes that the bride was not reluctant to get up, and that she immediately obeyed. While I agree with Mike that He comes to her as the Man of Sorrows, I do not agree that she immediately obeyed.

[27] To read more of Bobby Conner's amazing teachings or to purchase his books, go to www.bobbyconner.org or purchase video teachings from this conference at Royal Crown Publishing. https://secure.unasecure.net/rcfvl/store/comersus_listOneCategory.asp?.

[28] Mounce & Mounce. Greek and English Interlinear New Testament. Zondervan, 2008.

[29] This revelation was part of a larger message given by the Lord to intercessor Cathy Minnick. I share it here with gratitude for her continual stream of encouragements to me as I write this book.

[30] Helene Rudolph. "Bridal Preparation Series: Fragrance." Tal Zion Biblical Oils. www.tal-zion.org

Chapter 9

[31] Joyner, Rick. The Final Quest. Whitaker House, 1996.

Chapter 10

[32] The ESV for this verse contains a Hebrew text note, "causing the lips of sleepers to speak."

[33] Joyner, Rick. The Final Quest. Whitaker House, 1996. Page 147.

[34] Mike Bickle's teachings on Song of Solomon can be found on www.ihopkc.org

[35] In this one word, I deviated from the ESV translation. I chose to translate the Hebrew "dodai" (a plural form) as "my affections," which I believe is the more accurate meaning of this phrase, rather than, "my love." Some have taken "I will give

you my love" to express physical intimacy. "Dod" is the word where the name "David" comes from, and it means, "dearly beloved." It is a term of deep friendship and intimate affection, but not one of a physical relationship. In the Hebrew New Testament, this same root word is used by Yeshua, when He says that He lays down his life for His "friends." It is a term of deep affection, "y'didav." (see Jn. 15:13).

[36] To read extensive teachings about how to define, identify and walk in only the "pure streams of God," see my book, "The Seduction of Christianity." Order from any bookstore, or go to: www.coffeetalkswithmessiah.com

Chapter 11

[37] This awesome revelation about the Incarnation was shared with me by my dear friend and intercessor, Donna Greenberg. I am so thankful for this added dimension to the Song. Praise the Lord.

[38] This is the most literal translation of the Hebrew of verse 6, which I preferred to the other translations, as none of them say, "the very flame of YAH," which I believe is most correct.

Chapter 12

[39] In my book, "Israel's Prophetic Destiny," there is an in depth teaching on Romans 11, the olive tree and the relationship between the New Covenant believers and the Jewish people, both believing and unbelieving Israel.

[40] In my book, "The Seduction of Christianity," I wrote much about true worship versus strange fire, and how to guard our hearts and minds against mixture.

ABOUT THE AUTHOR

J ill Shannon is a Messianic Jewish Bible teacher, author and wor-shiper/songwriter. Growing up in a Jewish home, she accepted the Lord in 1973. In the 1980's, Jill and her husband immigrated to Israel, learned Hebrew and gave birth to three children.

She has authored five books, produced seven worship Cd's and one 12-part DVD teaching series. Her fourth book and DVD teaching series are called, *"Israel's Prophetic Destiny: If I Forget Jerusalem."* Check Jill's website for details. www.coffeetalkswith-messiah.com

Jill currently speaks and writes about the worship of Heaven, holy living, intimacy with the Lord, the biblical Feasts, Israel and the Church. Her newest worship CD is *"Song of the Beloved,"* which goes with this book. You can listen to clips of all her music on her website.

Jill presently resides in Israel with her husband and daughter. She has another daughter, a married son and daughter-in-law, and two grandchildren. To order or learn more about her books and listen to clips from her worship CD's, and to listen to free teachings, go to her website. To contact Jill, email: jill@coffeetalkswithmessiah.com

CPSIA information can be obtained at www.ICGtesting.com
Printed in the USA
BVOW05s1136270314

348914BV00005BA/9/P

9 781628 719666